BEGINNING
WITH
POEMS

⋞✱⋟

An Anthology

BEGINNING WITH POEMS

An Anthology

EDITED BY

Reuben A. Brower
HARVARD UNIVERSITY

Anne D. Ferry · David Kalstone
BOSTON COLLEGE   RUTGERS UNIVERSITY

W·W·NORTON & COMPANY·INC·

New York

To

our colleagues and students in Humanities 6
at Harvard University

Contents

WILLIAM SHAKESPEARE (1564–1616)

JOHN DONNE (1572–1631)

BEN JONSON (*1572–1637*)

GEORGE HERBERT (*1593–1633*)

JOHN MILTON (*1608–1674*)

HENRY VAUGHAN (1621–1695)

ANDREW MARVELL (1621–1678)

JOHN DRYDEN (1631–1700)

A Selection of Sixteenth- and Seventeenth-Century Poems

CHRISTOPHER MARLOWE (*1564–1593*)

SIR WALTER RALEIGH (*1552–1618*)

SAMUEL DANIEL (*1562–1619*)

MICHAEL DRAYTON (*1563–1631*)

THOMAS NASHE (*1567–1601*)

THOMAS CAMPION (*1567–1620*)

RICHARD CORBETT (*1582–1635*)

WILLIAM BLAKE (1757–1827)

WILLIAM WORDSWORTH (1770–1850)

A Selection of Eighteenth- and Early Nineteenth-Century Poems

A Selection of Later Nineteenth- and Twentieth-Century Poems

ROBERT BRIDGES (*1844–1930*)

ERNEST DOWSON (*1867–1900*)

EDWIN ARLINGTON ROBINSON (*1869–1935*)

DAVID HERBERT LAWRENCE (*1885–1930*)

WILLIAM CARLOS WILLIAMS (*1883–1963*)

MARIANNE MOORE (*b. 1887*)

Preface

AS THE title of this anthology indicates, the poems printed here have been selected for courses aimed at introducing readers to the study of literature. In making our choices we have kept in mind Arnold's remark that in studying poetry we are seeking "the benefit of clearly feeling and of deeply enjoying the really excellent." Our first principle has been to choose poems that we have liked and enjoyed, most of them poems we have read with students in a course we have been teaching for the past ten years.* In including or rejecting particular poems we have asked ourselves, "Is this a poem we would teach in a beginning course?" As readers will discover, this does not mean that we have limited ourselves to teachable poems—to those that offer a "job of work" for the teacher— or that we have looked for or avoided difficult writers whether old or new. We have looked rather for the excitement of poetry, trusting with Marianne Moore that

> Reading it, however, with a perfect contempt for it, one discovers
> in it after all, a place for the genuine.
>   Hands that can grasp, eyes
>   that can dilate, hair that can rise
>   if it must, these things are important not because a
>   high-sounding interpretation can be put upon them but because
>   they are
>   useful.

The usefulness, the good of poetry, depends on the excitement that leads to discovering the genuine. We can reach that goal only by full attention to the poem, to its words and their meanings. Many readers—all but a few—will feel that they have something to learn about improving their attentiveness, about ways of getting into a poet's language and of entering more fully into the life of the poem. For some suggestions as to the kind of reading we have in mind, see "Teaching Poetry in an Introductory Course" (p. xxvii).

We have accordingly included many poems that have proved especially valuable for guiding students to see how the poet's

---

* Humanities 6, Harvard University.

language works, and how the poem is composed for its particular expressive end. But though we necessarily read one poem at a time, no poem stands quite alone. As Frost has put it,

The way to read a poem in prose or verse is in the light of all the other poems ever written. We may begin everywhere . . . We read the second the better to read the third, the third the better to read the fourth, the fourth the better to read the fifth, the fifth the better to read the first again, or the second if it so happens.

Since it is often other poems by the same writer that provide the best comment on the poem we happen to be reading, the primary emphasis in this anthology has been placed on relatively generous selections of poems by a relatively small number of writers. We believe that these selections are large enough and representative enough for the single poem to be read in a context necessary for its full and peculiar value to emerge.

Though our preference is for large selections from a few poets, a glance at the Table of Contents will show that we have not rigidly kept to this principle. We have also included groups of single poems, or of two or three by a single author. Certain poems, we have felt, can be read with little or no knowledge of other verse by the same writer; they seem indeed to stand alone in the poetic memory-world of the individual reader. Good examples are Drayton's *Since there's no help* . . . and Waller's *Go lovely rose*. There are others, such as Shelley's *Ode to the West Wind* and Collins's *How sleep the brave*, which every reader should vividly possess if he is to be at home in the larger world of English poetry. His sense of quality and value in many other poems depends on his feeling that these poems are "there." All passionate addresses to nature of the "be-thou" variety (the adjective is Wallace Stevens's) are measured by Shelley's ode; and Collins's lyric quietly reminds us that a good patriotic poem, discreet and unforced in feeling, *can* be written.

In selecting single poems as in the choice of a number of poems by a single author, we have been guided in part, though never wholly, by our interest in training more responsive, more genuinely critical readers. We have wanted also to give students and teachers some sense of abundance, of more poems than they could possibly explore in a single course, of surprises met by the way. It is our hope that readers of this anthology will not find only the poems they expected to find.

Any assignment, any collection of poems is an expression of taste, and the present volume is no exception. A final assignment for students who use *Beginning with Poems* might be to send them to the complete works of one or two poets and ask them to write a critical essay on the selection made by the editors.

The poems are arranged in chronological order, so that the anthology may be used either in a course that goes on to the historical study of literature or in a course introducing various types of imaginative literature. In "Some Practical Suggestions"(p. xxvii),teachers will find suggested groupings of poems for study according to some single use of language or mode of expression. No one, we trust, will suppose that other uses of language or other modes of expression are of no importance in poems appearing in any one list. A poem that appears under the heading "Voice: Dramatic Uses of Language" could just as well appear under "Image" or "Metaphor," and all of the poems in the anthology could be listed under "Sound." The lists are intended as suggestions for using the anthology in one way—a way in which the editors have used similar anthologies in a course in close reading of literature.

Because of the fairly large selections of works by single poets, the anthology can also be used as a first step toward the important goal of reading the complete works of one poet. The student will have enough poems available to attempt a first essay on "The Poetry of ———." Or he may make a comparison between writers from the same or from distant periods: Donne and Herbert or Pope and Swift; Hardy and Frost or Tennyson and Yeats. "Practical Suggestions" also includes a list of pairs of poems that the editors have found particularly illuminating for the study of contrasts in modes of expression and in attitudes expressed. There are also enough examples of poems in certain genres for an introduction to the study of some major literary traditions: the pastoral, the heroic and the mock-heroic, the Roman satirical, the mythological and the symbolical, the Wordsworthian and the anti-Wordsworthian.

Teachers of courses beginning the study of literary history will find reasonably full selections of representative poets and types of poetry of all periods from the sixteenth century to the present (with the exception of long narrative poems). We have given more space than many anthologies to poetry of the later seventeenth and the eighteenth centuries, both because the poetry is of intrinsic value and because the Metaphysicals and the Romantics are often over fully represented at the sacrifice of the Augustan poets of wit and irony. The taste of students to whom these poems are offered, we have found, is in this respect in advance of that of the anthologists.

The choice of poets from the modern period presents a difficult problem for editors. In keeping with our basic principle of selection, we have chosen to include generous selections from four major writers—poets whom we have taught with pleasure and with some success in an introductory course. Of others we include only a small number, but we hope that students and teachers will want to make further explorations on their own. The success of an anthology—as of a course— can be measured by the degree to which it engenders fresh curiosity and increased power of discovery.

REUBEN A. BROWER
ANNE D. FERRY
DAVID KALSTONE

The editors wish to express their appreciation for the expert assistance of Mrs. Weld Henshaw in the preparation of the manuscript.

Some Practical Suggestions for Using this Anthology

EACH reader will use this anthology in his own way. While there is no preferred approach that a student or teacher might follow, one of the advantages of any collection of poems is that we can juxtapose them, can read them in a variety of illuminating combinations. This Note contains some suggested groupings like those which the editors have used in classroom discussions and for written assignments. We have found—to cite the simplest illustration—that certain poems in pairs provide interesting comments upon each other, that for example one may learn much from reading Keats's *Ode to a Nightingale* (p. 217) with Yeats's *Sailing to Byzantium* (p. 317). Or Frost's *Once by the Pacific* (p. 326) with Wordsworth's *It Is a Beauteous Evening* (p. 208); or Herbert's *The Collar* (p. 51) with Hopkins' *No Worst, There Is None* (p. 308); Donne's *The Apparition* (p. 32) with Campion's *When Thou Must Home to Shades of Underground* (p. 113); *The Young Housewife* by William Carlos Williams (p. 359) with Wordsworth's *The Solitary Reaper* (p. 208); Johnson's *On the Death of Dr. Robert Levet* (p. 186) with Milton's *On His Deceased Wife* (p. 63); Wyatt's *They Flee from Me* (p. 2) with *Non Sum Qualis . . .* by Ernest Dowson (p. 355); Herbert's *Death* (p. 54) with Nashe's *A Litany in Time of Plague* (p. 111).

Other groupings teach us about the structure of a poem, those controlling uses of language which create its total effect. Suggested below are combinations of poems directing the reader's attention to tone of voice, to image and metaphor, and to effects of sound.

TONE OF VOICE

Inviting a Friend to Supper (Jonson), p. 41
On the Death of Dr. Robert Levet (Johnson), p. 186
The Oven Bird (Frost), p. 325
To a Butterfly (Wordsworth), p. 207
They Flee from Me (Wyatt), p. 2

IMAGE

METAPHOR

EFFECTS OF SOUND

Poems may of course also be related to each other by their connections with literary tradition. For courses that include longer works in the heroic tradition—*Paradise Lost, The Faerie Queene, Absalom and Achitophel*—it is often useful to read also shorter poems that are linked to that tradition by allusion or by their adoption of an heroic tone. This anthology contains a number of examples, for instance:

HEROIC

Ulysses and the Siren (Daniel), p. 108
To William Roe (Jonson), p. 42
An Horatian Ode upon Cromwell's Return from Ireland (Marvell), p. 81
Mac Flecknoe (Dryden), p. 89
The Rape of the Lock (Pope), p. 144
On First Looking into Chapman's Homer (Keats), p. 213
Ulysses (Tennyson), p. 223
Coriolan: I. Triumphal March (Eliot), p. 350

Also in this anthology are a number of poems in the pastoral mode, using the word not only in its strict classical sense (e.g., *Lycidas*), but also to refer to poems that adopt pastoral attitudes and conventions:

PASTORAL

Epithalamion (Spenser), p. 7
The Passionate Shepherd to His Love (Marlowe), p. 105
To Penshurst (Jonson), p. 43
To Meadows (Herrick), p. 115
Lycidas (Milton), p. 56
The Garden, p. 79, and the Mower poems (Marvell)
To Richard Boyle . . . Of the Use of Riches (Pope), p. 171

Related to these are Wordsworth's reinterpretation of the pastoral tradition and the responses to it in nineteenth- and twentieth-century poetry. Some examples:

Wordsworth,
  Lines, Composed a Few Miles above Tintern Abbey, p. 202
  The Small Celandine, p. 210
  Composed by the Side of Grasmere Lake, p. 210
  On the Grasshopper and Cricket (Keats), p. 213
  The Scholar Gypsy (Arnold), p. 247

Other ways of grouping the poems in this collection will occur to the adventurous student. He may wish to juxtapose mythological poems from various periods: Keats's use of the Greek and Roman gods set against Spenser's, for example. Or he may pursue an interest in the effect of Roman satire on English poetry from Ben Jonson through the eighteenth century. These are the kinds of projects that may emerge as students become experienced readers of single poems.

Teaching Poetry in an Introductory Course

As NOTED in the Preface, this anthology has grown out of an actual course in which we start by reading short poems as a way of introducing students to more intelligent reading of imaginative literature. Our title suggests also that for most students the first reading of poetry is an initiation, "beginning with poems" in another sense. The paragraphs that follow * give some account of why we think the reading of poetry is the key to understanding and enjoying literature. We also give some examples of the kind of teaching we have practised in guiding students in the earlier—and the later—stages of their reading of poetry.

We begin with short poems because they offer literary experience in its purest form. By beginning with poems we can be reasonably sure that the student learns early to distinguish between life and literature without being unduly distracted by questions of biography and history or by social and psychological problems of the type raised so often by the novel. Most important, the student will learn at the outset to deal with *wholes,* since within the limits of a class-hour or a brief paper he can arrive at an interpretation of a whole literary expression. Poems may come to stand in his mind as Platonic forms of true and complete literary experience.

Beginning with poems has another advantage if students are to learn the value of attending closely to language and if they are to see the satisfactions that come from alert and accurate reading. In the small world of a sonnet, a reader can see how a single word may cause a shift in the equilibrium of feeling in the whole poem. So when Shakespeare says:

> For thy sweet love remembered such wealth brings
> That then I scorn to change my state with kings

"state" carries connotations of Elizabethan *state,* and as a result the speaker's voice takes on a tone of grandeur, a somewhat stagey grandeur that reminds us of gestures in a play. But the word "state" would hardly impart that quality with-

* Reprinted, with some small changes, from *In Defense of Reading,* ed. Reuben A. Brower and Richard Poirier (E. P. Dutton Co., 1962).

out the reference to "kings." This fairly simple example brings home the importance in interpretation of considering the context. A course in interpretation of literature is a course in definition by context, in seeing how words are given rich and precise meaning through their interrelations with other words. The student who acquires this habit of definition will be a better reader of philosophy or law or any other type of specialized discourse, and he may learn something about the art of writing, of how to control context in order to express oneself.

Reading poems also offers one of the best ways of lifting the student from adolescent to adult appreciation of literature. The adult reader realizes that reading a work of literature is at once a solitary and a social act. In reading we are alone, but we are also among the company of readers assumed by the poem or play or novel. The poem is more than a personal message, it invites us to move out of ourselves, to get into an "act," to be another self in a fictive drama. The sonnet of Shakespeare we have just quoted seems to call for a very simple identification of the actual reader with the imagined speaker,

> When in disgrace with fortune and men's eyes
> I all alone beweep my outcast state . . .

Yet even this simple if not sentimental sonnet asks something more of us in the end; it asks us to take on the demonstrative air of the theatrical lover, to protest in language we would never actually use in our most romantic moments.

We start by reading poems with no apparent method, or at least with method well concealed. We begin, as Frost says, with delight, to end in wisdom. "What is it *like*," we say rather crudely, "to read this poem?" "With what feeling are we left at its close?" "What sort of person is speaking?" "What is he *like*, and where does he reveal himself most clearly?" "In what line or phrase?" We may then ask if there is a key phrase or word in the poem, and we can begin to introduce the notion of the poem as a structure, as an ordered experience built up through various kinds of meaning controlled in turn by various uses of language.

Remembering our questions about the speaker, we first direct attention to dramatic uses of language, to the ways in which the words create a character speaking in a certain role. We may ask, for example, who is speaking in Keats' sonnet on Chapman's *Homer*. An alert student may point out that he is a traveler (many do not see this), and that he uses idioms with a medieval coloring: "realms," "goodly," "bards in fealty," "demesne." But the speaker does not continue to talk in this vein:

> Till I heard Chapman speak out loud and bold.

He has changed, and the drama moves into a second act. We hear a voice that is powerful and young, the voice of the New World discoverer and the Renaissance astronomer. We now point out to our young reader (if he is still listening) that the poem is indeed an "act." The poet is speaking *as if* he were a traveler-explorer, and the whole poem is built on a metaphor. So, while reading many poems, we may introduce a few basic notions of literary design and some useful critical terms. But our emphasis will always be on the term as a tool, as a device for calling attention to the poem and how it is made. In time we can turn to study of the poem as an experience of ordered sounds, but not, we hasten to add, of sounds divorced from sense. Our aim in talking about rhythmic pattern, as in considering dramatic and metaphorical design, is to show how the poem "works" and what it expresses. We see, for example, that as Keats's sonnet moves from the medieval to the modern speaker and as the metaphor also shifts, the rhythm changes from the "broken" couplets and inversions of the octave to the long and steady sweep of the sestet. The whole sonnet in its beautiful interaction of parts gives us the sense of discovery and release into a new world of literary and aesthetic experience.

The student who has had some practice in attentive reading of poetry of the kind we have been describing may discover that he has learned some ways of reading that will be useful when he turns to other forms of imaginative literature such as poetic drama, the long poem, the short story, and the novel. In reading a play by Shakespeare he can see, for example, that the man speaking in a poem corresponds to the character in a play, that Shakespeare has his large metaphors just as Keats has his smaller ones. The short story, like the poem, offers the reader literary experience in microcosm and makes it easier to detect analogies between fiction and poetry, to see that a tale by Hawthorne is the unfolding of a single metaphorical vision, or that the narrator in a story by Joyce controls our sense of being within the child's world, exiled from adult society. The novel, especially as we have it in its classic nineteenth-century form in Dickens or George Eliot, demands a very different reading from a Shakespearean drama, but by putting the same questions to both genres their likeness and unlikeness can be defined, and the exact quality of a particular work can be discovered. Thus alert reading of single poems may lead to full and precise response to these larger, but not necessarily more complex, literary forms.

BEGINNING
WITH
POEMS

≺☼≻

An Anthology

SIR THOMAS WYATT
(1503–1542)

·

WHOSO LIST TO HUNT

Whoso list to hunt, I know where is an hind,
But as for me, alas, I may no more;
The vain travail hath wearied me so sore.
I am of them that farthest cometh behind.
Yet may I by no means my wearied mind   5
Draw from the deer; but as she fleeth afore,
Fainting I follow. I leave off therefore,
Since in a net I seek to hold the wind.
Who list her hunt, I put him out of doubt,
As well as I may spend his time in vain;   10
And, graven with diamonds, in letters plain
There is written her fair neck round about:
"*Noli me tangere*, for Caesar's I am;
And wild for to hold, though I seem tame."

MY GALLEY CHARGED WITH
FORGETFULNESS

My galley chargéd with forgetfulness
Thorough sharp seas, in winter nights doth pass
'Tween rock and rock; and eke mine enemy, alas,
That is my lord, steereth with cruelness;
And every oar a thought in readiness,   5
As though that death were light in such a case.
And endless wind doth tear the sail apace
Of forcéd sighs and trusty fearfulness.
A rain of tears, a cloud of dark disdain,
Hath done the wearied cords great hinderance,   10
Wreathéd with error and eke with ignorance.
The stars be hid that led me to this pain;
Drownéd is reason that should me consort,
And I remain despairing of the port.

1. *list* wishes.
13. *Noli me tangere* touch me not
(traditional Latin motto, supposedly en-
graved on the collars of Caesar's
hounds); here also an ironic allusion

to Christ's words to Mary Magdalen
(*John* xx.17).

3. *eke* also; *enemy* Cupid.
13. *consort* accompany.

THEY FLEE FROM ME

They flee from me that sometime did me seek
With naked foot stalking in my chamber.
I have seen them gentle, tame, and meek
That now are wild and do not remember
That sometime they put themselves in danger   5
To take bread at my hand; and now they range
Busily seeking with a continual change.

Thankéd be Fortune, it hath been otherwise
Twenty times better; but once in special,
In thin array after a pleasant guise,   10
When her loose gown from her shoulders did fall,
And she me caught in her arms long and small;
And therewithall sweetly did me kiss,
And softly said, "Dear heart, how like you this?"

It was no dream; I lay broad waking.   15
But all is turned thorough my gentleness
Into a strange fashion of forsaking;
And I have leave to go of her goodness,
And she also to use newfangleness.
But since that I so kindely am served,   20
I fain would know what she hath deserved.

IN ETERNUM

In eternum I was once determed
For to have lovéd and my mind affirmed,
That with my heart it should be confirmed
      In eternum.

Forthwith I found the thing that I might like,   5
And sought with love to warm her heart alike,
For, as methought, I should not see the like
      In eternum.

To trace this dance I put myself in prese;
Vain hope did lead and bade I should not cease
To serve, to suffer, and still to hold my peace   10
      In eternum.

20. *kindely* in its early usage: according to nature; also understood ironically.

In Eternum forever and ever.
1. *determed* determined.
9. *prese* press, crowd.

With this first rule I furthered me apace,
That, as methought, my troth had taken place
With full assurance to stand in her grace   15
    In eternum.

It was not long ere I by proof had found
That feeble building is on feeble ground;
For in her heart this word did never sound,
    In eternum.   20

In eternum then from my heart I kest
That I had first determéd for the best;
Now in the place another thought doth rest,
    In eternum.

IS IT POSSIBLE

    Is it possible
    That so high debate,
  So sharp, so sore, and of such rate,
Should end so soon and was begun so late?
    Is it possible?   5

    Is it possible
    So cruel intent,
  So hasty heat and so soon spent,
From love to hate, and thence for to relent?
    Is it possible?   10

    Is it possible
    That any may find
  Within one heart so diverse mind,
To change or turn as weather and wind?
    Is it possible?   15

    Is it possible
    To spy it in an eye
  That turns as oft as chance on die?
The truth whereof can any try?
    Is it possible?   20

    Is it possible
    For to turn so oft,
  To bring that lowest that was most aloft,
And to fall highest yet to light soft;
    It is possible.   25

21. *kest*   cast.

All is possible
Who so list believe;
Trust therefore first, and after preve,
As men wed ladies by license and leave,
All is possible.

30

28. *preve* prove.

EDMUND SPENSER
(1552–1599)

·

FROM AMORETTI

13

In that proud port, which her so goodly graceth,
whiles her fair face she rears up to the sky;
and to the ground her eyelids low embaseth,
most goodly temperature ye may descry,
Mild humblesse mixed with awful majesty.   5
For looking on the earth whence she was born,
her mind remembreth her mortality,
what so is fairest shall to earth return.
But that same lofty countenance seems to scorn
base thing, and think how she to heaven may climb,   10
treading down earth as loathsome and forlorn,
that hinders heavenly thoughts with drossy slime.
Yet lowly still vouchsafe to look on me,
such lowliness shall make you lofty be.

23

Penelope for her Ulysses' sake,
Devised a web her wooers to deceive;
in which the work that she all day did make
the same at night she did again unreave:
Such subtile craft my damsel doth conceive,   5
th' importune suit of my desire to shun;
for all that I in many days do weave,
in one short hour I find by her undone.
So when I think to end that I begun,
I must begin and never bring to end;   10
for with one look she spills that long I spun,
and with one word my whole year's work doth rend.
Such labor like the spider's web I find,
whose fruitless work is broken with least wind.

3. *embaseth* lowers.   4. *unreave* disentangle.
4. *temperature* proportion.

35

My hungry eyes through greedy covetize,
still to behold the object of their pain,
with no contentment can themselves suffize,
but having pine and having not complain.
For lacking it they cannot life sustain,   5
and having it they gaze on it the more;
in their amazement like Narcissus vain
whose eyes him starved; so plenty makes me poor.
Yet are mine eyes so filléd with the store
of that fair sight, that nothing else they brook,   10
but loath the things which they did like before,
and can no more endure on them to look.
All this world's glory seemeth vain to me,
and all their shows but shadows saving she.

70

Fresh spring the herald of love's mighty king,
In whose coat armor richly are displayed
All sorts of flowers the which on earth do spring
In goodly colors gloriously arrayed.
Go to my love, where she is careless laid,   5
Yet in her winter's bower not well awake;
Tell her the joyous time will not be stayed
Unless she do him by the forelock take.
Bid her therefore herself soon ready make,
To wait on Love amongst his lovely crew;   10
Where every one that misseth then her make,
Shall be by him amerced with penance due.
Make haste therefore sweet love, whilst it is prime,
For none can call again the passéd time.

75

One day I wrote her name upon the strand,
But came the waves and washéd it away;
Again I wrote it with a second hand,
But came the tide, and made my pains his prey.

7. *Narcissus* the youth who admired
his own beauty so much that he pined
away for his reflection in a pool and
was metamorphosed into a flower.

2. *coat armor* tunic on which the

wearer's emblem or motto is displayed.
11. *make* mate.
12. *amerced* punished.
13. *prime* spring; also, the first hour
in the morning.

"Vain man," said she, "that dost in vain essay   5
A mortal thing so to immortalize,
For I myself shall like to this decay,
And eke my name be wipéd out likewise."
"Not so," quoth I; "let baser things devise
To die in dust, but you shall live by fame;   10
My verse your virtues rare shall eternize,
And in the heavens write your glorious name:
Where, whenas death shall all the world subdue,
Our love shall live, and later life renew."

.   .   .

EPITHALAMION

Ye learnéd sisters which have oftentimes
Been to me aiding, others to adorn,
Whom ye thought worthy of your graceful rimes,
That even the greatest did not greatly scorn
To hear their names sung in your simple lays,   5
But joyéd in their praise.
And when ye list your own mishaps to mourn,
Which death, or love, or fortune's wreck did raise,
Your string could soon to sadder tenor turn,
And teach the woods and waters to lament   10
Your doleful dreariment.
Now lay those sorrowful complaints aside,
And having all your heads with garland crowned,
Help me mine own love's praises to resound,
Ne let the same of any be envíed: 15
So Orpheus did for his own bride,
So I unto myself alone will sing,
The woods shall to me answer and my echo ring.

Early before the world's light-giving lamp
His golden beam upon the hills doth spread,   20
Having dispersed the night's uncheerful damp,
Do ye awake, and with fresh lustyhead,
Go to the bower of my belovéd love,
My truest turtle dove,
Bid her awake, for Hymen is awake,   25
And long since ready forth his mask to move,

8. *eke* also.

Epithalamion a marriage song or poem.
1. *learned sisters* Muses.
16. *Orpheus* husband of Eurydice, he charmed the spirits of Hades with the music of his lyre in order to regain her.
25. *Hymen* the god of marriage.

With his bright tead that flames with many a flake,
And many a bachelor to wait on him,
In their fresh garments trim.
Bid her awake therefore and soon her dight,   30
For lo the wishéd day is come at last,
That shall for all the pains and sorrows past,
Pay to her usury of long delight:
And whilst she doth her dight,
Do ye to her of joy and solace sing,   35
That all the woods may answer and your echo ring.

Bring with you all the nymphs that you can hear
Both of the rivers and the forests green,
And of the sea that neighbors to her near,
All with gay garlands goodly well beseen.   40
And let them also with them bring in hand
Another gay garland
For my fair love of lilies and of roses,
Bound truelove-wise with a blue silk riband.
And let them make great store of bridal posies,   45
And let them eke bring store of other flowers
To deck the bridal bowers.
And let the ground whereas her foot shall tread,
For fear the stones her tender foot should wrong
Be strewed with fragrant flowers all along,   50
And diapered like the discoloréd mead.
Which done, do at her chamber door await,
For she will waken straight,
The whiles do ye this song unto her sing,
The woods shall to you answer and your echo ring.   55

Ye nymphs of Mulla which with careful heed
The silver scaly trouts do tend full well,
And greedy pikes which use therein to feed,
(Those trouts and pikes all others do excel)
And ye likewise which keep the rushy lake,   60
Where none do fishes take,
Bind up the locks the which hang scattered light,
And in his waters, which your mirror make,
Behold your faces as the crystal bright,
That when you come whereas my love doth lie,   65
No blemish she may spy.

27. *tead* torch.   56. *Mulla* Irish river near Kilcoman,
51. *diapered* variegated; *discolored* Spenser's home.
variously colored.

And eke ye lightfoot maids which keep the deer,
That on the hoary mountain use to tower,
And the wild wolves which seek them to devour,
With your steel darts do chase from coming near   70
Be also present here,
To help to deck her and to help to sing,
That all the woods may answer and your echo ring.

Wake now, my love, awake; for it is time;
The rosy Morn long since left Tithone's bed,   75
All ready to her silver coach to climb,
And Phoebus 'gins to show his glorious head.
Hark, how the cheerful birds do chant their lays
And carol of love's praise!
The merry lark her matins sings aloft,   80
The thrush replies, the mavis descant plays,
The ousel shrills, the ruddock warbles soft,
So goodly all agree with sweet consent,
To this day's merriment.
Ah my dear love why do ye sleep thus long,   85
When meeter were that ye should now awake,
T'await the coming of your joyous make,
And hearken to the birds' love-learnéd song,
The dewy leaves among.
For they of joy and pleasance to you sing,   90
That all the woods them answer and their echo ring.

My love is now awake out of her dreams,
And her fair eyes like stars that dimméd were
With darksome cloud, now show their goodly beams
More bright than Hesperus his head doth rear.   95
Come now ye damsels, daughters of delight,
Help quickly her to dight,
But first come ye fair Hours which were begot
In Jove's sweet paradise, of Day and Night,
Which do the seasons of the year allot,   100
And all that ever in this world is fair
Do make and still repair.
And ye three handmaids of the Cyprian queen,
The which do still adorn her beauty's pride,
Help to adorn my beautifulest bride;   105
And as ye her array, still throw between

75. *Tithone* (Tithonus) beloved by
Aurora, the dawn. She secured for him
the gift of immortality, but not eternal
youth.

77. *Phoebus* Apollo, the sun.
95. *Hesperus* the evening star.
103. *Cyprian queen* Venus.

Some graces to be seen,
And as ye use to Venus, to her sing,
The whiles the woods shall answer and your echo ring.

Now is my love all ready forth to come,   110
Let all the virgins therefore well await,
And ye fresh boys that tend upon her groom,
Prepare yourselves; for he is coming straight.
Set all your things in seemly good array
Fit for so joyful day,   115
The joyful'st day that ever sun did see.
Fair Sun, show forth thy favorable ray,
And let thy lifeful heat not fervent be
For fear of burning her sunshiny face,
Her beauty to disgrace.   120
O fairest Phoebus, father of the Muse,
If ever I did honor thee aright,
Or sing the thing, that mote thy mind delight,
Do not thy servant's simple boon refuse,
But let this day, let this one day be mine,   125
Let all the rest be thine.
Then I thy sovereign praises loud will sing,
That all the woods shall answer and their echo ring.

Hark how the minstrels 'gin to shrill aloud
Their merry music that resounds from far,   130
The pipe, the tabor, and the trembling croud,
That well agree withouten breach or jar.
But most of all the damsels do delight,
When they their timbrels smite,
And thereunto do dance and carol sweet,   135
That all the senses they do ravish quite,
The whiles the boys run up and down the street,
Crying aloud with strong confuséd noise,
As if it were one voice.
"Hymen io Hymen, Hymen," they do shout,   140
That even to the heavens their shouting shrill
Doth reach, and all the firmament doth fill;
To which the people, standing all about,
As in approvance do thereto applaud
And loud advance her laud,   145
And evermore they "Hymen, Hymen" sing,
That all the woods them answer and their echo ring.

131. *croud*   a violin or fiddle.

Lo where she comes along with portly pace
Like Phoebe from her chamber of the East,
Arising forth to run her mighty race   150
Clad all in white, that seems a virgin best.
So well it her beseems that ye would ween
Some angel she had been.
Her long loose yellow locks like golden wire,
Sprinkled with pearl, and pearling flowers atween,   155
Do like a golden mantle her attire,
And being crownéd with a garland green,
Seem like some maiden queen.
Her modest eyes abashéd to behold
So many gazers as on her do stare,   160
Upon the lowly ground affixéd are.
Ne dare lift up her countenance too bold,
But blush to hear her praises sung so loud,
So far from being proud.
Nathless do ye still loud her praises sing,   165
That all the woods may answer and your echo ring.

Tell me, ye merchants' daughters, did ye see
So fair a creature in your town before,
So sweet, so lovely, and so mild as she,
Adorned with beauty's grace and virtue's store;   170
Her goodly eyes like sapphires shining bright,
Her forehead ivory white,
Her cheeks like apples which the sun hath ruddied,
Her lips like cherries charming men to bite,
Her breast like to a bowl of cream uncrudded,   175
Her paps like lilies budded,
Her snowy neck like to a marble tower,
And all her body like a palace fair,
Ascending up with many a stately stair,
To honor's seat and chastity's sweet bower.   180
Why stand ye still ye virgins in amaze,
Upon her so to gaze,
Whiles ye forget your former lay to sing,
To which the woods did answer and your echo ring.

But if ye saw that which no eyes can see,   185
The inward beauty of her lively spright,
Garnished with heavenly gifts of high degree,
Much more then would ye wonder at that sight,

149. *Phoebe* Diana, a goddess of the   186. *spright* spirit.
moon.

And stand astonished like to those which read
Medusa's mazeful head.   190
There dwells sweet love and constant chastity,
Unspotted faith and comely womanhood,
Regard of honor and mild modesty;
There virtue reigns as queen in royal throne,
And giveth laws alone,   195
The which the base affections do obey,
And yield their services unto her will,
Ne thought of thing uncomely ever may
Thereto approach to tempt her mind to ill.
Had ye once seen these her celestial treasures,   200
And unrevealéd pleasures,
Then would ye wonder and her praises sing,
That all the woods should answer and your echo ring.

Open the temple gates unto my love,
Open them wide that she may enter in,   205
And all the posts adorn as doth behove,
And all the pillars deck with garlands trim,
For to receive this saint with honor due,
That cometh in to you.
With trembling steps and humble reverence,   210
She cometh in before th' Almighty's view;
Of her, ye virgins, learn obedience,
When so ye come into those holy places,
To humble your proud faces:
Bring her up to the high altar, that she may   215
The sacred ceremonies there partake,
The which do endless matrimony make,
And let the roaring organs loudly play
The praises of the Lord in lively notes,
The whiles with hollow throats   220
The choristers the joyous anthem sing,
That all the woods may answer and their echo ring.

Behold whiles she before the altar stands
Hearing the holy priest that to her speaks
And blesseth her with his two happy hands,   225
How the red roses flush up in her cheeks,
And the pure snow with goodly vermil stain,
Like crimson dyed in grain,
That even th' angels which continually

190. *Medusa* one of the Gorgons; any who looked at her head were turned to
stone.

About the sacred altar do remain,   230
Forget their service and about her fly,
Oft peeping in her face that seems more fair,
The more they on it stare.
But her sad eyes, still fastened on the ground,
Are governéd with goodly modesty,   235
That suffers not one look to glance awry,
Which may let in a little thought unsound.
Why blush ye, love, to give to me your hand,
The pledge of all our band?
Sing ye sweet angels, Allelujah sing,   240
That all the woods may answer and your echo ring.

Now all is done; bring home the bride again,
Bring home the triumph of our victory,
Bring home with you the glory of her gain,
With joyance bring her and with jollity.   245
Never had man more joyful day than this,
Whom heaven would heap with bliss.
Make feast therefore now all this live-long day;
This day forever to me holy is;
Pour out the wine without restraint or stay,   250
Pour not by cups, but by the belly full,
Pour out to all that wull,
And sprinkle all the posts and walls with wine,
That they may sweat, and drunken be withal.
Crown ye God Bacchus with a coronal,   255
And Hymen also crown with wreaths of vine;
And let the Graces dance unto the rest;
For they can do it best:
The whiles the maidens do their carol sing,
To which the woods shall answer and their echo ring.   260

Ring ye the bells, ye young men of the town,
And leave your wonted labors for this day.
This day is holy; do ye write it down,
That ye forever it remember may.
This day the sun is in his chiefest height,   265
With Barnaby the bright,
From whence declining daily by degrees,
He somewhat loseth of his heat and light,
Whence once the Crab behind his back he sees.
But for this time it ill ordainéd was,   270

266. *Barnaby* St. Barnabas on whose feast day (June 11) this wedding takes place.

To choose the longest day in all the year,
And shortest night, when longest fitter were;
Yet never day so long but late would pass.
Ring ye the bells, to make it wear away,
And bonfires make all day,   275
And dance about them, and about them sing:
That all the woods may answer and your echo ring.

Ah when will this long weary day have end,
And lend me leave to come unto my love?
How slowly do the hours their numbers spend?   280
How slowly does sad Time his feathers move?
Haste thee O fairest planet to thy home
Within the western foam;
Thy tiréd steeds long since have need of rest.
Long though it be, at last I see it gloom,   285
And the bright evening star with golden crest
Appear out of the East.
Fair child of beauty, glorious lamp of love,
That all the host of heaven in ranks dost lead,
And guidest lovers through the nightés dread,   290
How cheerfully thou lookest from above,
And seemst to laugh atween thy twinkling light
As joying in the sight
Of these glad many which for joy do sing,
That all the woods them answer and their echo ring.   295

Now cease, ye damsels, your delights forepast;
Enough is it that all the day was yours;
Now day is done, and night is nighing fast;
Now bring the bride into the bridal bowers.
Now night is come, now soon her disarray,   300
And in her bed her lay;
Lay her in lilies and in violets,
And silken curtains over her display,
And odored sheets, and Arras coverlets.
Behold how goodly my fair love does lie   305
In proud humility;
Like unto Maia, when as Jove her took,
In Tempe, lying on the flowery grass,
Twixt sleep and wake, after she weary was,
With bathing in the Acidalian brook.   310
Now it is night, ye damsels may be gone,

307. *Maia*   mother of Hermes by Zeus (Jove).

And leave my love alone,
And leave likewise your former lay to sing:
The woods no more shall answer, nor your echo ring.

Now welcome night, thou night so long expected,   315
That long day's labor dost at last defray,
And all my cares, which cruel love collected,
Hast summed in one, and canceléd for aye;
Spread thy broad wing over my love and me,
That no man may us see,   320
And in thy sable mantle us enwrap,
From fear of peril and foul horror free.
Let no false treason seek us to entrap,
Nor any dread disquiet once annoy
The safety of our joy;   325
But let the night be calm and quietsome,
Without tempestuous storms or sad affray:
Like as when Jove with fair Alcmena lay,
When he begot the great Tirynthian groom;
Or like as when he with thyself did lie,   330
And begot Majesty.
And let the maids and youngmen cease to sing:
Ne let the woods them answer, nor their echo ring.

Let no lamenting cries, nor doleful tears,
Be heard all night within nor yet without;   335
Ne let false whispers, breeding hidden fears,
Break gentle sleep with misconceivéd doubt.
Let no deluding dreams, nor dreadful sights
Make sudden sad affrights;
Ne let house-fires, nor lightning's helpless harms,   340
Ne let the Pouke, nor other evil sprights,
Ne let mischievous witches with their charms,
Ne let hobgoblins, names whose sense we see not,
Fray us with things that be not.
Let not the shriek-owl, nor the stork be heard,   345
Nor the night raven that still deadly yells,
Nor damnéd ghosts called up with mighty spells,
Nor grisly vultures make us once afeard;
Ne let the unpleasant choir of frogs still croaking
Make us to wish their choking.   350
Let none of these their dreary accents sing;
Ne let the woods them answer, nor their echo ring.

328. *Alcmena*   mother of Hercules by Zeus.

But let still silence true night watches keep,
That sacred peace may in assurance reign,
And timely sleep, when it is time to sleep, 355
May pour his limbs forth on your pleasant plain,
The whiles an hundred little wingéd loves,
Like divers feathered doves,
Shall fly and flutter round about your bed,
And in the secret dark, that none reproves, 360
Their pretty stealths shall work, and snares shall spread
To filch away sweet snatches of delight,
Concealed through covert night.
Ye sons of Venus, play your sports at will,
For greedy pleasure, careless of your toys, 365
Thinks more upon her paradise of joys,
Than what ye do, all be it good or ill.
All night therefore attend your merry play,
For it will soon be day;
Now none doth hinder you, that say or sing, 370
Ne will the woods now answer, nor your echo ring.

Who is the same, which at my window peeps?
Or whose is that fair face, that shines so bright?
Is it not Cynthia, she that never sleeps,
But walks about high heaven all the night? 375
O fairest goddess, do thou not envy
My love with me to spy;
For thou likewise didst love, though now unthought,
And for a fleece of wool, which privily
The Latmian shepherd once unto thee brought, 380
His pleasures with thee wrought.
Therefore to us be favorable now;
And sith of women's labors thou hast charge,
And generation goodly dost enlarge,
Incline thy will to effect our wishful vow, 385
And the chaste womb inform with timely seed,
That may our comfort breed;
Till which we cease our hopeful hap to sing,
Ne let the woods us answer, nor our echo ring.

And thou, great Juno, which with awful might 390
The laws of wedlock still dost patronize,
And the religion of the faith first plight

374. *Cynthia* a goddess of the moon;
also, Lucina who presides over child-
birth.

380. *Latmian shepherd* Endymion, so
beautiful that the chaste Cynthia
(Diana) fell in love with him.

With sacred rites hast taught to solemnize,
And eke for comfort often calléd art
Of women in their smart,   395
Eternally bind thou this lovely band,
And all thy blessings unto us impart.
And thou glad Genius, in whose gentle hand,
The bridal bower and genial bed remain,
Without blemish or stain,   400
And the sweet pleasures of their love's delight
With secret aid dost succor and supply,
Till they bring forth the fruitful progeny,
Send us the timely fruit of this same night.
And thou, fair Hebe, and thou Hymen free,   405
Grant that it may so be.
Till which we cease your further praise to sing,
Ne any woods shall answer, nor your echo ring.

And ye high heavens, the temple of the gods,
In which a thousand torches flaming bright   410
Do burn, that to us wretched earthly clods,
In dreadful darkness lend desiréd light;
And all ye powers which in the same remain,
More than we men can feign,
Pour out your blessing on us plenteously,   415
And happy influence upon us rain,
That we may raise a large posterity,
Which from the earth, which they may long possess,
With lasting happiness,
Up to your haughty palaces may mount,   420
And for the guerdon of their glorious merit
May heavenly tabernacles there inherit,
Of blessed saints for to increase the count.
So let us rest, sweet love, in hope of this,
And cease till then our timely joys to sing,   425
The woods no more us answer, nor our echo ring.

Song made in lieu of many ornaments,
With which my love should duly have been decked,
Which cutting off through hasty accidents,
Ye would not stay your due time to expect,   430
But promised both to recompense,
Be unto her a goodly ornament,
And for short time an endless monument.

⤙ ☼ ⤚

SIR PHILIP SIDNEY
(*1554–1586*)

·

FROM ARCADIA

YE GOATHERD GODS

STREPHON. Ye goatherd gods, that love the grassy mountains,
Ye nymphs that haunt the springs in pleasant valleys,
Ye satyrs joyed with free and quiet forests,
Vouchsafe your silent ears to plaining music,
Which to my woes give still an early morning,   5
And draws the dolor on till weary evening.

KLAIUS. O Mercury, foregoer to the evening,
O heavenly huntress of the savage mountains,
O lovely star, entitled of the morning,
While that my voice doth fill these woeful valleys,   10
Vouchsafe your silent ears to plaining music,
Which oft hath echo tired in secret forests.

STREPHON. I that was once free-burgess of the forests,
Where shade from sun, and sport I sought at evening,
I that was once esteemed for pleasant music,   15
Am banished now among the monstrous mountains
Of huge despair, and foul affliction's valleys,
Am grown a shriek-owl to myself each morning.

KLAIUS. I that was once delighted every morning,
Hunting the wild inhabiters of forests,   20
I that was once the music of these valleys,
So darkened am, that all my day is evening,
Heartbroken so, that molehills seem high mountains,
And fill the vales with cries instead of music.

STREPHON. Long since alas, my deadly swannish music   25
Hath made itself a crier of the morning,
And hath with wailing strength climbed highest moun-
    tains;
Long since my thoughts more desert be than forests;

8. *heavenly huntress* Diana, goddess of the moon.
9. *star* Venus.

25. *swannish* refers to a traditional view that the swan sang only at the point of death.

18

Long since I see my joys come to their evening,
And state thrown down to overtrodden valleys.   30

KLAIUS.   Long since the happy dwellers of these valleys,
Have prayed me leave my strange exclaiming music,
Which troubles their day's work and joys of evening;
Long since I hate the night, more hate the morning;
Long since my thoughts chase me like beasts in
          forests,   35
And make me wish myself laid under mountains.

STREPHON.   Meseems I see the high and stately mountains
Transform themselves to low dejected valleys;
Meseems I hear in these ill-changéd forests
The nightingales do learn of owls their music;   40
Meseems I feel the comfort of the morning
Turned to the mortal serene of an evening.

KLAIUS.   Meseems I see a filthy cloudy evening
As soon as sun begins to climb the mountains;
Meseems I feel a noisome scent, the morning   45
When I do smell the flowers of these valleys;
Meseems I hear, when I do hear sweet music,
The dreadful cries of murdered men in forests.

STREPHON.   I wish to fire the trees of all those forests;
I give the sun a last farewell each evening;   50
I curse the fiddling finders-out of music;
With envy I do hate the lofty mountains,
And with despite despise the humble valleys;
I do detest night, evening, day, and morning.

KLAIUS.   Curse to myself my prayer is, the morning;   55
My fire is more than can be made with forests,
My state more base, than are the basest valleys.
I wish no evenings more to see, each evening;
Shaméd, I hate myself in sight of mountains,
And stop mine ears, lest I grow mad with music.   60

STREPHON.   For she, whose parts maintained a perfect music,
Whose beauty shined more than the blushing morning,
Who much did pass in state the stately mountains,
In straightness passed the cedars of the forests,
Hath cast me, wretch, into eternal evening,   65
By taking her two suns from these dark valleys.

42. *mortal serene*   a deadly dew.

KLAIUS.   For she, with whom compared, the Alps are valleys,
        She, whose least word brings from the spheres their
           music,
        At whose approach the sun rose in the evening,
        Who, where she went, bare in her forehead morning,   70
        Is gone, is gone, from these our spoiléd forests,
        Turning to deserts our best pastured mountains.

STREPHON. These mountains witness shall, so shall these valleys,
KLAIUS.   These forests eke, made wretched by our music,
        Our morning hymn this is, and song at evening.   75

FROM ASTROPHEL AND STELLA

1

Loving in truth, and fain in verse my love to show,
That she, dear she, might take some pleasure of my pain,
Pleasure might cause her read, reading might make her know,
Knowledge might pity win, and pity grace obtain,
I sought fit words to paint the blackest face of woe,   5
Studying inventions fine, her wits to entertain,
Oft turning others' leaves, to see if thence would flow
Some fresh and fruitful showers upon my sunburnt brain.
But words came halting forth, wanting Invention's stay;
Invention, Nature's child, fled stepdame Study's blows;   10
And others' feet still seemed but strangers in my way.
Thus, great with child to speak, and helpless in my throes,
Biting my truant pen, beating myself for spite,
"Fool," said my Muse to me, "look in thy heart and write."

31

With how sad steps, O Moon, thou climb'st the skies,
How silently, and with how wan a face,
What, may it be that even in heavenly place
That busy archer his sharp arrows tries?
Sure, if that long-with-love-acquainted eyes   5
Can judge of love, thou feel'st a lover's case;
I read it in thy looks, thy languished grace,
To me, that feel the like, thy state descries.
Then, even of fellowship, O Moon, tell me
Is constant love deemed there but want of wit?   10
Are beauties there as proud as here they be?
Do they above love to be loved, and yet
Those lovers scorn whom that love doth possess?
Do they call virtue there ungratefulness?

38

This night while sleep begins with heavy wings
To hatch mine eyes, and that unbitted thought
Doth fall to stray, and my chief powers are brought
To leave the scepter of all subject things,
The first that straight my fancy's error brings   5
Unto my mind, is Stella's image, wrought
By Love's own self, but with so curious draught,
That she, me thinks, not only shines but sings.
I start, look, hark, but what in closed-up sense
Was held, in opened sense it flies away,   10
Leaving me nought but wailing eloquence;
I, seeing better sights in sight's decay,
Called it anew, and wooéd sleep again;
But him her host that unkind guest had slain.

71

Who will in fairest book of Nature know,
How virtue may best lodged in beauty be,
Let him but learn of love to read in thee,
Stella, those fair lines, which true goodness show.
There shall he find all vices' overthrow,   5
Not by rude force, but sweetest sovereignty
Of reason, from whose light those night-birds fly,
That inward sun in thine eyes shineth so.
And not content to be perfection's heir
Thy self, doest strive all minds that way to move,   10
Who mark in thee what is in thee most fair.
So while thy beauty draws the heart to love,
As fast thy virtue bends that love to good:
"But ah," Desire still cries, "give me some food."

. . .

THOU BLIND MAN'S MARK

Thou blind man's mark, thou fool's self-chosen snare,
Fond fancy's scum, and dregs of scattered thought,
Band of all evils, cradle of causeless care,
Thou web of will, whose end is never wrought;
Desire, desire I have too dearly bought,   5
With price of mangled mind, thy worthless ware;

2. *hatch* close. *unbitted* removed the   7. *draught* i.e., draftsmanship.
bit; term from horsemanship.

Too long, too long, asleep thou hast me brought,
Who should my mind to higher things prepare.
But yet in vain thou hast my ruin sought,
In vain thou madest me to vain things aspire,   10
In vain thou kindlest all thy smoky fire;
For virtue hath this better lesson taught,
Within myself to seek my only hire,
Desiring naught but how to kill desire.

LEAVE ME O LOVE

Leave me O Love, which reachest but to dust,
And thou my mind aspire to higher things;
Grow rich in that which never taketh rust;
Whatever fades, but fading pleasure brings.
Draw in thy beams, and humble all thy might,   5
To that sweet yoke, where lasting freedoms be;
Which breaks the clouds and opens forth the light,
That doth both shine and give us sight to see.
O take fast hold; let that light be thy guide,
In this small course which birth draws out to death,   10
And think how evil becometh him to slide,
Who seeketh heaven, and comes of heavenly breath.
Then farewell world, thy uttermost I see;
Eternal Love, maintain thy life in me.

IN WONTED WALKS

In wonted walks, since wonted fancies change,
Some cause there is, which of strange cause doth rise;
For in each thing whereto mine eye doth range,
Part of my pain me seems engravéd lies.
The rocks which were of constant mind the mark   5
In climbing steep, now hard refusal show;
The shading woods seem now my sun to dark,
And stately hills disdain to look so low.
The restful caves now restless visions give,
In dales I see each way a hard ascent,   10
Like late mown meads, late cut from joy I live.
Alas sweet brooks do in my tears augment;
Rocks, woods, hills, caves, dales, meads, brooks, answer me,
Infected minds infect each thing they see.

WILLIAM SHAKESPEARE
(1564–1616)

·

FROM SONNETS

3

Look in thy glass and tell the face thou viewest,
Now is the time that face should form another,
Whose fresh repair if now thou not renewest,
Thou dost beguile the world, unbless some mother.
For where is she so fair whose uneared womb   5
Disdains the tillage of thy husbandry?
Or who is he so fond will be the tomb
Of his self-love, to stop posterity?
Thou art thy mother's glass and she in thee
Calls back the lovely April of her prime;   10
So thou through windows of thine age shalt see,
Despite of wrinkles, this thy golden time.
But if thou live remember'd not to be,
Die single and thine image dies with thee.

15

When I consider every thing that grows
Holds in perfection but a little moment,
That this huge stage presenteth nought but shows
Whereon the stars in secret influence comment;
When I perceive that men as plants increase,   5
Cheeréd and checked even by the self-same sky,
Vaunt in their youthful sap, at height decrease,
And wear their brave state out of memory;
Then the conceit of this inconstant stay
Sets you most rich in youth before my sight,   10
Where wasteful time debateth with decay
To change your day of youth to sullied night,
And all in war with time for love of you,
As he takes from you I engraft you new.

18

Shall I compare thee to a summer's day?
Thou art more lovely and more temperate;

5. *uneared* untilled.   9. *conceit* idea.
7. *fond* foolish.

Rough winds do shake the darling buds of May,
And summer's lease hath all too short a date;
Sometime too hot the eye of heaven shines,   5
And often is his gold complexion dimmed,
And every fair from fair sometimes declines,
By chance or nature's changing course untrimmed;
But thy eternal summer shall not fade,
Nor lose possession of that fair thou ow'st,   10
Nor shall death brag thou wander'st in his shade,
When in eternal lines to time thou grow'st;
So long as men can breathe or eyes can see,
So long lives this and this gives life to thee.

19

Devouring Time, blunt thou the lion's paws,
And make the earth devour her own sweet brood;
Pluck the keen teeth from the fierce tiger's jaws,
And burn the long-lived phœnix in her blood;
Make glad and sorry seasons as thou fleet'st,   5
And do whate'er thou wilt, swift-footed Time,
To the wide world and all her fading sweets;
But I forbid thee one most heinous crime:
O, carve not with thy hours my love's fair brow,
Nor draw no lines there with thine antique pen;   10
Him in thy course untainted do allow
For beauty's pattern to succeeding men.
Yet do thy worst, old Time, despite thy wrong,
My love shall in my verse ever live young.

29

When, in disgrace with fortune and men's eyes,
I all alone beweep my outcast state,
And trouble deaf heaven with my bootless cries,
And look upon myself and curse my fate;
Wishing me like to one more rich in hope,   5
Featured like him, like him with friends possessed,
Desiring this man's art, and that man's scope,
With what I most enjoy contented least;
Yet in these thoughts myself almost despising,
Haply I think on thee, and then my state,   10

10. *ow'st* own.

4. *phœnix* the legendary bird which. after a long life, is consumed in flames and reborn from its own ashes.

10. *antique* (1) old; (2) antic, grotesque.

6. *like him, like him* like one man, like another man.

Like to the lark at break of day arising
From sullen earth, sings hymns at heaven's gate;
For thy sweet love remembered such wealth brings
That then I scorn to change my state with kings.

33

Full many a glorious morning have I seen
Flatter the mountain-tops with sovereign eye,
Kissing with golden face the meadows green,
Gilding pale streams with heavenly alchemy;
Anon permit the basest clouds to ride,   5
With ugly rack on his celestial face,
And from the forlorn world his visage hide
Stealing unseen to west with this disgrace;
Even so my sun one early morn did shine,
With all-triumphant splendor on my brow;   10
But, out, alack, he was but one hour mine,
The region cloud hath masked him from me now.
Yet him for this my love no whit disdaineth,
Suns of the world may stain, when heaven's sun staineth.

49

Against that time, if ever that time come,
When I shall see thee frown on my defects,
When as thy love hath cast his utmost sum,
Called to that audit by advised respects;
Against that time when thou shalt strangely pass,   5
And scarcely greet me with that sun, thine eye,
When love converted from the thing it was
Shall reasons find of settled gravity;
Against that time do I ensconce me here
Within the knowledge of mine own desert,   10
And this my hand, against myself uprear,
To guard the lawful reasons on thy part;
To leave poor me, thou hast the strength of laws,
Since why to love, I can allege no cause.

53

What is your substance, whereof are you made,
That millions of strange shadows on you tend?
Since every one hath, every one, one shade,
And you but one, can every shadow lend;

4. *respects* points of view.

Describe Adonis and the counterfeit   5
Is poorly imitated after you;
On Helen's cheek all art of beauty set,
And you in Grecian tires are painted new;
Speak of the spring and foison of the year,
The one doth shadow of your beauty show,   10
The other as your bounty doth appear,
And you in every blessed shape we know.
In all external grace you have some part,
But you like none, none you for constant heart.

55

Not marble, nor the gilded monuments
Of princes shall outlive this powerful rhyme,
But you shall shine more bright in these contents
Than unswept stone, besmeared with sluttish time.
When wasteful war shall statues overturn,   5
And broils root out the work of masonry,
Nor Mars his sword, nor war's quick fire shall burn
The living record of your memory.
'Gainst death, and all oblivious enmity
Shall you pace forth; your praise shall still find room,   10
Even in the eyes of all posterity
That wear this world out to the ending doom.
So, till the judgment that yourself arise,
You live in this, and dwell in lovers' eyes.

60

Like as the waves make towards the pebbled shore,
So do our minutes hasten to their end,
Each changing place with that which goes before,
In sequent toil all forwards do contend.
Nativity once in the main of light   5
Crawls to maturity, wherewith being crown'd,
Crooked eclipses 'gainst his glory fight,
And Time that gave, doth now his gift confound.
Time doth transfix the flourish set on youth,
And delves the parallels in beauty's brow,   10
Feeds on the rarities of nature's truth,
And nothing stands but for his scythe to mow.
And yet to times in hope my verse shall stand
Praising thy worth, despite his cruel hand.

8. *tires* attire.   13. *judgment that* Judgment Day
9. *foison* harvest, abundance.   when.

64

When I have seen by Time's fell hand defaced
The rich-proud cost of outworn buried age;
When sometime lofty towers I see down-razed,
And brass eternal slave to mortal rage;
When I have seen the hungry ocean gain   5
Advantage on the kingdom of the shore,
And the firm soil win of the wat'ry main,
Increasing store with loss, and loss with store;
When I have seen such interchange of state,
Or state itself confounded, to decay,   10
Ruin hath taught me thus to ruminate
That Time will come and take my love away.
This thought is as a death which cannot choose
But weep to have that which it fears to lose.

65

Since brass, nor stone, nor earth, nor boundless sea,
But sad mortality o'er-sways their power,
How with this rage shall beauty hold a plea,
Whose action is no stronger than a flower?
O how shall summer's honey breath hold out,   5
Against the wrackful siege of battering days,
When rocks impregnable are not so stout,
Nor gates of steel so strong but Time decays?
O fearful meditation, where, alack,
Shall Time's best jewel from Time's chest lie hid?   10
Or what strong hand can hold his swift foot back,
Or who his spoil of beauty can forbid?
O none, unless this miracle have might,
That in black ink my love may still shine bright.

73

That time of year thou mayst in me behold,
When yellow leaves, or none, or few, do hang
Upon those boughs which shake against the cold,
Bare ruined choirs, where late the sweet birds sang.
In me thou see'st the twilight of such day,   5
As after sunset fadeth in the west,
Which by and by black night doth take away,
Death's second self that seals up all in rest.
In me thou see'st the glowing of such fire,

That on the ashes of his youth doth lie,   10
As the deathbed, whereon it must expire,
Consumed with that which it was nourished by.
This thou perceiv'st, which makes thy love more strong,
To love that well, which thou must leave ere long.

87

Farewell, thou art too dear for my possessing,
And like enough thou know'st thy estimate;
The charter of thy worth gives thee releasing;
My bonds in thee are all determinate.
For how do I hold thee but by thy granting,   5
And for that riches where is my deserving?
The cause of this fair gift in me is wanting,
And so my patent back again is swerving.
Thyself thou gavest, thy own worth then not knowing,
Or me to whom thou gavest it, else mistaking;   10
So thy great gift, upon misprision growing,
Comes home again, on better judgment making.
Thus have I had thee as a dream doth flatter,
In sleep a king, but waking no such matter.

94

They that have power to hurt, and will do none,
That do not do the thing they most do show,
Who moving others, are themselves as stone,
Unmovéd, cold, and to temptation slow;
They rightly do inherit heaven's graces,   5
And husband nature's riches from expense;
They are the lords and owners of their faces,
Others, but stewards of their excellence.
The summer's flower is to the summer sweet,
Though to itself, it only live and die,   10
But if that flower with base infection meet,
The basest weed outbraves his dignity;
For sweetest things turn sourest by their deeds,
Lilies that fester smell far worse than weeds.

98

From you have I been absent in the spring,
When proud-pied April, dress'd in all his trim,

---

11. *misprision* misunderstanding.   2. *pied* parti-colored.

Hath put a spirit of youth in every thing,
That heavy Saturn laughed and leaped with him.
Yet nor the lays of birds, nor the sweet smell   5
Of different flowers in odor and in hue,
Could make me any summer's story tell,
Or from their proud lap pluck them where they grew;
Nor did I wonder at the lily's white,
Nor praise the deep vermilion in the rose;   10
They were but sweet, but figures of delight,
Drawn after you, you pattern of all those.
Yet seem'd it winter still, and, you away,
As with your shadow I with these did play.

104

To me, fair friend, you never can be old,
For as you were when first your eye I eyed,
Such seems your beauty still. Three winters' cold
Have from the forests shook three summers' pride;
Three beauteous springs to yellow autumn turned,   5
In process of the seasons have I seen;
Three April perfumes in three hot Junes burned,
Since first I saw you fresh which yet are green.
Ah yet doth beauty like a dial-hand
Steal from his figure, and no pace perceived;   10
So your sweet hue, which methinks still doth stand
Hath motion, and mine eye may be deceived.
For fear of which, hear this thou age unbred;
Ere you were born was beauty's summer dead.

121

'Tis better to be vile than vile esteemed,
When not to be, receives reproach of being,
And the just pleasure lost, which is so deemed,
Not by our feeling, but by others' seeing.
For why should others' false adulterate eyes   5
Give salutation to my sportive blood?
Or on my frailties why are frailer spies,
Which in their wills count bad what I think good?
No, I am that I am, and they that level
At my abuses, reckon up their own;   10
I may be straight, though they themselves be bevel;
By their rank thoughts, my deeds must not be shown

---

4. *Saturn* the melancholy planet.   11. *bevel* oblique, hence crooked.

Unless this general evil they maintain,
All men are bad and in their badness reign.

129

Th' expense of spirit in a waste of shame
Is lust in action, and till action, lust
Is perjured, murderous, bloody, full of blame,
Savage, extreme, rude, cruel, not to trust,
Enjoyed no sooner but despiséd straight,   5
Past reason hunted, and no sooner had
Past reason hated as a swallowed bait,
On purpose laid to make the taker mad:
Mad in pursuit and in possession so,
Had, having, and in quest to have, extreme;   10
A bliss in proof and proved a very woe,
Before a joy proposed, behind a dream;
All this the world well knows yet none knows well,
To shun the heaven that leads men to this hell.

146

Poor soul the center of my sinful earth,
[Thrall to] these rebel powers that thee array,
Why dost thou pine within and suffer dearth
Painting thy outward walls so costly gay?
Why so large cost having so short a lease,   5
Dost thou upon thy fading mansion spend?
Shall worms inheritors of this excess
Eat up thy charge? Is this thy body's end?
Then soul live thou upon thy servant's loss,
And let that pine to aggravate thy store;   10
Buy terms divine in selling hours of dross;
Within be fed, without be rich no more;
So shalt thou feed on death, that feeds on men,
And death once dead, there's no more dying then.

‐< ☼ >‐

JOHN DONNE
(1572–1631)

·

THE CANONIZATION

For God's sake hold your tongue, and let me love,
    Or chide my palsy, or my gout,
My five gray hairs, or ruined fortune flout,
      With wealth your state, your mind with arts improve,
        Take you a course, get you a place,   5
        Observe his honor, or his grace,
Or the king's real, or his stampéd face;
    Contemplate, what you will approve,
    So you will let me love.

Alas, alas, who's injured by my love?   10
    What merchant's ships have my sighs drowned?
Who says my tears have overflowed his ground?
    When did my colds a forward spring remove?
      When did the heats which my veins fill
      Add one more to the plaguey bill?   15
Soldiers find wars, and lawyers find out still
    Litigious men, which quarrels move,
    Though she and I do love.

Call us what you will, we are made such by love;
    Call her one, me another fly,   20
We are tapers too, and at our own cost die,
    And we in us find the eagle and the dove.
      The phoenix riddle hath more wit
      By us, we two being one, are it.
So to one neutral thing both sexes fit,   25
    We die and rise the same, and prove
    Mysterious by this love.

We can die by it, if not live by love,
    And if unfit for tombs and hearse
Our legend be, it will be fit for verse;   30
    And if no piece of chronicle we prove,
      We'll build in sonnets pretty rooms;
      As well a well-wrought urn becomes

23. *phoenix* a mythological bird, of which only one existed, that rose from its
own ashes.

The greatest ashes, as half-acre tombs,
  And by these hymns, all shall approve   35
  Us canonized for love;

And thus invoke us: you whom reverend love
  Made one another's hermitage;
You, to whom love was peace, that now is rage;
  Who did the whole world's soul contract, and drove   40
    Into the glasses of your eyes
    (So made such mirrors, and such spies,
That they did all to you epitomize),
  Countries, towns, courts; beg from above
  A pattern of your love!   45

THE APPARITION

When by thy scorn, O murderess, I am dead,
And that thou thinkst thee free
From all solicitation from me,
Then shall my ghost come to thy bed,
And thee, feigned vestal, in worse arms shall see;   5
Then thy sick taper will begin to wink,
And he, whose thou art then, being tired before,
Will, if thou stir, or pinch to wake him, think
    Thou call'st for more,
And in false sleep will from thee shrink,   10
And then poor aspen wretch, neglected thou
Bathed in a cold quicksilver sweat wilt lie
    A verier ghost than I;
What I will say, I will not tell thee now,
Lest that preserve thee; and since my love is spent,   15
I had rather thou shouldst painfully repent,
Than by my threatenings rest still innocent.

A VALEDICTION: FORBIDDING MOURNING

As virtuous men pass mildly away,
  And whisper to their souls, to go,
Whilst some of their sad friends do say,
  The breath goes now, and some say, No;

So let us melt, and make no noise,   5
    No tear-floods, nor sigh-tempests move,
'Twere profanation of our joys
    To tell the laity our love.

Moving of th' earth brings harms and fears,
    Men reckon what it did and meant,   10
But trepidation of the spheres,
    Though greater far, is innocent.

Dull sublunary lovers' love
    (Whose soul is sense) cannot admit
Absence, because it doth remove   15
    Those things which elemented it.

But we by a love, so much refined,
    That our selves know not what it is,
Inter-assuréd of the mind,
    Care less, eyes, lips, and hands to miss.   20

Our two souls therefore, which are one,
    Though I must go, endure not yet
A breach, but an expansion,
    Like gold to airy thinness beat.

If they be two, they are two so   25
    As stiff twin compasses are two;
Thy soul the fixed foot makes no show
    To move, but doth, if the other do.

And though it in the center sit,
    Yet when the other far doth roam,   30
It leans, and hearkens after it,
    And grows erect, as that comes home.

Such wilt thou be to me, who must
    Like th' other foot, obliquely run;
Thy firmness makes my circle just,   35
    And makes me end, where I begun.

THE SUN RISING

    Busy old fool, unruly sun,
    Why dost thou thus,
Through windows and through curtains call on us?

Must to thy motions lovers' seasons run?
    Saucy, pedantic wretch, go chide   5
    Late schoolboys, and sour prentices,
  Go tell court huntsmen that the king will ride,
  Call country ants to harvest offices;
Love, all alike, no season knows nor clime,
Nor hours, days, months, which are the rags of time.   10

    Thy beams, so reverend and strong,
    Why shouldst thou think?
I could eclipse and cloud them with a wink,
But that I would not lose her sight so long;
    If her eyes have not blinded thine,   15
    Look, and tomorrow late, tell me
  Whether both the Indias of spice and mine
  Be where thou left'st them, or lie here with me.
Ask for those kings whom thou saw'st yesterday,
And thou shalt hear, all here in one bed lay.   20

    She is all states, and all princes, I;
    Nothing else is.
Princes do but play us; compared to this,
All honor's mimic, all wealth alchemy.
    Thou sun art half as happy as we,   25
    In that the world's contracted thus;
  Thine age asks ease, and since thy duties be
  To warm the world, that's done in warming us.
Shine here to us, and thou art everywhere;
This bed thy center is, these walls thy sphere.   30

AIR AND ANGELS

Twice or thrice had I loved thee,
Before I knew thy face or name;
So in a voice, so in a shapeless flame,
Angels affect us oft, and worshiped be;
    Still when, to where thou wert, I came,   5
Some lovely glorious nothing I did see.
    But since my soul, whose child love is,
Takes limbs of flesh, and else could nothing do,
    More subtle than the parent is,

17. *Indias of spice and mine* East Indies of spices and West Indies of gold
mines.

Love must not be, but take a body too,   10
    And therefore what thou wert, and who,
        I bid Love ask, and now
That it assume thy body, I allow,
And fix itself in thy lip, eye, and brow.

Whilst thus to ballast love, I thought,   15
And so more steadily to have gone,
With wares which would sink admiration,
I saw I had love's pinnace overfraught;
    Every thy hair for love to work upon
Is much too much, some fitter must be sought;   20
    For, nor in nothing, nor in things
Extreme, and scatt'ring bright, can love inhere;
    Then as an angel, face and wings
Of air, not pure as it, yet pure doth wear,
    So thy love may be my love's sphere;   25
        Just such disparity
As is 'twixt air and angels' purity,
'Twixt women's love and men's will ever be.

A VALEDICTION: OF WEEPING

        Let me pour forth
My tears before thy face, whilst I stay here,
For thy face coins them, and thy stamp they bear,
And by this mintage they are something worth,
        For thus they be   5
        Pregnant of thee;
Fruits of much grief they are, emblems of more—
When a tear falls, that thou fall'st which it bore,
So thou and I are nothing then, when on a diverse shore.

        On a round ball   10
A workman that hath copies by, can lay
An Europe, Afric, and an Asia,
And quickly make that, which was nothing, all;
        So doth each tear
        Which thee doth wear,   15
A globe, yea world by that impression grow,
Till thy tears mixed with mine do overflow
This world, by waters sent from thee, my heaven dissolvéd so.

O more than moon,
Draw not up seas to drown me in thy sphere,   20
Weep me not dead, in thine arms, but forbear
To teach the sea what it may do too soon;
      Let not the wind
      Example find
To do me more harm than it purposeth;   25
Since thou and I sigh one another's breath,
Whoe'er sighs most is cruelest, and hastes the other's death.

THE FUNERAL

Whoever comes to shroud me, do not harm
      Nor question much
That subtle wreath of hair which crowns my arm;
The mystery, the sign you must not touch,
      For 'tis my outward soul,   5
Viceroy to that, which then to heaven being gone,
      Will leave this to control,
And keep these limbs, her provinces, from dissolution.

For if the sinewy thread my brain lets fall
      Through every part   10
Can tie those parts, and make me one of all;
These hairs which upward grew, and strength and art
      Have from a better brain,
Can better do it; except she meant that I
      By this should know my pain,   15
As prisoners then are manacled, when they are condemned
      to die.

Whate'er she meant by it, bury it with me,
      For since I am
Love's martyr, it might breed idolatry,
If into others' hands these relics came;   20
      As 'twas humility
To afford to it all that a soul can do,
      So, 'tis some bravery
That since you would save none of me, I bury some of you.

FROM HOLY SONNETS

1

Thou hast made me, and shall thy work decay?
Repair me now, for now mine end doth haste,

I run to death, and death meets me as fast,
And all my pleasures are like yesterday;
I dare not move my dim eyes any way,   5
Despair behind, and death before doth cast
Such terror, and my feeble flesh doth waste
By sin in it, which it towards hell doth weigh;
Only thou art above, and when towards thee
By thy leave I can look, I rise again;   10
But our old subtle foe so tempteth me,
That not one hour myself I can sustain;
Thy grace may wing me to prevent his art,
And thou like adamant draw mine iron heart.

7

At the round earth's imagined corners, blow
Your trumpets, angels; and arise, arise
From death, you numberless infinities
Of souls, and to your scattered bodies go,
All whom the flood did, and fire shall, o'erthrow,   5
All whom war, dearth, age, agues, tyrannies,
Despair, law, chance hath slain, and you whose eyes
Shall behold God, and never taste death's woe.
But let them sleep, Lord, and me mourn a space,
For, if above all these, my sins abound,   10
'Tis late to ask abundance of thy grace
When we are there; here on this lowly ground,
Teach me how to repent; for that's as good
As if thou hadst sealed my pardon with thy blood.

10

Death, be not proud, though some have callèd thee
Mighty and dreadful, for thou art not so;
For those whom thou think'st thou dost overthrow
Die not, poor death, nor yet canst thou kill me.
From rest and sleep, which but thy pictures be,   5
Much pleasure; then from thee much more must flow,
And soonest our best men with thee do go,
Rest of their bones, and soul's delivery.
Thou art slave to fate, chance, kings, and desperate men,
And dost with poison, war, and sickness dwell,   10
And poppy or charms can make us sleep as well,
And better than thy stroke; why swell'st thou then?
One short sleep past, we wake eternally,
And death shall be no more; death, thou shalt die.

14

Batter my heart, three-personed God; for you
As yet but knock, breathe, shine, and seek to mend;
That I may rise, and stand, o'erthrow me, and bend
Your force to break, blow, burn, and make me new.
I, like an usurped town, to another due,   5
Labor to admit you, but O, to no end;
Reason, your viceroy in me, me should defend,
But is captived, and proves weak or untrue.
Yet dearly I love you, and would be lovéd fain,
But am betrothed unto your enemy.   10
Divorce me, untie, or break that knot again;
Take me to you, imprison me, for I,
Except you enthrall me, never shall be free,
Nor ever chaste, except you ravish me.

. . .

HYMN TO GOD MY GOD,
IN MY SICKNESS

Since I am coming to that holy room,
   Where, with thy choir of saints for evermore,
I shall be made thy music; as I come
    I tune the instrument here at the door,
    And what I must do then, think here before.   5

Whilst my physicians by their love are grown
   Cosmographers, and I their map, who lie
Flat on this bed, that by them may be shown
    That this is my southwest discovery
    Per fretum febris, by these straits to die,   10

I joy, that in these straits, I see my West,
   For, though their currents yield return to none,
What shall my West hurt me? As West and East
    In all flat maps (and I am one) are one,
    So death doth touch the Resurrection.   15

Is the Pacific sea my home? Or are
   The Eastern riches? Is Jerusalem?
Anyan, and Magellan, and Gibraltar,
    All straits, and none but straits, are ways to them,
    Whether where Japhet dwelt, or Cham, or Shem.   20

10. *per fretum febris* through the strait of fever.
20. *Japhet, Cham, Shem* the sons of Noah whose offspring overspread the earth.

We think that Paradise and Calvary,
    Christ's cross, and Adam's tree, stood in one place;
Look Lord, and find both Adams met in me;
    As the first Adam's sweat surrounds my face,
    May the last Adam's blood my soul embrace.   25

So, in his purple wrapped, receive me, Lord;
    By these his thorns give me his other crown;
And, as to others' souls I preached thy word,
    Be this my text, my sermon to mine own,
    Therefore that he may raise the Lord throws down.   30

BEN JONSON
(1572–1637)

·

ON MY FIRST SON

Farewell, thou child of my right hand, and joy;
My sin was too much hope of thee, loved boy,
Seven years thou wert lent to me, and I thee pay,
Exacted by thy fate, on the just day.
O, could I lose all father now. For why   5
Will man lament the state he should envy?
To have so soon 'scaped world's and flesh's rage,
And, if no other misery, yet age?
Rest in soft peace, and, asked, say, "Here doth lie
Ben Jonson his best piece of poetry."   10
For whose sake henceforth all his vows be such,
As what he loves may never like too much.

ON LUCY, COUNTESS OF BEDFORD

This morning, timely rapt with holy fire,
    I thought to form unto my zealous Muse
What kind of creature I could most desire
    To honor, serve, and love, as poets use.
I meant to make her fair and free and wise,   5
    Of greatest blood, and yet more good than great;
I meant the day-star should not brighter rise,
    Nor lend like influence from his lucent seat.
I meant she should be courteous, facile, sweet,
    Hating that solemn vice of greatness, pride;   10
I meant each softest virtue there should meet,
    Fit in that softer bosom to reside.
Only a learnéd and a manly soul
    I purposed her, that should, with even powers,
The rock, the spindle, and the shears control   15
    Of destiny, and spin her own free hours.
Such when I meant to feign, and wished to see,
    My Muse bade, Bedford write, and that was she.

1. *child of my right hand*   Hebrew meaning of the name Benjamin.

INVITING A FRIEND TO SUPPER

Tonight, grave sir, both my poor house and I
Do equally desire your company;
Not that we think us worthy such a guest,
But that your worth will dignify our feast,
With those that come, whose grace may make that seem   5
Something, which else could hope for no esteem.
It is the fair acceptance, sir, creates
The entertainment perfect, not the cates.
Yet shall you have, to rectify your palate,
An olive, capers, or some better salad   10
Ushering the mutton; with a short-legged hen,
If we can get her, full of eggs; and then,
Lemons, and wine for sauce: to these, a cony
Is not to be despaired of for our money;
And though fowl now be scarce, yet there are clerks,   15
The sky not falling, think we may have larks.
I'll tell you of more, and lie, so you will come:
Of partridge, pheasant, woodcock, of which some
May yet be there; and godwit if we can:
Gnat, rail, and ruff, too. Howsoe'er, my man   20
Shall read a piece of Virgil, Tacitus,
Livy, or of some better book to us,
Of which we'll speak our minds, amidst our meat;
And I'll profess no verses to repeat:
To this, if aught appear, which I not know of,   25
That will the pastry, not my paper, show of.
Digestive cheese, and fruit there sure will be;
But that which most doth take my muse and me,
Is a pure cup of rich Canary wine,
Which is the Mermaid's now, but shall be mine: 30
Of which had Horace, or Anacreon tasted,
Their lives, as do their lines, till now had lasted.
Tobacco, nectar, or the Thespian spring,
Are all but Luther's beer, to this I sing.
Of this we will sup free, but moderately,   35
And we will have no Pooly or Parrot by;
Nor shall our cups make any guilty men,
But at our parting, we will be as when
We innocently met. No simple word

30. *Mermaid's* Mermaid Tavern.
36. *Pooly or Parrot* probably two state informers.

That shall be uttered at our mirthful board   40
Shall make us sad next morning, or affright
The liberty that we'll enjoy tonight.

EPITAPH ON S. P., A CHILD OF QUEEN ELIZABETH'S CHAPEL

Weep with me all you that read
   This little story;
And know, for whom a tear you shed,
   Death's self is sorry.
'Twas a child, that so did thrive   5
   In grace and feature,
As Heaven and Nature seemed to strive
   Which owned the creature.
Years he numbered scarce thirteen
   When Fates turned cruel,   10
Yet three filled zodiacs had he been
   The stage's jewel;
And did act (what now we moan)
   Old men so duly,
As, sooth, the Parcae thought him one,   15
   He played so truly.
So, by error, to his fate
   They all consented;
But viewing him since (alas, too late)
   They have repented.   20
And have sought, to give new birth,
   In baths to steep him;
But, being so much too good for earth,
   Heaven vows to keep him.

TO WILLIAM ROE

Roe (and my joy to name) th'art now to go
Countries, and climes, manners, and men to know,
T'extract, and choose the best of all these known,
And those to turn to blood, and make thine own.
May winds as soft as breath of kissing friends   5
Attend thee hence; and there, may all thy ends,
As the beginnings here, prove purely sweet,
And perfect in a circle always meet.
So, when we, blest with thy return, shall see

15. *Parcae*   the Fates.

Thyself, with thy first thoughts, brought home by thee,   10
We each to other may this voice inspire;
This is that good Aeneas passed through fire,
Through seas, storms, tempests: and embarked for hell,
Came back untouched. This man hath travailed well.

TO PENSHURST

Thou art not, Penshurst, built to envious show,
Of touch, or marble; nor canst boast a row
Of polished pillars, or a roof of gold:
Thou hast no lantern, whereof tales are told;
Or stair, or courts; but stand'st an ancient pile,   5
And these grudged at, art reverenced the while.
Thou joy'st in better marks, of soil, of air,
Of wood, of water: therein thou art fair.
Thou hast thy walks for health, as well as sport:
Thy mount, to which the Dryads do resort,   10
Where Pan and Bacchus their high feasts have made,
Beneath the broad beech, and the chestnut shade;
That taller tree, which of a nut was set,
At his great birth, where all the Muses met.
There, in the writhéd bark, are cut the names   15
Of many a sylvan, taken with his flames.
And thence, the ruddy Satyrs oft provoke
The lighter Fauns, to reach thy lady's oak.
Thy copse, too, named of Gamage, thou hast there,
That never fails to serve thee seasoned deer,   20
When thou would'st feast, or exercise thy friends.
The lower land, that to the river bends,
Thy sheep, thy bullocks, kine, and calves do feed:
The middle grounds thy mares, and horses breed.
Each bank doth yield thee conies and the tops   25
Fertile of wood, Ashore, and Sydney's copse,
To crown thy open table, doth provide
The purpled pheasant, with the speckled side:
The painted partridge lies in every field,
And, for thy mess, is willing to be killed.   30
And if the high swol'n Medway fail thy dish,
Thou hast thy ponds, that pay thee tribute fish,
Fat, aged carps, that run into thy net.
And pikes, now weary their own kind to eat,
As loath, the second draught, or cast to stay,   35
Officiously, at first, themselves betray.

Bright eels, that emulate them, and leap on land,
Before the fisher, or into his hand.
Then hath thy orchard fruit, thy garden flowers,
Fresh as the air, and new as are the hours.   40
The early cherry, with the later plum,
Fig, grape, and quince, each in his time doth come:
The blushing apricot, and woolly peach
Hang on thy walls, that every child may reach.
And though thy walls be of the country stone,   45
They are reared with no man's ruin, no man's groan,
There's none, that dwell about them, wish them down;
But all come in, the farmer, and the clown:
And no one empty-handed, to salute
Thy lord, and lady, though they have no suit.   50
Some bring a capon, some a rural cake,
Some nuts, some apples; some that think they make
The better cheeses, bring them; or else send
By their ripe daughters, whom they would commend
This way to husbands; and whose baskets bear   55
An emblem of themselves, in plum, or pear.
But what can this (more than express their love)
Add to thy free provisions, far above
The need of such? whose liberal board doth flow,
With all, that hospitality doth know!   60
Where comes no guest, but is allowed to eat,
Without his fear, and of the lord's own meat:
Where the same beer, and bread, and self-same wine,
That is his lordship's, shall be also mine.
And I not fain to sit (as some, this day,   65
At great men's tables) and yet dine away.
Here no man tells my cups; nor, standing by,
A waiter doth my gluttony envy:
But gives me what I call, and lets me eat,
He knows, below, he shall find plenty of meat,   70
Thy tables hoard not up for the next day,
Nor, when I take my lodging, need I pray
For fire, or lights, or livory: all is there;
As if thou, then, wert mine, or I reigned here:
There's nothing I can wish, for which I stay.   75
That found King James, when hunting late, this way,
With his brave son, the Prince, they saw thy fires
Shine bright on every hearth as the desires
Of thy Penates had been set on flame,
To entertain them; or the country came,   80

73. *livory* provision.   79. *Penates* household gods.

With all their zeal, to warm their welcome here.
What (great, I will not say, but) sudden cheer
Did'st thou, then, make them! and what praise was heaped
On thy good lady, then! who, therein, reaped
The just reward of her high huswifery;   85
To have her linen, plate, and all things nigh,
When she was far: and not a room, but dressed,
As if it had expected such a guest!
These, Penshurst, are thy praise, and yet not all.
Thy lady's noble, fruitful, chaste withall.   90
His children thy great lord may call his own:
A fortune, in this age, but rarely known.
They are, and have been taught religion: thence
Their gentler spirits have sucked innocence.
Each morn, and even, they are taught to pray,   95
With the whole household, and may, every day,
Read, in their virtuous parents' noble parts,
The mysteries of manners, arms, and arts.
Now, Penshurst, they that will proportion thee
With other edifices, when they see   100
Those proud, ambitious heaps, and nothing else,
May say, their lords have built, but thy lord dwells.

AN ELEGY

Though beauty be the mark of praise,
   And yours of whom I sing be such
   As not the world can praise too much,
Yet is't your virtue now I raise.

A virtue, like allay, so gone   5
   Throughout your form as, though that move
   And draw and conquer all men's love,
This subjects you to love of one.

Wherein you triumph yet; because
   'Tis of yourself, and that you use   10
   The noblest freedom, not to choose
Against or faith or honor's laws.

But who should less expect from you,
   In whom alone Love lives again?
   By whom he is restored to men,   15
And kept, and bred, and brought up true.

5. *allay* alloy.

His falling temples you have reared,
  The withered garlands ta'en away;
  His altars kept from the decay
That envy wished, and nature feared;   20

And on them burn so chaste a flame,
  With so much loyalty's expense,
  As Love, t'acquit such excellence,
Is gone himself into your name.

And you are he, the deity   25
  To whom all lovers are designed
  That would their better objects find;
Among which faithful troop am I.

Who, as an offering at your shrine,
  Have sung this hymn, and here entreat   30
  One spark of your diviner heat
To light upon a love of mine.

Which, if it kindle not, but scant
  Appear, and that to shortest view,
  Yet give me leave t'adore in you   35
What I, in her, am grieved to want.

AN ODE

  High spirited friend,
I send nor balms, nor cor'sives to your wound;
  Your fate hath found
A gentler, and more agile hand, to tend
The cure of that, which is but corporal,   5
And doubtful days (which were named critical)
  Have made their fairest flight,
  And now are out of sight.
Yet doth some wholesome physic for the mind,
  Wrapped in this paper lie,   10
Which in the taking if you misapply,
  You are unkind.

  Your covetous hand,
Happy in that fair honor it hath gained,
  Must now be reined.   15

2. *cor'sives* corrosives.

True valor doth her own renown command
In one full action; nor have you now more
To do, than be a husband of that store.
  Think but how dear you bought
  This same which you have caught, 20
Such thoughts will make you more in love with truth.
  'Tis wisdom, and that high,
For men to use their fortune reverently,
    Even in youth.

TO HEAVEN

Good and great God, can I not think of thee,
But it must straight my melancholy be?
Is it interpreted in me disease,
That, laden with my sins, I seek for ease?
O, be thou witness, that the reins dost know 5
And hearts of all, if I be sad for show,
And judge me after, if I dare pretend
To aught but grace, or aim at other end.
As thou art all, so be thou all to me,
First, midst, and last, converted one and three; 10
My faith, my hope, my love; and in this state,
My judge, my witness, and my advocate.
Where have I been this while exiled from thee?
And whither rapt, now thou but stoop'st to me?
Dwell, dwell here still: O, being everywhere, 15
How can I doubt to find thee ever, here?
I know my state, both full of shame and scorn,
Conceived in sin, and unto labor born,
Standing with fear, and must with horror fall,
And destined unto judgment, after all. 20
I feel my griefs too, and there scarce is ground
Upon my flesh t'inflict another wound.
Yet dare I not complain or wish for death
With holy Paul, lest it be thought the breath
Of discontent; or that these prayers be 25
For weariness of life, not love of thee.

GEORGE HERBERT
(*1593–1633*)

·

REDEMPTION

Having been tenant long to a rich lord,
Not thriving, I resolved to be bold,
And make a suit unto him, to afford
A new small-rented lease, and cancel th' old.
In heaven at his manor I him sought:
They told me there, that he was lately gone
About some land, which he had dearly bought
Long since on earth, to take possession.
I straight returned, and knowing his great birth,
Sought him accordingly in great resorts,
In cities, theaters, gardens, parks, and courts.
At length I heard a ragged noise and mirth
Of thieves and murderers: there I him espied,
Who straight, *Your suit is granted*, said, and died.

AFFLICTION (I)

When first thou didst entice to thee my heart,
             I thought the service brave;
So many joys I writ down for my part,
             Besides what I might have
Out of my stock of natural delights,
Augmented with thy gracious benefits.

I lookéd on thy furniture so fine,
             And made it fine to me;
Thy glorious household-stuff did me entwine,
             And 'tice me unto thee.
Such stars I counted mine: both heaven and earth
Paid me my wages in a world of mirth.

What pleasures could I want, whose king I served,
             Where joys my fellows were?
Thus argued into hopes, my thoughts reserved
             No place for grief or fear.
Therefore my sudden soul caught at the place,
And made her youth and fierceness seek thy face.

At first thou gav'st me milk and sweetnesses;
            I had my wish and way.   20
My days were straw'd with flowers and happiness;
            There was no month but May.
But with my years sorrow did twist and grow,
And made a party unawares for woe.

My flesh began unto my soul in pain,   25
            Sicknesses cleave my bones;
Consuming agues dwell in every vein,
            And tune my breath to groans.
Sorrow was all my soul; I scarce believed,
Till grief did tell me roundly, that I lived.   30

When I got health, thou took'st away my life,
            And more; for my friends die.
My mirth and edge was lost; a blunted knife
            Was of more use than I.
Thus thin and lean without a fence or friend,   35
I was blown through with every storm and wind.

Whereas my birth and spirit rather took
            The way that takes the town;
Thou didst betray me to a lingering book,
            And wrap me in a gown.   40
I was entangled in the world of strife,
Before I had the power to change my life.

Yet, for I threatened oft the siege to raise,
            Not simpering all mine age,
Thou often didst with academic praise   45
            Melt and dissolve my rage.
I took thy sweetened pill, till I came where
I could not go away, nor persevere.

Yet lèst perchance I should too happy be
            In my unhappiness,   50
Turning my purge to food, thou throwest me
            Into more sicknesses.
Thus doth thy power cross-bias me, not making
Thine own gift good, yet me from my ways taking.

Now I am here, what thou wilt do with me   55
            None of my books will show.

53. *cross-bias me* give me an inclination other than my own (a term in the
game of bowls).

I read, and sigh, and wish I were a tree;
            For sure then I should grow
To fruit or shade: at least some bird would trust
Her household to me, and I should be just.   60

Yet, though thou troublest me, I must be meek;
            In weakness must be stout.
Well, I will change the service, and go seek
            Some other master out.
Ah my dear God! though I am clean forgot,   65
Let me not love thee, if I love thee not.

THE WINDOWS

Lord, how can man preach thy eternal word?
            He is a brittle crazy glass;
Yet in thy temple thou dost him afford
            This glorious and transcendent place,
            To be a window, through thy grace.   5

But when thou dost anneal in glass thy story,
            Making thy life to shine within
The holy preachers, then the light and glory
            More reverend grows, and more doth win,
            Which else shows waterish, bleak, and thin.   10

Doctrine and life, colors and light, in one
            When they combine and mingle, bring
A strong regard and awe; but speech alone
            Doth vanish like a flaring thing,
            And in the ear, not conscience ring.   15

VIRTUE

Sweet day, so cool, so calm, so bright,
The bridal of the earth and sky;
The dew shall weep thy fall tonight,
            For thou must die.

Sweet rose, whose hue angry and brave   5
Bids the rash gazer wipe his eye;
Thy root is ever in its grave,
            And thou must die.

6. *anneal*   fix the colors by heating.

Sweet spring, full of sweet days and roses,
A box where sweets compacted lie;   10
My music shows ye have your closes,
    And all must die.

Only a sweet and virtuous soul,
Like seasoned timber, never gives;
But though the whole world turn to coal,   15
    Then chiefly lives.

LIFE

I made a posy, while the day ran by;
Here will I smell my remnant out, and tie
    My life within this band.
But Time did beckon to the flowers, and they
By noon most cunningly did steal away,   5
    And withered in my hand.

My hand was next to them, and then my heart;
I took, without more thinking, in good part
    Time's gentle admonition:
Who did so sweetly death's sad taste convey,   10
Making my mind to smell my fatal day;
    Yet sugaring the suspicion.

Farewell, dear flowers, sweetly your time ye spent,
Fit, while ye lived, for smell or ornament,
    And after death for cures.   15
I follow straight without complaints or grief,
Since if my scent be good, I care not if
    It be as short as yours.

THE COLLAR

I struck the board, and cried, "No more.
    I will abroad.
What, shall I ever sigh and pine?
My lines and life are free; free as the road,
  Loose as the wind, as large as store.   5
    Shall I be still in suit?
  Have I no harvest but a thorn
  To let me blood, and not restore
What I have lost with cordial fruit?
    Sure there was wine   10

Before my sighs did dry it; there was corn
    Before my tears did drown it.
Is the year only lost to me?
    Have I no bays to crown it?
No flowers, no garlands gay? all blasted?   15
      All wasted?
  Not so, my heart; but there is fruit,
    And thou hast hands.
    Recover all thy sigh-blown age
On double pleasures; leave thy cold dispute   20
Of what is fit, and not. Forsake thy cage,
    Thy rope of sands,
Which petty thoughts have made, and made to thee
  Good cable, to enforce and draw,
    And be thy law,   25
  While thou didst wink and wouldst not see.
    Away; take heed;
    I will abroad.
Call in thy death's head there; tie up thy fears.
    He that forbears   30
  To suit and serve his need,
    Deserves his load."
But as I raved and grew more fierce and wild
    At every word,
Methought I heard one calling, *Child!*   35
    And I replied, *My Lord.*

THE FLOWER

  How fresh, oh Lord, how sweet and clean
Are thy returns! even as the flowers in spring;
    To which, besides their own demesne,
The late-past frosts tributes of pleasure bring.
         Grief melts away
        Like snow in May,   5
  As if there were no such cold thing.

  Who would have thought my shriveled heart
Could have recovered greenness? It was gone
    Quite underground; as flowers depart   10
To see their mother-root, when they have blown,
        Where they together
        All the hard weather,
  Dead to the world, keep house unknown.

These are thy wonders, Lord of power,   15
Killing and quickening, bringing down to hell
    And up to heaven in an hour,
Making a chiming of a passing-bell.
            We say amiss,
            This or that is;   20
    Thy word is all, if we could spell.

Oh that I once past changing were,
Fast in thy Paradise, where no flower can wither!
    Many a spring I shoot up fair,
Offering at heaven, growing and groaning thither;   25
            Nor doth my flower
            Want a spring shower,
    My sins and I joining together.

But while I grow in a straight line,
Still upwards bent, as if heaven were mine own,   30
    Thy anger comes, and I decline;
What frost to that? what pole is not the zone,
            Where all things burn,
            When thou dost turn,
    And the least frown of thine is shown?   35

And now in age I bud again,
After so many deaths I live and write;
    I once more smell the dew and rain,
And relish versing: Oh my only light,
            It cannot be   40
            That I am he
    On whom thy tempests fell all night.

These are thy wonders, Lord of love,
To make us see we are but flowers that glide;
    Which when we once can find and prove,   45
Thou hast a garden for us, where to bide;
            Who would be more,
            Swelling through store,
    Forfeit their Paradise by their pride.

44. *glide* slip away imperceptibly.

DEATH

Death, thou wast once an uncouth hideous thing,
      Nothing but bones,
    The sad effect of sadder groans;
Thy mouth was open, but thou couldst not sing.

For we considered thee as at some six   5
      Or ten years hence,
    After the loss of life and sense,
Flesh being turned to dust, and bones to sticks.

We looked on this side of thee, shooting short;
      Where we did find   10
    The shells of fledge souls left behind,
Dry dust, which sheds no tears, but may extort.

But since our Saviour's death did put some blood
      Into thy face;
    Thou art grown fair and full of grace,   15
Much in request, much sought for as a good.

For we do now behold thee gay and glad,
      As at doomsday;
    When souls shall wear their new array,
And all thy bones with beauty shall be clad.   20

Therefore we can go die as sleep, and trust
      Half that we have
    Unto an honest faithful grave;
Making our pillows either down, or dust.

LOVE (III)

Love bade me welcome; yet my soul drew back,
      Guilty of dust and sin.
But quick-eyed Love, observing me grow slack
      From my first entrance in,
Drew nearer to me, sweetly questioning,   5
      If I lacked anything.

11. *fledge* furnished for flight (as with feathers).

"A guest," I answered, "worthy to be here";
    Love said, "You shall be he."
"I the unkind, ungrateful? Ah my dear,
    I cannot look on thee."   10
Love took my hand, and smiling did reply,
    "Who made the eyes but I?"

"Truth, Lord, but I have marred them; let my shame
    Go where it doth deserve."
"And know you not," says Love, "who bore the blame?"   15
    "My dear, then I will serve."
"You must sit down," says Love, "and taste my meat."
    So I did sit and eat.

JOHN MILTON
(1608–1674)

·

ON TIME

Fly envious Time, till thou run out thy race,
Call on the lazy leaden-stepping hours,
Whose speed is but the heavy plummet's pace;
And glut thy self with what thy womb devours,
Which is no more than what is false and vain,   5
And merely mortal dross;
So little is our loss,
So little is thy gain.
For when as each thing bad thou hast entombed,
And last of all, thy greedy self consumed,   10
Then long eternity shall greet our bliss
With an individual kiss;
And joy shall overtake us as a flood,
When every thing that is sincerely good
And perfectly divine,   15
With truth, and peace, and love shall ever shine
About the supreme throne
Of him, to whose happy-making sight alone,
When once our heavenly-guided soul shall climb,
Then all this earthy grossness quit,   20
Attired with stars, we shall forever sit,
     Triumphing over death, and chance, and thee O Time.

LYCIDAS

*In this monody the author bewails a learned friend, unfortunately
drowned in his passage from Chester on the Irish Seas, 1637; and by
occasion, foretells the ruin of our corrupted clergy, then in their height.*

Yet once more, O ye laurels, and once more
Ye myrtles brown, with ivy never sere,
I come to pluck your berries harsh and crude,
And with forced fingers rude,
Shatter your leaves before the mellowing year.   5
Bitter constraint, and sad occasion dear,
Compels me to disturb your season due;
For Lycidas is dead, dead ere his prime,

56

Young Lycidas, and hath not left his peer.
Who would not sing for Lycidas? he knew   10
Himself to sing, and build the lofty rhyme.
He must not float upon his watery bier
Unwept, and welter to the parching wind,
Without the meed of some melodious tear.
    Begin, then, Sisters of the sacred well,   15
That from beneath the seat of Jove doth spring,
Begin, and somewhat loudly sweep the string.
Hence with denial vain, and coy excuse,
So may some gentle Muse
With lucky words favor my destined urn,   20
And as he passes turn,
And bid fair peace be to my sable shroud.
For we were nursed upon the self-same hill,
Fed the same flock, by fountain, shade, and rill.
    Together both, ere the high lawns appeared   25
Under the opening eyelids of the morn,
We drove a-field, and both together heard
What time the grey-fly winds her sultry horn,
Battening our flocks with the fresh dews of night,
Oft till the star that rose, at evening, bright   30
Toward heaven's descent had sloped his westering wheel.
Meanwhile the rural ditties were not mute,
Tempered to th' oaten flute,
Rough Satyrs danced, and Fauns with cloven heel,
From the glad sound would not be absent long,   35
And old Damaetas loved to hear our song.
    But o the heavy change, now thou art gone,
Now thou art gone and never must return!
Thee, Shepherd, thee the woods and desert caves,
With wild thyme and the gadding vine o'ergrown,   40
And all their echoes mourn.
The willows, and the hazel copses green,
Shall now no more be seen,
Fanning their joyous leaves to thy soft lays.
As killing as the canker to the rose,   45
Or taint-worm to the weanling herds that graze,
Or frost to flowers, that their gay wardrobe wear,
When first the white-thorn blows;
Such, Lycidas, thy loss to shepherd's ear.
    Where were ye, Nymphs, when the remorseless deep   50
Closed o'er the head of your loved Lycidas?
For neither were ye playing on the steep

15. *Sisters of the sacred well*   the Muses.

Where your old bards, the famous Druids, lie,
Nor on the shaggy top of Mona high,
Nor yet where Deva spreads her wizard stream.   55
Ay me, I fondly dream!
Had ye been there—for what could that have done?
What could the Muse herself that Orpheus bore,
The Muse herself, for her enchanting son,
Whom universal nature did lament,   60
When by the rout that made the hideous roar,
His gory visage down the stream was sent,
Down the swift Hebrus to the Lesbian shore?
    Alas! what boots it with uncessant care
To tend the homely, slighted, shepherd's trade,   65
And strictly meditate the thankless Muse?
Were it not better done as others use,
To sport with Amaryllis in the shade,
Or with the tangles of Neaera's hair?
Fame is the spur that the clear spirit doth raise   70
(That last infirmity of noble mind)
To scorn delights, and live laborious days;
But the fair guerdon when we hope to find,
And think to burst out into sudden blaze,
Comes the blind Fury with th' abhorréd shears,   75
And slits the thin-spun life. "But not the praise,"
Phoebus replied, and touched my trembling ears:
"Fame is no plant that grows on mortal soil,
Nor in the glistering foil
Set off to the world, nor in broad rumor lies,   80
But lives and spreads aloft by those pure eyes
And perfect witness of all-judging Jove;
As he pronounces lastly on each deed,
Of so much fame in Heaven expect thy meed."
    O fountain Arethuse, and thou honored flood,   85
Smooth-sliding Mincius, crowned with vocal reeds,
That strain I heard was of a higher mood;
But now my oat proceeds,
And listens to the Herald of the Sea
That came in Neptune's plea.   90
He asked the waves, and asked the felon winds,
What hard mishap hath doomed this gentle swain?
And questioned every gust of rugged wings

---

58. *Orpheus* Thracian poet, son of Calliope, the Muse of epic poetry, who was torn to pieces by the Bacchantes. 75. *blind Fury* a combined reference to the Furies and to blind Atropos, one of the three Fates, who cut the threads of human lives woven by her sisters. 85–86. *Arethuse, Mincius* rivers associated with pastoral poetry. 89. *Herald of the Sea* Triton, Neptune's representative.

That blows from off each beakèd promontory;
They knew not of his story, 95
And sage Hippotades their answer brings,
That not a blast was from his dungeon strayed;
The air was calm, and on the level brine,
Sleek Panopé with all her sisters played.
It was that fatal and perfidious bark, 100
Built in th' eclipse, and rigged with curses dark,
That sunk so low that sacred head of thine.
      Next, Camus, reverend sire, went footing slow,
His mantle hairy, and his bonnet sedge,
Inwrought with figures dim, and on the edge 105
Like to that sanguine flower inscribed with woe.
"Ah! who hath reft," quoth he, "my dearest pledge?"
Last came, and last did go,
The Pilot of the Galilean Lake;
Two massy keys he bore of metals twain 110
(The golden opes, the iron shuts amain).
He shook his mitred locks, and stern bespake,
"How well could I have spared for thee, young swain,
Enow of such as for their bellies' sake
Creep and intrude and climb into the fold? 115
Of other care they little reckoning make,
Than how to scramble at the shearers' feast,
And shove away the worthy bidden guest.
Blind mouths! that scarce themselves know how to hold
A sheep-hook, or have learnt aught else the least 120
That to the faithful herdman's art belongs!
What recks it them? What need they? They are sped;
And when they list, their lean and flashy songs
Grate on their scrannel pipes of wretched straw;
The hungry sheep look up, and are not fed, 125
But swoln with wind, and the rank mist they draw,
Rot inwardly, and foul contagion spread;
Besides what the grim wolf with privy paw
Daily devours apace, and nothing said,
But that two-handed engine at the door 130
Stands ready to smite once, and smite no more."
      Return, Alpheus, the dread voice is past
That shrunk thy streams; return, Sicilian Muse,

96. *Hippotades* Aeolus, god of winds.
103. *Camus* god of the river Cam in Cambridge.
106. *that sanguine flower* the hyacinth, which has red markings said to resemble the Greek word *ai* (alas), inscribed to Apollo who turned the youth Hyacinthus into a flower.
109. *Pilot of the Galilean Lake* St. Peter.
123. *list* wish.
132. *Alpheus* river associated with pastoral poetry, lover of Arethuse.

And call the vales, and bid them hither cast
Their bells and flowerets of a thousand hues.   135
Ye valleys low where the mild whispers use
Of shades, and wanton winds, and gushing brooks,
On whose fresh lap the swart star sparely looks,
Throw hither all your quaint enameled eyes,
That on the green turf suck the honeyed showers,   140
And purple all the ground with vernal flowers.
Bring the rathe primrose that forsaken dies,
The tufted crow-toe, and pale jessamine,
The white pink, and the pansy freaked with jet,
The glowing violet,   145
The musk rose, and the well-attired woodbine,
With cowslips wan that hang the pensive head,
And every flower that sad embroidery wears;
Bid amaranthus all his beauty shed,
And daffodillies fill their cups with tears,   150
To strew the laureate hearse where Lycid lies.
For so to interpose a little ease,
Let our frail thoughts dally with false surmise.
Ay me! whilst thee the shores and sounding seas
Wash far away, where'er thy bones are hurled,   155
Whether beyond the stormy Hebrides,
Where thou perhaps under the whelming tide
Visit'st the bottom of the monstrous world;
Or whether thou to our moist vows denied,
Sleep'st by the fable of Bellerus old,   160
Where the great vision of the guarded mount
Looks toward Namancos and Bayona's hold;
Look homeward, Angel, now, and melt with ruth.
And, O ye dolphins, waft the hapless youth.
      Weep no more, woeful shepherds, weep no more,   165
For Lycidas, your sorrow, is not dead,
Sunk though he be beneath the watery floor,
So sinks the day-star in the ocean bed,
And yet anon repairs his drooping head,
And tricks his beams, and with new-spangled ore   170
Flames in the forehead of the morning sky:
So Lycidas sunk low, but mounted high,
Through the dear might of him that walked the waves,
Where other groves and other streams along,
With nectar pure his oozy locks he laves,   175
And hears the unexpressive nuptial song,

139. *quaint* intricately designed.
142. *rathe* early.
164. *the hapless youth* Arion, thrown
overboard by sailors, was carried safely
to shore by dolphins who had been
charmed by his song.

In the blest kingdoms meek of joy and love.
There entertain him all the saints above,
In solemn troops, and sweet societies
That sing, and singing in their glory move,   180
And wipe the tears for ever from his eyes.
Now, Lycidas, the shepherds weep no more;
Henceforth thou art the genius of the shore,
In thy large recompense, and shalt be good
To all that wander in that perilous flood.   185
     Thus sang the uncouth swain to th' oaks and rills,
While the still morn went out with sandals grey;
He touched the tender stops of various quills,
With eager thought warbling his Doric lay;
And now the sun had stretched out all the hills,   190
And now was dropped into the western bay;
At last he rose, and twitched his mantle blue:
Tomorrow to fresh woods, and pastures new.

ON HIS HAVING ARRIVED AT THE AGE OF TWENTY-THREE

How soon hath Time, the subtle thief of youth,
Stoln on his wing my three and twentieth year!
My hasting days fly on with full career,
But my late spring no bud or blossom show'th.
Perhaps my semblance might deceive the truth,   5
That I to manhood am arrived so near,
And inward ripeness doth much less appear,
That some more timely-happy spirits endu'th.
Yet be it less or more, or soon or slow,
It shall be still in strictest measure even   10
To that same lot, however mean, or high,
Toward which Time leads me, and the will of Heaven;
All is, if I have grace to use it so,
As ever in my great taskmaster's eye.

TO A VIRTUOUS YOUNG LADY

Lady that in the prime of earliest youth,
Wisely hast shunned the broad way and the green,
And with those few art eminently seen,
That labor up the hill of heavenly truth,
The better part with Mary, and with Ruth,   5

8. *endu'th*   endoweth.

Chosen thou hast, and they that overween,
And at thy growing virtues fret their spleen,
No anger find in thee, but pity and ruth.
Thy care is fixed and zealously attends
To fill thy odorous lamp with deeds of light,   10
And hope that reaps not shame. Therefore be sure
Thou, when the Bridegroom with his feastful friends
Passes to bliss at the mid hour of night,
Hast gained thy entrance, virgin wise and pure.

ON THE LATE MASSACRE
IN PIEDMONT

Avenge O Lord thy slaughtered saints, whose bones
Lie scattered on the Alpine mountains cold,
Even them who kept thy truth so pure of old
When all our fathers worshiped stocks and stones,
Forget not; in thy book record their groans   5
Who were thy sheep and in their ancient fold
Slain by the bloody Piemontese that rolled
Mother with infant down the rocks. Their moans
The vales redoubled to the hills, and they
To Heaven. Their martyred blood and ashes sow   10
O'er all th' Italian fields where still doth sway
The triple tyrant; that from these may grow
A hundredfold, who having learnt thy way
Early may fly the Babylonian woe.

ON HIS BLINDNESS

When I consider how my light is spent,
Ere half my days, in this dark world and wide,
And that one talent which is death to hide,
Lodged with me useless, though my soul more bent
To serve therewith my Maker, and present   5
My true account, lest he returning chide;
Doth God exact day-labor, light denied?
I fondly ask; but Patience, to prevent
That murmur, soon replies, "God doth not need
Either man's work or his own gifts; who best   10
Bear his mild yoke, they serve him best; his state

12. *Bridegroom* referring to the parable (*Matt.* xxv.1–13) of the wise virgins who prepared for the coming of the Bridegroom (Christ) by filling their lamps.

12. *triple tyrant* the Pope.

Is kingly; thousands at his bidding speed,
And post o'er land and ocean without rest;
They also serve who only stand and wait."

TO MR. CYRIACK SKINNER
UPON HIS BLINDNESS

Cyriack, this three years' day these eyes, though clear
To outward view, of blemish or of spot,
Bereft of light their seeing have forgot,
Nor to their idle orbs doth sight appear
Of sun or moon or star throughout the year,   5
Or man or woman. Yet I argue not
Against heaven's hand or will, nor bate a jot
Of heart or hope; but still bear up and steer
Right onward. What supports me, dost thou ask?
The conscience, Friend, to have lost them overplied   10
In liberty's defense, my noble task,
Of which all Europe talks from side to side.
This thought might lead me through the world's vain
        mask
Content though blind, had I no better guide.

ON HIS DECEASED WIFE

Methought I saw my late espousèd saint
Brought to me like Alcestis from the grave,
Whom Jove's great son to her glad husband gave,
Rescued from death by force, though pale and faint.
Mine as whom washed from spot of child-bed taint,   5
Purification in the Old Law did save,
And such, as yet once more I trust to have
Full sight of her in Heaven without restraint,
Came vested all in white, pure as her mind;
Her face was veiled, yet to my fancied sight,   10
Love, sweetness, goodness, in her person shined
So clear, as in no face with more delight.
But O, as to embrace me she inclined,
I waked, she fled, and day brought back my night.

2. *Alcestis* wife of Admetus, who offered to die for her husband, but was
rescued from death by Hercules.

HENRY VAUGHAN
(1621–1695)

THE RETREAT

Happy those early days! when I
Shined in my angel infancy,
Before I understood this place
Appointed for my second race,
Or taught my soul to fancy aught   5
But a white, celestial thought;
When yet I had not walked above
A mile, or two, from my first love,
And looking back (at that short space)
Could see a glimpse of His bright face;   10
When on some gilded cloud or flower
My gazing soul would dwell an hour,
And in those weaker glories spy
Some shadows of eternity;
Before I taught my tongue to wound   15
My conscience with a sinful sound,
Or had the black art to dispense
A several sin to every sense,
But felt through all this fleshly dress
Bright shoots of everlastingness.   20
   O how I long to travel back,
And tread again that ancient track!
That I might once more reach that plain,
Where first I left my glorious train,
From whence th' enlightened spirit sees   25
That shady city of palm trees;
But, ah! my soul with too much stay
Is drunk, and staggers in the way.
Some men a forward motion love,
But I by backward steps would move,   30
And when this dust falls to the urn
In that state I came return.

PEACE

My soul, there is a country
  Far beyond the stars,
Where stands a wingéd sentry
  All skillful in the wars;
There above noise and danger   5
  Sweet Peace sits crowned with smiles,
And one born in a manger
  Commands the beauteous files;
He is thy gracious friend,
  And (O my soul, awake!)   10
Did in pure love descend
  To die here for thy sake;
If thou canst get but thither,
  There grows the flower of peace,
The rose that cannot wither,   15
  Thy fortress, and thy ease;
Leave then thy foolish ranges;
  For none can thee secure,
But one, who never changes,
  Thy God, thy life, thy cure.   20

MAN

Weighing the steadfastness and state
Of some mean things which here below reside,
Where birds like watchful clocks the noiseless date
  And intercourse of times divide,
Where bees at night get home and hive, and flowers   5
    Early, as well as late,
Rise with the sun and set in the same bowers;

I would (said I) my God would give
The staidness of these things to man! for these
To his divine appointments ever cleave,   10
  And no new business breaks their peace;
The birds nor sow nor reap, yet sup and dine;
    The flowers without clothes live,
Yet Solomon was never dressed so fine.

Man hath still either toys or care;   15
He hath no root, nor to one place is tied,

But ever restless and irregular
   About this earth doth run and ride;
He knows he hath a home, but scarce knows where,
     He says it is so far   20
That he hath quite forgot how to go there.

He knocks at all doors, strays and roams,
Nay, hath not so much wit as some stones have
Which in the darkest nights point to their homes,
   By some hid sense their Maker gave;   25
Man is the shuttle, to whose winding quest
     And passage through these looms
God ordered motion, but ordained no rest.

THE NIGHT

John iii.2

Through that pure virgin-shrine,
That sacred veil drawn o'er thy glorious noon
That men might look and live as glowworms shine,
     And face the moon;
    Wise Nicodemus saw such light   5
    As made him know his God by night.

Most blest believer he!
Who in that land of darkness and blind eyes
Thy long-expected healing wings could see,
     When thou didst rise,   10
    And what can never more be done,
    Did at midnight speak with the sun!

O who will tell me, where
He found thee at that dead and silent hour!
What hallowed solitary ground did bear   15
     So rare a flower,
    Within whose sacred leaves did lie
    The fullness of the Deity.

No mercy-seat of gold,
No dead and dusty cherub, nor carved stone,   20
But his own living works did my Lord hold
     And lodge alone;

5. *Nicodemus* the Pharisee who (according to *John* iii) recognized Jesus, the light of the world, as sent from God.

Where trees and herbs did watch and peep
And wonder, while the Jews did sleep.

Dear night! this world's defeat;   25
The stop to busy fools; care's check and curb;
The day of spirits; my soul's calm retreat
   Which none disturb!
  Christ's progress, and his prayer time;
  The hours to which high Heaven doth chime;   30

God's silent, searching flight;
When my Lord's head is filled with dew, and all
His locks are wet with the clear drops of night;
   His still, soft call;
  His knocking time; the soul's dumb watch,   35
  When spirits their fair kindred catch.

Were all my loud, evil days
Calm and unhaunted as is thy dark tent,
Whose peace but by some angel's wing or voice
   Is seldom rent;   40
  Then I in heaven all the long year
  Would keep, and never wander here.

But living where the sun
Doth all things wake, and where all mix and tire
Themselves and others, I consent and run   45
   To every mire,
  And by this world's ill-guiding light,
  Err more than I can do by night.

There is in God (some say)
A deep, but dazzling darkness; as men here   50
Say it is late and dusky, because they
   See not all clear;
  O for that night! where I in him
  Might live invisible and dim.

THE WATERFALL

With what deep murmurs through time's silent stealth
Doth thy transparent, cool and watery wealth
    Here flowing fall,
    And chide, and call,

As if his liquid, loose retinue stayed   5
Lingering, and were of this steep place afraid,
                    The common pass
                    Where, clear as glass,
                    All must descend
                    Not to an end;   10
But quick'ned by this deep and rocky grave,
Rise to a longer course more bright and brave.

    Dear stream! dear bank, where often I
    Have sat, and pleased my pensive eye,
    Why, since each drop of thy quick store   15
    Runs thither, whence it flowed before,
    Should poor souls fear a shade or night,
    Who came (sure) from a sea of light?
    Or since those drops are all sent back
    So sure to thee, that none doth lack,   20
    Why should frail flesh doubt any more
    That what God takes, he'll not restore?
    O useful element and clear!
    My sacred wash and cleanser here,
    My first consigner unto those   25
    Fountains of life, where the Lamb goes?
    What sublime truths, and wholesome themes,
    Lodge in thy mystical, deep streams!
    Such as dull man can never find
    Unless that Spirit lead his mind,   30
    Which first upon thy face did move,
    And hatched all with his quickening love.
    As this loud brook's incessant fall
    In streaming rings restagnates all,
    Which reach by course the bank, and then   35
    Are no more seen, just so pass men.
    O my invisible estate,
    My glorious liberty, still late!
    Thou art the channel my soul seeks,
    Not this with cataracts and creeks.   40

                    QUICKNESS

    False life! a foil and no more, when
                    Wilt thou be gone?
    Thou foul deception of all men
    That would not have the true come on.

34. *restagnates* overflows.

Thou art a moon-like toil; a blind   5
                    Self-posing state;
A dark contest of waves and wind;
A mere tempestuous debate.

Life is a fixed, discerning light,
                    A knowing joy;   10
No chance, or fit: but ever bright,
And calm and full, yet doth not cloy.

'Tis such a blissful thing, that still
                    Doth vivify,
And shine and smile, and hath the skill   15
To please without eternity.

Thou art a toilsome mole, or less,
                    A moving mist,
But life is, what none can express,
A quickness, which my God hath kissed.   20

THE WORLD

I saw eternity the other night
Like a great ring of pure and endless light,
          All calm, as it was bright,
And round beneath it, time, in hours, days, years,
          Driven by the spheres   5
Like a vast shadow moved, in which the world
          And all her train were hurled;
The doting lover in his quaintest strain
          Did there complain;
Near him, his lute, his fancy, and his flights,   10
          Wit's sour delights,
With gloves and knots, the silly snares of pleasure,
          Yet his dear treasure,
All scattered lay, while he his eyes did pour
          Upon a flower.   15

The darksome statesman hung with weights and woe,
Like a thick midnight fog moved there so slow
          He did nor stay, nor go;
Condemning thoughts (like sad eclipses) scowl
          Upon his soul,   20
And clouds of crying witnesses without
          Pursued him with one shout.

Yet digged the mole, and lest his ways be found
    Worked underground,
Where he did clutch his prey; but one did see   25
    That policy,
Churches and altars fed him, perjuries
    Were gnats and flies,
It rained about him blood and tears, but he
    Drank them as free.   30

The fearful miser on a heap of rust
Sat pining all his life there, did scarce trust
    His own hands with the dust,
Yet would not place one piece above, but lives
    In fear of thieves.   35
Thousands there were as frantic as himself
    And hugged each one his pelf,
The downright epicure placed heaven in sense
    And scorned pretense
While others, slipped into a wide excess,   40
    Said little less;
The weaker sort, slight, trivial wares enslave,
    Who think them brave;
And poor, despiséd truth sat counting by
    Their victory.   45

Yet some, who all this while did weep and sing,
And sing, and weep, soared up into the ring,
    But most would use no wing.
O fools (said I) thus to prefer dark night
    Before true light,   50
To live in grots, and caves, and hate the day
    Because it shows the way,
The way which from this dead and dark abode
    Leads up to God,
A way where you might tread the sun, and be   55
    More bright than he.
But as I did their madness so discuss
    One whispered thus,
This ring the Bridegroom did for none provide
    But for his bride.   60

59. *Bridegroom*   Christ.

ANDREW MARVELL
(1621–1678)

·

ON A DROP OF DEW

See how the orient dew,
Shed from the bosom of the morn
  Into the blowing roses,
Yet careless of its mansion new;
For the clear region where 'twas born   5
  Round in itself encloses;
  And in its little globe's extent,
Frames as it can its native element.
  How it the purple flower does slight,
    Scarce touching where it lies,   10
  But gazing back upon the skies,
    Shines with a mournful light;
      Like its own tear,
Because so long divided from the sphere.
  Restless it rolls and unsecure,   15
    Trembling lest it grow impure;
  Till the warm sun pity its pain,
And to the skies exhale it back again.
    So the soul, that drop, that ray
Of the clear fountain of eternal day,   20
Could it within the human flower be seen,
    Remembering still its former height,
    Shuns the sweet leaves and blossoms green;
    And, recollecting its own light,
Does, in its pure and circling thoughts, express   25
The greater heaven in an heaven less.
    In how coy a figure wound,
    Every way it turns away;
    So the world excluding round,
    Yet receiving in the day.   30
    Dark beneath, but bright above;
    Here disdaining, there in love,
  How loose and easy hence to go;
  How girt and ready to ascend.
  Moving but on a point below,   35
  It all about does upwards bend.
Such did the manna's sacred dew distill;

White, and entire, though congealed and chill.
Congealed on earth; but does, dissolving, run
Into the glories of the almighty Sun.   40

TO HIS COY MISTRESS

Had we but world enough, and time,
This coyness, lady, were no crime.
We would sit down, and think which way
To walk, and pass our long love's day.
Thou by the Indian Ganges' side   5
Shouldst rubies find; I by the tide
Of Humber would complain. I would
Love you ten years before the flood,
And you should, if you please, refuse
Till the conversion of the Jews.   10
My vegetable love should grow
Vaster than empires, and more slow.
An hundred years should go to praise
Thine eyes, and on thy forehead gaze.
Two hundred to adore each breast,   15
But thirty thousand to the rest.
An age at least to every part,
And the last age should show your heart.
For, lady, you deserve this state,
Nor would I love at lower rate.   20
    But at my back I always hear
Time's wingéd chariot hurrying near;
And yonder all before us lie
Deserts of vast eternity.
Thy beauty shall no more be found;   25
Nor, in thy marble vault, shall sound
My echoing song; then worms shall try
That long-preserved virginity;
And your quaint honor turn to dust,
And into ashes all my lust.   30
The grave's a fine and private place,
But none, I think, do there embrace.
    Now therefore, while the youthful hue
Sits on thy skin like morning dew,
And while thy willing soul transpires
At every pore with instant fires,   35
Now let us sport us while we may;
And now, like amorous birds of prey,

Rather at once our time devour,
Than languish in his slow-chapped power.   40
Let us roll all our strength, and all
Our sweetness, up into one ball;
And tear our pleasures with rough strife,
Thorough the iron gates of life.
Thus, though we cannot make our sun   45
Stand still, yet we will make him run.

THE DEFINITION OF LOVE

My love is of a birth as rare
As 'tis for object strange and high;
It was begotten by despair
Upon impossibility.

Magnanimous despair alone   5
Could show me so divine a thing,
Where feeble hope could ne'er have flown
But vainly flapped its tinsel wing.

And yet I quickly might arrive
Where my extended soul is fixed,   10
But Fate does iron wedges drive,
And always crowds itself betwixt.

For Fate with jealous eye does see
Two perfect loves, nor lets them close;
Their union would her ruin be,   15
And her tyrannic power depose.

And therefore her decrees of steel
Us as the distant poles have placed,
(Though love's whole world on us doth wheel)
Not by themselves to be embraced.   20

Unless the giddy heaven fall,
And earth some new convulsion tear,
And, us to join, the world should all
Be cramped into a planisphere.

As lines, so loves oblique may well   25
Themselves in every angle greet;
But ours so truly parallel
Though infinite can never meet.

40. *slow-chapped power*   power of jaws moving slowly.

Therefore the love which us doth bind,
But fate so enviously debars,   30
Is the conjunction of the mind,
And opposition of the stars.

THE PICTURE OF LITTLE T. C. IN
A PROSPECT OF FLOWERS

See with what simplicity
This nymph begins her golden days!
In the green grass she loves to lie,
And there with her fair aspect tames
The wilder flowers, and gives them names;   5
But only with the roses plays,
      And then does tell
What color best becomes them, and what smell.

Who can foretell for what high cause
This darling of the gods was born!
Yet this is she whose chaster laws   10
The wanton Love shall one day fear,
And, under her command severe,
See his bow broke and ensigns torn.
      Happy, who can
Appease this virtuous enemy of man!   15

O then let me in time compound,
And parley with those conquering eyes;
Ere they have tried their force to wound,
Ere, with their glancing wheels, they drive
In triumph over hearts that strive,   20
And them that yield but more despise.
      Let me be laid,
Where I may see thy glories from some shade.

Meantime, whilst every verdant thing
Itself does at thy beauty charm,   25
Reform the errors of the spring;
Make that the tulips may have share
Of sweetness, seeing they are fair,
And roses of their thorns disarm;
      But most procure   30
That violets may a longer age endure.

But O, young beauty of the woods,
Whom nature courts with fruits and flowers,
Gather the flowers, but spare the buds;
Lest Flora, angry at thy crime,   35
To kill her infants in their prime,
Do quickly make th' example yours;
      And, ere we see,
Nip in the blossom all our hopes and thee.

THE MOWER, AGAINST GARDENS

Luxurious man, to bring his vice in use,
   Did after him the world seduce;
And from the fields the flowers and plants allure
   Where nature was most plain and pure.
He first enclosed within the garden's square   5
   A dead and standing pool of air;
And a more luscious earth for them did knead,
   Which stupefied them while it fed.
The pink grew then as double as his mind;
   The nutriment did change the kind.   10
With strange perfumes he did the roses taint,
   And flowers themselves were taught to paint.
The tulip, white, did for complexion seek,
   And learned to interline its cheek;
Its onion root they then so high did hold,   15
   That one was for a meadow sold.
Another world was searched, through oceans new,
   To find the Marvel of Peru.
And yet these rarities might be allowed,
   To man, that sovereign thing and proud,   20
Had he not dealt between the bark and tree,
   Forbidden mixtures there to see.
No plant now knew the stock from which it came;
   He grafts upon the wild the tame,
That the uncertain and adulterate fruit   25
   Might put the palate in dispute.
His green seraglio has its eunuchs too,
   Lest any tyrant him outdo.
And in the cherry he does nature vex,
   To procreate without a sex.   30
'Tis all enforced, the fountain and the grot,
   While the sweet fields do lie forgot;

18. *Marvel of Peru*   a species of plant.

Where willing nature does to all dispense
  A wild and fragrant innocence;
And fauns and fairies do the meadows till   35
  More by their presence than their skill.
Their statues polished by some ancient hand,
  May to adorn the gardens stand;
But howsoe'er the figures do excel,
  The gods themselves with us do dwell.   40

DAMON THE MOWER

Hark how the mower Damon sung,
With love of Juliana stung!
While everything did seem to paint
The scene more fit for his complaint.
Like her fair eyes the day was fair,   5
But scorching like his am'rous care.
Sharp like his scythe his sorrow was,
And withered like his hopes the grass.

"Oh what unusual heats are here,
Which thus our sunburned meadows sear!   10
The grasshopper its pipe gives o'er,
And hamstring'd frogs can dance no more.
But in the brook the green frog wades,
And grasshoppers seek out the shades.
Only the snake, that kept within,   15
Now glitters in its second skin.

"This heat the sun could never raise,
Nor Dog-star so inflames the days.
It from an higher beauty grow'th,
Which burns the fields and mower both;   20
Which made the Dog, and makes the sun
Hotter than his own Phaeton.
Not July causeth these extremes,
But Juliana's scorching beams.

"Tell me where I may pass the fires   25
Of the hot day, or hot desires.
To what cool cave shall I descend,
Or to what gelid fountain bend?
Alas! I look for ease in vain,
When remedies themselves complain.   30

No moisture but my tears do rest,
Nor cold but in her icy breast.

"How long wilt thou, fair shepherdess,
Esteem me, and my presents less?
To thee the harmless snake I bring,   35
Disarmed of its teeth and sting.
To thee chameleons changing hue,
And oak leaves tipped with honey dew.
Yet thou ungrateful hast not sought
Nor what they are, nor who them brought.   40

"I am the mower Damon, known
Through all the meadows I have mown.
On me the morn her dew distills
Before her darling daffodils.
And, if at noon my toil me heat,   45
The sun himself licks off my sweat.
While, going home, the evening sweet
In cowslip-water bathes my feet.

"What, though the piping shepherd stock
The plains with an unnumbered flock,   50
This scythe of mine discovers wide
More ground than all his sheep do hide.
With this the golden fleece I shear
Of all these closes every year.
And though in wool more poor than they,   55
Yet am I richer far in hay.

"Nor am I so deformed to sight,
If in my scythe I lookéd right;
In which I see my picture done,
As in a crescent moon the sun.   60
The deathless fairies take me oft
To lead them in their dances soft;
And, when I tune my self to sing,
About me they contract their ring.

"How happy might I still have mowed,   65
Had not Love here his thistles sowed!
But now I all the day complain,
Joining my labor to my pain;
And with my scythe cut down the grass,
Yet still my grief is where it was;   70

But, when the iron blunter grows,
Sighing I whet my scythe and woes."

While thus he threw his elbow round,
Depopulating all the ground,
And, with his whistling scythe, does cut   75
Each stroke between the earth and root,
The edged steel by careless chance
Did into his own ankle glance;
And there among the grass fell down,
By his own scythe, the mower mown.   80

"Alas!" said he, "these hurts are slight
To those that die by Love's despite.
With shepherds-purse, and Clowns-all-heal,
The blood I staunch, and wound I seal.
Only for him no cure is found,   85
Whom Juliana's eyes do wound.
'Tis death alone that this must do:
For Death thou art a mower too."

THE MOWER TO THE GLOWWORMS

Ye living lamps, by whose dear light
The nightingale doth sit so late,
And studying all the summer night,
Her matchless songs does meditate;

Ye country comets that portend   5
No war, nor prince's funeral,
Shining unto no higher end
Than to presage the grass's fall;

Ye glowworms, whose officious flame
To wandering mowers shows the way,   10
That in the night have lost their aim,
And after foolish fires do stray;

Your courteous lights in vain you waste,
Since Juliana here is come;
For she my mind hath so displaced   15
That I shall never find my home.

THE MOWER'S SONG

My mind was once the true survey
Of all these meadows fresh and gay;
And in the greenness of the grass
Did see its hopes as in a glass;
When Juliana came, and she   5
What I do to the grass, does to my thoughts and me.

But these, while I with sorrow pine,
Grew more luxuriant still and fine;
That not one blade of grass you spied,
But had a flower on either side;   10
When Juliana came, and she
What I do to the grass, does to my thoughts and me.

Unthankful meadows, could you so
A fellowship so true forego,
And in your gaudy May-games meet,   15
While I lay trodden under feet?
When Juliana came, and she
What I do to the grass, does to my thoughts and me.

But what you in compassion ought,
Shall now by my revenge be wrought;   20
And flowers, and grass, and I, and all,
Will in one common ruin fall.
For Juliana comes, and she
What I do to the grass, does to my thoughts and me.

And thus, ye meadows, which have been   25
Companions of my thoughts more green,
Shall now the heraldry become
With which I shall adorn my tomb;
For Juliana comes, and she
What I do to the grass, does to my thoughts and me.   30

THE GARDEN

How vainly men themselves amaze
To win the palm, the oak, or bays;
And their incessant labors see
Crowned from some single herb or tree;

Whose short and narrow-vergéd shade   5
Does prudently their toils upbraid;
While all flowers and all trees do close
To weave the garlands of repose.

Fair Quiet, have I found thee here,
And Innocence, thy sister dear!   10
Mistaken long, I sought you then
In busy companies of men.
Your sacred plants, if here below,
Only among the plants will grow.
Society is all but rude   15
To this delicious solitude.

No white nor red was ever seen
So am'rous as this lovely green.
Fond lovers, cruel as their flame,
Cut in these trees their mistress' name.   20
Little, alas, they know, or heed,
How far these beauties hers exceed!
Fair trees! wheresoe'er your barks I wound,
No name shall but your own be found.

When we have run our passion's heat,   25
Love hither makes his best retreat.
The gods, that mortal beauty chase,
Still in a tree did end their race:
Apollo hunted Daphne so,
Only that she might laurel grow.   30
And Pan did after Syrinx speed,
Not as a nymph, but for a reed.

What wondrous life in this I lead!
Ripe apples drop about my head;
The luscious clusters of the vine   35
Upon my mouth do crush their wine;
The nectarine, and curious peach,
Into my hands themselves do reach;
Stumbling on melons, as I pass,
Insnared with flowers, I fall on grass.   40

Meanwhile the mind, from pleasure less,
Withdraws into its happiness;
The mind, that ocean where each kind
Does straight its own resemblance find;

Yet it creates, transcending these,   45
Far other worlds, and other seas;
Annihilating all that's made
To a green thought in a green shade.

Here at the fountain's sliding foot,
Or at some fruit tree's mossy root,   50
Casting the body's vest aside,
My soul into the boughs does glide;
There like a bird it sits, and sings,
Then whets, and combs its silver wings;
And, till prepared for longer flight,   55
Waves in its plumes the various light.

Such was that happy garden-state,
While man there walked without a mate;
After a place so pure, and sweet,
What other help could yet be meet!   60
But 'twas beyond a mortal's share
To wander solitary there;
Two paradises 'twere in one
To live in paradise alone.

How well the skillful gardener drew   65
Of flowers and herbs this dial new;
Where, from above, the milder sun
Does through a fragrant zodiac run;
And, as it works, th' industrious bee
Computes its time as well as we.   70
How could such sweet and wholesome hours
Be reckoned but with herbs and flowers!

AN HORATIAN ODE UPON CROMWELL'S RETURN FROM IRELAND

The forward youth that would appear
Must now forsake his muses dear,
   Nor in the shadows sing
   His numbers languishing.

'Tis time to leave the books in dust,   5
And oil the unused armor's rust,
   Removing from the wall
   The corselet of the hall.

So restless Cromwell could not cease
In the inglorious arts of peace,   10
   But through adventurous war
   Urgéd his active star.

And, like the three-forked lightning, first
Breaking the clouds where it was nursed,
   Did thorough his own side   15
   His fiery way divide.

For 'tis all one to courage high,
The emulous, or enemy;
   And with such to inclose,
   Is more than to oppose.   20

Then burning through the air he went,
And palaces and temples rent;
   And Caesar's head at last
   Did through his laurels blast.

'Tis madness to resist or blame   25
The force of angry heaven's flame;
   And, if we would speak true,
   Much to the man is due.

Who, from his private gardens, where
He lived reservéd and austere,   30
   As if his highest plot
   To plant the bergamot,

Could by industrious valor climb
To ruin the great work of time,
   And cast the kingdom old,   35
   Into another mold.

Though Justice against Fate complain,
And plead the ancient rights in vain;
   But those do hold or break,
   As men are strong or weak.   40

Nature that hateth emptiness,
Allows of penetration less;
   And therefore must make room
   Where greater spirits come.

32. *bergamot*   a kind of pear, also known as "the king's pear."

What field of all the civil wars,   45
Where his were not the deepest scars?
　　And Hampton shows what part
　　He had of wiser art.

Where, twining subtle fears with hope,
He wove a net of such a scope,   50
　　That Charles himself might chase
　　To Carisbrooke's narrow case.

That thence the royal actor borne
The tragic scaffold might adorn;
　　While round the armèd bands   55
　　Did clap their bloody hands.

He nothing common did or mean
Upon that memorable scene;
　　But with his keener eye
　　The axe's edge did try;   60

Nor called the gods with vulgar spite
To vindicate his helpless right,
　　But bowed his comely head,
　　Down as upon a bed.

This was that memorable hour   65
Which first assured the forcèd power.
　　So when they did design
　　The Capitol's first line,

A bleeding head where they begun,
Did fright the architects to run;   70
　　And yet in that the state
　　Foresaw its happy fate.

And now the Irish are ashamed
To see themselves in one year tamed;
　　So much one man can do,   75
　　That does both act and know.

They can affirm his praises best,
And have, though overcome, confessed
　　How good he is, how just,
　　And fit for highest trust;   80

47. *Hampton* referring to the report that Cromwell frightened the king into his flight from Hampton Court to Carisbrooke.

Nor yet grown stiffer with command,
But still in the Republic's hand;
   How fit he is to sway
   That can so well obey.

He to the Commons' feet presents   85
A kingdom, for his first year's rents;
   And, what he may, forbears
   His fame to make it theirs;

And has his sword and spoils ungirt,
To lay them at the public's skirt.   90
   So when the falcon high
   Falls heavy from the sky,

She, having killed, no more does search,
But on the next green bough to perch;
   Where, when he first does lure,   95
   The falconer has her sure.

What may not then our isle presume
While victory his crest does plume!
   What may not others fear
   If thus he crowns each year!   100

A Caesar he ere long to Gaul,
To Italy an Hannibal,
   And to all states not free
   Shall climacteric be.

The Pict no shelter now shall find   105
Within his parti-colored mind;
   But from this valor sad
   Shrink underneath the plaid;

Happy if in the tufted brake
The English hunter him mistake;   110
   Nor lay his hounds in near
   The Caledonian deer.

But thou, the war's and fortune's son
March indefatigably on;
   And for the last effect   115
   Still keep thy sword erect;

104. *climacteric* critical.

Besides the force it has to fright
The spirits of the shady night,
  The same arts that did gain
  A power must it maintain.

120

JOHN DRYDEN
(1631–1700)

·

EPILOGUE TO *TYRANNIC LOVE*
SPOKEN BY MRS. ELLEN, WHEN SHE WAS TO BE
CARRIED OFF DEAD BY THE BEARERS

To the Bearer. Hold, are you mad? you damned confounded dog,
I am to rise, and speak the epilogue.
   To the Audience. I come, kind gentlemen, strange news to tell ye,
I am the ghost of poor departed Nelly.
Sweet ladies, be not frighted, I'll be civil;   5
I'm what I was, a little harmless devil:
For after death, we sprites have just such natures
We had for all the world, when human creatures;
And therefore, I that was an actress here,
Play all my tricks in hell, a goblin there.   10
Gallants, look to it, you say there are no sprites;
But I'll come dance about your beds at nights.
And faith you'll be in a sweet kind of taking,
When I surprise you between sleep and waking.
To tell you true, I walk because I die   15
Out of my calling in a tragedy.
O poet, damned dull poet, who could prove
So senseless! to make Nelly die for love!
Nay, what's yet worse, to kill me in the prime
Of Easter term, in tart and cheese-cake time!   20
I'll fit the fop, for I'll not one word say
To excuse his godly out-of-fashion play:
A play, which if you dare but twice sit out,
You'll all be slandered, and be thought devout.
But farewell, gentlemen, make haste to me;   25
I'm sure ere long to have your company.
As for my epitaph, when I am gone,
I'll trust no poet, but will write my own:

Here Nelly lies, who, though she lived a slattern,
Yet died a princess, acting in St. Cathar'n.   30

Mrs. Ellen Nell Gwyn, famous actress, mistress of Charles II.   30. *St. Cathar'n* Saint Catherine, heroine of Dryden's *Tyrannic Love.*

PROLOGUE TO
THE UNIVERSITY OF OXFORD, 1674
SPOKEN BY MR. HART

Poets, your subjects, have their parts assigned
T'unbend, and to divert their sovereign's mind:
When tired with following nature, you think fit
To seek repose in the cool shades of wit,
And from the sweet retreat, with joy survey   5
What rests, and what is conquered, of the way.
Here, free yourselves from envy, care, and strife,
You view the various turns of human life:
Safe in our scene, through dangerous courts you go,
And, undebauched, the vice of cities know.   10
Your theories are here to practice brought,
As in mechanic operations wrought;
And man, the little world, before you set,
As once the sphere of crystal showed the great.
Blest sure are you above all mortal kind,   15
If to your fortunes you can suit your mind:
Content to see, and shun, those ills we show,
And crimes on theaters alone to know,
With joy we bring what our dead authors writ,
And beg from you the value of their wit: 20
That Shakespeare's, Fletcher's, and great Jonson's claim
May be renewed from those who gave them fame.
None of our living poets dare appear;
For Muses so severe are worshipped here,
That, conscious of their faults, they shun the eye,   25
And, as profane, from sacred places fly,
Rather than see th' offended God, and die.
We bring no imperfections but our own;
Such faults as made are by the makers shown:
And you have been so kind, that we may boast,   30
The greatest judges still can pardon most.
Poets must stoop, when they would please our pit,
Debased even to the level of their wit;
Disdaining that which yet they know will take,
Hating themselves what their applause must make.   35
But when to praise from you they would aspire,
Though they like eagles mount, your Jove is higher.
So far your knowledge all their pow'r transcends
As what *should* be, beyond what *is*, extends.

PROLOGUE TO *AURENG-ZEBE*

Our author by experience finds it true,
'Tis much more hard to please himself than you;
And out of no feigned modesty, this day
Damns his laborious trifle of a play:
Not that it's worse than what before he writ,   5
But he has now another taste of wit;
And to confess a truth (though out of time)
Grows weary of his long-loved mistress, Rhyme.
Passion's too fierce to be in fetters bound,
And nature flies him like enchanted ground.   10
What verse can do, he has performed in this,
Which he presumes the most correct of his;
But spite of all his pride a secret shame
Invades his breast at Shakespeare's sacred name:
Awed when he hears his godlike Romans rage,   15
He, in a just despair, would quit the stage;
And to an age less polished, more unskilled,
Does, with disdain, the foremost honors yield.
As with the greater dead he dares not strive,
He would not match his verse with those who live: 20
Let him retire, betwixt two ages cast,
The first of this, and hindmost of the last.
A losing gamester, let him sneak away;
He bears no ready money from the play.
The fate which governs poets thought it fit   25
He should not raise his fortunes by his wit.
The clergy thrive, and the litigious bar;
Dull heroes fatten with the spoils of war.
All southern vices, Heav'n be praised, are here;
But wit's a luxury you think too dear.   30
When you to cultivate the plant are loth,
'Tis a shrewd sign 'twas never of your growth;
And wit in northern climates will not blow,
Except, like orange trees, 'tis housed from snow.
There needs no care to put a playhouse down,   35
'Tis the most desert place of all the town:
We and our neighbors, to speak proudly, are,
Like monarchs, ruined with expensive war;
While, like wise English, unconcerned you sit,
And see us play the tragedy of wit.   40

37. *neighbors*   a rival theatrical company.

MAC FLECKNOE

OR, A SATIRE UPON THE TRUE-BLUE-PROTESTANT POET, T. S.

All human things are subject to decay,
And when fate summons, monarchs must obey.
This Flecknoe found, who, like Augustus, young
Was called to empire, and had governed long;
In prose and verse, was owned, without dispute,   5
Through all the realms of Nonsense, absolute.
This aged prince, now flourishing in peace,
And blessed with issue of a large increase,
Worn out with business, did at length debate
To settle the succession of the State;   10
And, pond'ring which of all his sons was fit
To reign, and wage immortal war with wit,
Cried: " 'Tis resolved; for nature pleads, that he
Should only rule, who most resembles me.
Sh—— alone my perfect image bears,   15
Mature in dullness from his tender years:
Sh—— alone, of all my sons, is he
Who stands confirmed in full stupidity.
The rest to some faint meaning make pretense,
But Sh—— never deviates into sense.   20
Some beams of wit on other souls may fall,
Strike through, and make a lucid interval;
But Sh——'s genuine night admits no ray,
His rising fogs prevail upon the day.
Besides, his goodly fabric fills the eye,   25
And seems designed for thoughtless majesty;
Thoughtless as monarch oaks that shade the plain,
And, spread in solemn state, supinely reign.
Heywood and Shirley were but types of thee,
Thou last great prophet of tautology.   30
Even I, a dunce of more renown than they,
Was sent before but to prepare thy way;
And coarsely clad in Norwich drugget came
To teach the nations in thy greater name.
My warbling lute, the lute I whilom strung,   35
When to King John of Portugal I sung,
Was but the prelude to that glorious day,
When thou on silver Thames didst cut thy way,
With well-timed oars before the royal barge,

3. *Flecknoe* pretended father of Mac
Flecknoe, Thomas Shadwell, a writer
of comedy of "humors" in the manner
of Ben Jonson (see lines 187–190).

Swelled with the pride of thy celestial charge;   40
And big with hymn, commander of a host,
The like was ne'er in Epsom blankets tossed.
Methinks I see the new Arion sail,
The lute still trembling underneath thy nail.
At thy well-sharpened thumb from shore to shore   45
The treble squeaks for fear, the basses roar;
Echoes from Pissing Alley Sh—— call,
And Sh—— they resound from A—— Hall.
About thy boat the little fishes throng,
As at the morning toast that floats along.   50
Sometimes, as prince of thy harmonious band,
Thou wield'st thy papers in thy threshing hand.
St. André's feet ne'er kept more equal time,
Not ev'n the feet of thy own *Psyche's* rhyme;
Though they in number as in sense excel: 55
So just, so like tautology, they fell,
That, pale with envy, Singleton forswore
The lute and sword, which he in triumph bore,
And vowed he ne'er would act Villerius more."
Here stopped the good old sire, and wept for joy   60
In silent raptures of the hopeful boy.
All arguments, but most his plays, persuade,
That for anointed dullness he was made.
    Close to the walls which fair Augusta bind,
(The fair Augusta much to fears inclined)   65
An ancient fabric raised t'inform the sight,
There stood of yore, and Barbican it hight:
A watchtower once; but now, so fate ordains,
Of all the pile an empty name remains.
From its old ruins brothel-houses rise,   70
Scenes of lewd loves, and of polluted joys,
Where their vast courts the mother-strumpets keep,
And, undisturbed by watch, in silence sleep.
Near these a nursery erects its head,
Where queens are formed, and future heroes bred;   75
Where unfledged actors learn to laugh and cry,
Where infant punks their tender voices try,
And little Maximins the gods defy.
Great Fletcher never treads in buskins here,
Nor greater Jonson dares in socks appear;   80
But gentle Simkin just reception finds

48. *A—— Hall* Aston Hall; not iden-
tified.
54. *Psyche* play by Shadwell; other
plays and characters of Shadwell men-
tioned also in lines 91–93, 149, 168, 180.

74. *nursery* school for young actors.
78. *Maximin* hero of *Tyrannic Love.*
81. *Simkin* a simpleton, a character
in a contemporary farce.

Amidst this monument of vanished minds:
Pure clinches the suburbian Muse affords,
And Panton waging harmless war with words.
Here Flecknoe, as a place to fame well known,   85
Ambitiously designed his Sh——'s throne;
For ancient Dekker prophesied long since,
That in this pile should reign a mighty prince,
Born for a scourge of wit, and flail of sense;
To whom true dullness should some *Psyches* owe,   90
But worlds of *Misers* from his pen should flow;
Humorists and *Hypocrites* it should produce,
Whole Raymond families, and tribes of Bruce.
   Now Empress Fame had published the renown
Oh Sh——'s coronation through the town.   95
Roused by report of Fame, the nations meet,
From near Bunhill, and distant Watling Street.
No Persian carpets spread th' imperial way,
But scattered limbs of mangled poets lay;
From dusty shops neglected authors come,   100
Martyrs of pies, and relics of the bum.
Much Heywood, Shirley, Ogleby there lay,
But loads of Sh—— almost choked the way.
Bilked stationers for yeomen stood prepared,
And Herringman was captain of the guard.   105
The hoary prince in majesty appeared,
High on a throne of his own labors reared.
At his right hand our young Ascanius sate,
Rome's other hope, and pillar of the state.
His brows thick fogs, instead of glories, grace,   110
And lambent dullness played around his face.
As Hannibal did to the altars come,
Sworn by his sire a mortal foe to Rome;
So Sh—— swore, nor should his vow be vain,
That he till death true dullness would maintain;   115
And, in his father's right, and realm's defense,
Ne'er to have peace with wit, nor truce with sense.
The king himself the sacred unction made,
As king by office, and as priest by trade.
In his sinister hand, instead of ball,   120
He placed a mighty mug of potent ale;
Love's Kingdom to his right he did convey,
At once his scepter, and his rule of sway;

108. *Ascanius*   the   son   of   Aeneas.   vine flame comes down on Ascanius'
(Two   scenes   from   the   *Aeneid*   are   head.)
blended in lines 106–111: one, a sacri-   122. *Love's Kingdom*   play by Fleck-
fice; the other, the moment when a di-   noe.

Whose righteous lore the prince had practiced young,
And from whose loins recorded *Psyche* sprung.   125
His temples, last, with poppies were o'erspread,
That nodding seemed to consecrate his head.
Just at that point of time, if fame not lie,
On his left hand twelve reverend owls did fly.
So Romulus, 'tis sung, by Tiber's brook,   130
Presage of sway from twice six vultures took.
Th' admiring throng loud acclamations make,
And omens of his future empire take.
The sire then shook the honors of his head,
And from his brows damps of oblivion shed   135
Full on the filial dullness: long he stood,
Repelling from his breast the raging god;
At length burst out in this prophetic mood:
   "Heavens bless my son, from Ireland let him reign
To far Barbadoes on the western main;   140
Of his dominion may no end be known,
And greater than his father's be his throne;
Beyond *Love's Kingdom* let him stretch his pen!"
He paused, and all the people cried, "Amen."
Then thus continued he: "My son, advance   145
Still in new impudence, new ignorance.
Success let others teach, learn thou from me
Pangs without birth, and fruitless industry.
Let *Virtuosos* in five years be writ;
Yet not one thought accuse thy toil of wit.   150
Let gentle George in triumph tread the stage,
Make Dorimant betray, and Loveit rage;
Let Cully, Cockwood, Fopling, charm the pit,
And in their folly show the writer's wit.
Yet still thy fools shall stand in thy defense,   155
And justify their author's want of sense.
Let 'em be all by thy own model made
Of dullness, and desire no foreign aid;
That they to future ages may be known,
Not copies drawn, but issue of thy own.   160
Nay, let thy men of wit too be the same,
All full of thee, and differing but in name.
But let no alien S—dl—y interpose,
To lard with wit thy hungry *Epsom* prose.
And when false flowers of rhetoric thou wouldst cull,   165
Trust nature, do not labor to be dull;
But write thy best, and top; and, in each line,

163. *S—dl—y* Sedley (see p. 127).

Sir Formal's oratory will be thine:
Sir Formal, though unsought, attends thy quill,
And does thy northern dedications fill.   170
Nor let false friends seduce thy mind to fame,
By arrogating Jonson's hostile name.
Let father Flecknoe fire thy mind with praise,
And uncle Ogleby thy envy raise.
Thou art my blood, where Jonson has no part: 175
What share have we in nature, or in art?
Where did his wit on learning fix a brand,
And rail at arts he did not understand?
Where made he love in Prince Nicander's vein,
Or swept the dust in *Psyche's* humble strain?   180
Where sold he bargains, "whip-stitch, kiss my arse,"
Promised a play and dwindled to a farce?
When did his Muse from Fletcher scenes purloin,
As thou whole Eth'rege dost transfuse to thine?
But so transfused, as oil on water's flow,   185
His always floats above, thine sinks below.
This is thy province, this thy wondrous way,
New humors to invent for each new play:
This is that boasted bias of thy mind,
By which one way, to dullness, 'tis inclined;   190
Which makes thy writings lean on one side still,
And, in all changes, that way bends thy will.
Nor let thy mountain-belly make pretense
Of likeness; thine's a tympany of sense.
A tun of man in thy large bulk is writ,   195
But sure thou'rt but a kilderkin of wit.
Like mine, thy gentle numbers feebly creep;
Thy tragic Muse gives smiles, thy comic sleep.
With whate'er gall thou set'st thyself to write,
Thy inoffensive satires never bite.   200
In thy felonious heart though venom lies,
It does but touch thy Irish pen, and dies.
Thy genius calls thee not to purchase fame
In keen iambics, but mild anagram.
Leave writing plays, and choose for thy command   205
Some peaceful province in acrostic land.
There thou may'st wings display and altars raise,
And torture one poor word ten thousand ways.
Or, if thou wouldst thy diff'rent talents suit,
Set thy own songs, and sing them to thy lute."   210

181. *sold . . . bargains*   answered   196. *kilderkin* a quarter of a "tun"
questions with vulgar replies like these.   (cask).

He said: but his last words were scarcely heard;
For Bruce and Longvil had a trap prepared,
And down they sent the yet declaiming bard.
Sinking he left his drugget robe behind,
Borne upwards by a subterranean wind.   215
The mantle fell to the young prophet's part,
With double portion of his father's art.

TO THE MEMORY OF MR. OLDHAM

Farewell, too little and too lately known,
Whom I began to think and call my own;
For sure our souls were near allied, and thine
Cast in the same poetic mold with mine.
One common note on either lyre did strike,   5
And knaves and fools we both abhorred alike.
To the same goal did both our studies drive;
The last set out the soonest did arrive.
Thus Nisus fell upon the slippery place,
While his young friend performed and won the race.   10
O early ripe! to thy abundant store
What could advancing age have added more?
It might (what nature never gives the young)
Have taught the numbers of thy native tongue.
But satire needs not those, and wit will shine   15
Through the harsh cadence of a rugged line.
A noble error, and but seldom made,
When poets are by too much force betrayed.
Thy generous fruits, though gathered ere their prime,
Still showed a quickness; and maturing time   20
But mellows what we write to the dull sweets of rhyme.
Once more, hail and farewell; farewell, thou young,
But ah too short, Marcellus of our tongue;
Thy brows with ivy, and with laurels bound;
But fate and gloomy night encompass thee around.   25

AGAINST THE FEAR OF DEATH

What has this bugbear death to frighten man,
If souls can die, as well as bodies can?

Mr. Oldham John Oldham, a writer of satire.
9. *Nisus* Nisus, in Virgil's *Aeneid,* fell and tripped the man following him, and so helped his friend to win the race.

23. *Marcellus* nephew of the emperor Augustus, who died at twenty.

Against the Fear of Death translation of the latter part of the third book of Lucretius, *On the Nature of Things.*

For, as before our birth we felt no pain
When Punic arms infested land and main,
When heav'n and earth were in confusion hurled   5
For the debated empire of the world,
Which awed with dreadful expectation lay,
Sure to be slaves, uncertain who should sway:
So, when our mortal frame shall be disjoined,
The lifeless lump, uncoupled from the mind,   10
From sense of grief and pain we shall be free;
We shall not feel, because we shall not *be*.
Though earth in seas, and seas in heav'n were lost,
We should not move, we only should be tossed.
Nay, ev'n suppose when we have suffered Fate,   15
The soul could feel in her divided state,
What's that to us, for we are only we
While souls and bodies in one frame agree?
Nay, though our atoms should revolve by chance,
And matter leap into the former dance;   20
Though time our life and motion could restore,
And make our bodies what they were before,
What gain to us would all this bustle bring,
The new made man would be another thing;
When once an interrupting pause is made,   25
That individual being is decayed.
We, who are dead and gone, shall bear no part
In all the pleasures, nor shall feel the smart,
Which to that other mortal shall accrue,
Whom of our matter time shall mold anew.   30
For backward if you look, on that long space
Of ages past, and view the changing face
Of matter, tossed and variously combined
In sundry shapes, 'tis easy for the mind
From thence t'infer that seeds of things have been   35
In the same order as they now are seen:
Which yet our dark remembrance cannot trace,
Because a pause of life, a gaping space
Has come betwixt, where memory lies dead,
And all the wand'ring motions from the sense are fled.   40
For whosoe'er shall in misfortunes live
Must *be*, when those misfortunes shall arrive;
And since the man who *is* not, feels not woe,
(For death exempts him, and wards off the blow,
Which we, the living, only feel and bear)   45
What is there left for us in death to fear?
When once that pause of life has come between,

'Tis just the same as we had never been.
   And therefore if a man bemoan his lot,
That after death his mold'ring limbs shall rot,   50
Or flames, or jaws of beasts devour his mass,
Know he's an unsincere, unthinking ass.
A secret sting remains within his mind,
The fool is to his own cast offals kind;
He boasts no sense can after death remain,   55
Yet makes himself a part of life again:
As if some other he could feel the pain.
If, while he live, this thought molest his head,
What wolf or vulture shall devour me dead,
He wastes his days in idle grief, nor can   60
Distinguish 'twixt the body and the man:
But thinks himself can still himself survive;
And what when dead he feels not, feels alive.
Then he repines that he was born to die,
Nor knows in death there is no other he,   65
No living he remains his grief to vent,
And o'er his senseless carcass to lament.
If after death 'tis painful to be torn
By birds and beasts, then why not so to burn,
Or drenched in floods of honey to be soaked,   70
Imbalmed to be at once preserved and choked;
Or on an ayery mountain's top to lie
Exposed to cold and heav'n's inclemency,
Or crowded in a Tomb to be oppressed
With monumental marble on thy breast?   75
But to be snatched from all thy household joys,
From thy chaste wife, and thy dear prattling boys,
Whose little arms about thy legs are cast
And climbing for a kiss prevent their Mothers hast,
Inspiring secret pleasure through thy breast,   80
All these shall be no more: thy friends oppressed,
Thy care and courage now no more shall free:
Ah wretch, thou cry'st, ah! miserable me,
One woeful day sweeps children, friends, and wife,
And all the brittle blessings of my life!   85
Add one thing more, and all thou say'st is true;
Thy want and wish of them is vanished too,
Which well considered were a quick relief,
To all thy vain imaginary grief.
For thou shalt sleep and never wake again,   90
And quitting life, shall quit thy living pain.
But we thy friends shall all those sorrows find,

Which in forgetful death thou leav'st behind,
No time shall dry our tears, nor drive thee from our mind.
The worst that can befall thee, measured right, 95
Is a sound slumber, and a long good night.
Yet thus the fools, that would be thought the wits,
Disturb their mirth with melancholy fits,
When healths go round, and kindly brimmers flow,
Till the fresh garlands on their foreheads glow, 100
They whine, and cry, let us make haste to live,
Short are the joys that human life can give.
Eternal preachers, that corrupt the draught,
And pall the God that never thinks, with thought;
Idiots with all that thought, to whom the worst 105
Of death, is want of drink, and endless thirst,
Or any fond desire as vain as these.
For ev'n in sleep, the body wrapped in ease,
Supinely lies, as in the peaceful grave,
And wanting nothing, nothing can it crave. 110
Were that sound sleep eternal it were death;
Yet the first atoms then, the seeds of breath,
Are moving near to sense; we do but shake
And rouse that sense, and straight we are awake.
Then death to us, and death's anxiety 115
Is less than nothing, if a less could be.
For then our atoms, which in order lay,
Are scattered from their heap, and puffed away,
And never can return into their place,
When once the pause of life has left an empty space. 120
    And last, suppose Great Nature's voice should call
To thee, or me, or any of us all,
"What dost thou mean, ungrateful wretch, thou vain,
Thou mortal thing, thus idly to complain,
And sigh and sob, that thou shalt be no more? 125
For if thy life were pleasant heretofore,
If all the bounteous blessings I could give
Thou hast enjoyed, if thou hast known to live,
And pleasure not leaked through thee like a sieve,
Why dost thou not give thanks as at a plenteous feast 130
Crammed to the throat with life, and rise and take thy rest?
But if my blessings thou hast thrown away,
If indigested joys passed through and would not stay,
Why dost thou wish for more to squander still?
If life be grown a load, a real ill, 135
And I would all thy cares and labors end,
Lay down thy burden fool, and know thy friend.

To please thee I have emptied all my store;
I can invent, and can supply no more;
But run the round again, the round I ran before.   140
Suppose thou art not broken yet with years,
Yet still the self same scene of things appears,
And would be ever, could'st thou ever live;
For life is still but life, there's nothing new to give."
What can we plead against so just a bill?   145
We stand convicted, and our cause goes ill.
But if a wretch, a man oppressed by fate,
Should beg of Nature to prolong his date,
She speaks aloud to him with more disdain,
"Be still thou martyr fool, thou covetous of pain."   150
But if an old decrepit sot lament;
"What thou" (she cries) "who hast outlived content!
Dost thou complain, who hast enjoyed my store?
But this is still th' effect of wishing more!
Unsatisfied with all that Nature brings;   155
Loathing the present, liking absent things;
From hence it comes thy vain desires at strife
Within themselves, have tantalized thy life,
And ghastly death appeared before thy sight
Ere thou hadst gorged thy soul, and senses with delight. 160
Now leave those joys unsuiting to thy age,
To a fresh comer, and resign the stage."
   Is Nature to be blamed if thus she chide?
No, sure; for 'tis her business to provide,
Against this ever changing frame's decay,   165
New things to come, and old to pass away.
One being worn, another being makes;
Changed but not lost; for Nature gives and takes:
New matter must be found for things to come,
And these must waste like those, and follow Nature's doom. 170
All things, like thee, have time to rise and rot;
And from each other's ruin are begot;
For life is not confined to him or thee;
'Tis giv'n to all for use; to none for property.
Consider former ages past and gone,   175
Whose circles ended long ere thine begun,
Then tell me fool, what part in them thou hast?
Thus may'st thou judge the future by the past.
What horror seest thou in that quiet state,
What bugbear dreams to fright thee after fate?   180
No ghost, no goblins, that still passage keep,
But all is there serene, in that eternal sleep.

For all the dismal tales that poets tell,
Are verified on earth, and not in hell.
No Tantalus looks up with fearful eye,   185
Or dreads th' impending rock to crush him from on high:
But fear of chance on earth disturbs our easy hours:
Or vain imagined wrath of vain imagined pow'rs.
No Tityus torn by vultures lies in Hell;
Nor could the lobes of his rank liver swell   190
To that prodigious mass for their eternal meal.
Not though his monstrous bulk had covered o'er
Nine spreading acres, or nine thousand more;
Not though the globe of earth had been the giants' floor.
Nor in eternal torments could he lie;   195
Nor could his corpse sufficient food supply.
But he's the Tityus, who by love oppressed,
Or tyrant passion preying on his breast,
And ever anxious thoughts, is robbed of rest.
The Sisiphus is he, whom noise and strife   200
Seduce from all the soft retreats of life,
To vex the government, disturb the laws;
Drunk with the fumes of popular applause,
He courts the giddy crowd to make him great,
And sweats and toils in vain, to mount the sovereign seat.   205
For still to aim at pow'r, and still to fail,
Ever to strive and never to prevail,
What is it, but in reason's true account
To heave the stone against the rising mount;
Which urged, and labored, and forced up with pain,   210
Recoils and rolls impetuous down, and smokes along the plain.
Then still to treat thy ever craving mind
With ev'ry blessing, and of ev'ry kind,
Yet never fill thy rav'ning appetite;
Though years and seasons vary thy delight,   215
Yet nothing to be seen of all the store,
But still the wolf within thee barks for more;
This is the fable's moral, which they tell
Of fifty foolish virgins damned in Hell
To leaky vessels, which the liquor spill;   220
To vessels of their sex, which none could ever fill.
As for the Dog, the Furies, and their snakes,
The gloomy caverns, and the burning lakes,
And all the vain infernal trumpery,

---

189. *Tityus* gigantic son of Earth,   222. *Dog* Cerberus, who guards the
punished in Hades by vultures who   entrance to Hades.
feed on his liver.

They neither are, nor were, nor e'er can be.   225
But here on earth the guilty have in view
The mighty pains to mighty mischiefs due:
Racks, prisons, poisons, the Tarpeian Rock,
Stripes, hangmen, pitch, and suffocating smoke,
And last, and most, if these were cast behind,   230
Th' avenging horror of a conscious mind,
Whose deadly fear anticipates the blow,
And sees no end of punishment and woe:
But looks for more, at the last gasp of breath:
This makes a hell on earth, and life a death.   235
    Meantime, when thoughts of death disturb thy head;
Consider, Ancus great and good is dead;
Ancus thy better far, was born to die,
And thou, dost thou bewail mortality?
So many monarchs with their mighty state,   240
Who ruled the world, were overruled by fate.
That haughty king, who lorded o'er the main,
And whose stupendous bridge did the wild waves restrain,
(In vain they foamed, in vain they threatened wreck,
While his proud legions marched upon their back)   245
Him death, a greater monarch, overcame;
Nor spared his guards the more, for their immortal name.
The Roman chief, the Carthaginian dread,
Scipio the thunderbolt of war is dead,
And like a common slave, by fate in triumph led.   250
The founders of invented arts are lost;
And wits who made eternity their boast;
Where now is Homer who possessed the throne?
Th' immortal work remains, the mortal author's gone.
Democritus perceiving age invade,   255
His body weakened, and his mind decayed,
Obeyed the summons with a cheerful face;
Made haste to welcome death, and met him half the race.
That stroke, ev'n Epicurus could not bar,
Though he in wit surpassed mankind, as far   260
As does the midday sun, the midnight star.
And thou, dost thou disdain to yield thy breath,
Whose very life is little more than death?
More than one half by lazy sleep possessed;
And when awake, thy soul but nods at best,   265
Daydreams and sickly thoughts revolving in thy breast.

228. *Tarpeian Rock* a cliff in Rome, where criminals were thrown to their death.
237. *Ancus* an early king of Rome.

242. *king* Xerxes, king of Persia (see *The Vanity of Human Wishes*, p. 177, lines 223–240).

Eternal troubles haunt thy anxious mind,
Whose cause and cure thou never hop'st to find;
But still uncertain, with thy self at strife,
Thou wander'st in the labyrinth of life.   270
   O, if the foolish race of man, who find
A weight of cares still pressing on their mind,
Could find as well the cause of this unrest,
And all this burden lodged within the breast,
Sure they would change their course; nor live as now,   275
Uncertain what to wish or what to vow.
Uneasy both in country and in town,
They search a place to lay their burden down.
One restless in his palace, walks abroad,
And vainly thinks to leave behind the load.   280
But straight returns; for he's as restless there;
And finds there's no relief in open air.
Another to his villa would retire,
And spurs as hard as if it were on fire;
No sooner entered at his country door,   285
But he begins to stretch, and yawn, and snore;
Or seeks the city which he left before.
Thus every man o'er works his weary will,
To shun himself, and to shake off his ill;
The shaking fit returns and hangs upon him still.   290
No prospect of repose, nor hope of ease;
The wretch is ignorant of his disease;
Which known would all his fruitless trouble spare;
For he would know the world not worth his care;
Then would he search more deeply for the cause;   295
And study nature well, and nature's laws:
For in this moment lies not the debate;
But on our future, fixed, eternal state;
That never changing state which all must keep
Whom death has doomed to everlasting sleep.   300
   Why are we then so fond of mortal life,
Beset with dangers and maintained with strife?
A life which all our care can never save;
One fate attends us; and one common grave.
Besides, we tread but a perpetual round,   305
We ne'er strike out, but beat the former ground,
And the same mawkish joys in the same track are found.
For still we think an absent blessing best;
Which cloys, and is no blessing when possessed;
A new arising wish expells it from the breast.   310
The fev'rish thirst of life increases still;

We call for more and more and never have our fill,
Yet know not what tomorrow we shall try,
What dregs of life in the last draught may lie.
Nor, by the longest life we can attain, 315
One moment from the length of death we gain;
For all behind belongs to his eternal reign.
When once the Fates have cut the mortal thread,
The man as much to all intents is dead,
Who dies today, and will as long be so, 320
As he who died a thousand years ago.

A SONG FOR ST. CECILIA'S DAY, 1687

I

From harmony, from heav'nly harmony,
This universal frame began:
When Nature underneath a heap
Of jarring atoms lay,
And could not heave her head, 5
The tuneful voice was heard from high:
"Arise, ye more than dead."
Then cold, and hot, and moist, and dry
In order to their stations leap,
And Music's power obey. 10
From harmony, from heav'nly harmony,
This universal frame began:
From harmony to harmony
Through all the compass of the notes it ran,
The diapason closing full in Man. 15

II

What passion cannot Music raise and quell!
When Jubal struck the chorded shell,
His list'ning brethren stood around,
And wond'ring, on their faces fell
To worship that celestial sound. 20
Less than a god they thought there could not dwell
Within the hollow of that shell
That spoke so sweetly and so well.
What passion cannot Music raise and quell!

III

The trumpet's loud clangor 25
Excites us to arms

With shrill notes of anger
    And mortal alarms.
  The double double double beat
    Of the thund'ring drum   30
    Cries: "Hark! the foes come;
Charge, charge, 'tis too late to retreat!"

IV

The soft complaining flute
    In dying notes discovers
    The woes of hopeless lovers,   35
Whose dirge is whispered by the warbling lute.

V

Sharp violins proclaim
Their jealous pangs, and desperation,
Fury, frantic indignation,
Depth of pains, and height of passion,   40
  For the fair, disdainful dame.

VI

  But oh! what art can teach,
  What human voice can reach
The sacred organ's praise?
Notes inspiring holy love,   45
Notes that wing their heav'nly ways
  To mend the choirs above.

VII

Orpheus could lead the savage race;
And trees unrooted left their place,
  Sequacious of the lyre;   50
But bright Cecilia raised the wonder higher:
When to her organ vocal breath was given,
An angel heard, and straight appeared,
  Mistaking earth for heaven.

GRAND CHORUS

As from the power of sacred lays   55
  The spheres began to move,
And sung the great Creator's praise
  To all the bless'd above;
So when the last and dreadful hour
This crumbling pageant shall devour,   60
The trumpet shall be heard on high,
The dead shall live, the living die,
And Music shall untune the sky.

SONG TO A FAIR, YOUNG LADY, GOING OUT OF THE TOWN IN THE SPRING

Ask not the cause, why sullen Spring
   So long delays her flow'rs to bear;
Why warbling birds forget to sing,
   And winter storms invert the year?
Chloris is gone; and fate provides   5
To make it spring, where she resides.

Chloris is gone, the cruel fair;
   She cast not back a pitying eye,
But left her lover in despair;
   To sigh, to languish, and to die: 10
Ah, how can those fair eyes endure
To give the wounds they will not cure!

Great god of love, why hast thou made
   A face that can all hearts command,
That all religions can invade,   15
   And change the laws of ev'ry land?
Where thou hadst placed such pow'r before,
Thou shouldst have made her mercy more.

When Chloris to the temple comes,
   Adoring crowds before her fall;   20
She can restore the dead from tombs,
   And ev'ry life but mine recall.
I only am by Love designed
To be the victim for mankind.

A Selection of Sixteenth- and Seventeenth-Century Poems

CHRISTOPHER MARLOWE
(1564–1593)

THE PASSIONATE SHEPHERD
TO HIS LOVE

Come live with me and be my love,
And we will all the pleasures prove
That valleys, groves, hills, and fields,
Woods, or steepy mountain yields.

And we will sit upon the rocks,   5
Seeing the shepherds feed their flocks
By shallow rivers, to whose falls
Melodious birds sing madrigals.

And I will make thee beds of roses
And a thousand fragrant posies,   10
A cap of flowers, and a kirtle
Embroidered all with leaves of myrtle;

A gown made of the finest wool
Which from our pretty lambs we pull,
Fair linéd slippers for the cold,   15
With buckles of the purest gold;

A belt of straw and ivy buds
With coral clasps and amber studs:
And if these pleasures may thee move,
Come live with me, and be my love.   20

The shepherds' swains shall dance and sing
For thy delight each May morning.
If these delights thy mind may move,
Then live with me and be my love.

SIR WALTER RALEIGH
(1552–1618)

·

THE NYMPH'S REPLY TO
THE SHEPHERD

If all the world and love were young,
And truth in every shepherd's tongue,
These pretty pleasures might me move
To live with thee, and be thy love.

Time drives the flocks from field to fold,   5
When rivers rage, and rocks grow cold,
And Philomel becometh dumb,
The rest complains of cares to come.

The flowers do fade, and wanton fields
To wayward winter reckoning yields,   10
A honey tongue, a heart of gall,
Is fancy's spring, but sorrow's fall.

Thy gowns, thy shoes, thy beds of roses,
Thy cap, thy kirtle, and thy posies
Soon break, soon wither, soon forgotten,   15
In folly ripe, in reason rotten.

Thy belt of straw and ivy buds,
Thy coral clasps and amber studs,
All these in me no means can move
To come to thee, and be thy love.   20

But could youth last, and love still breed,
Had joys no date, nor age no need,
Then these delights my mind might move
To live with thee, and be thy love.

7. *Philomel*   mythological name for the nightingale.

TO HIS SON

Three things there be that prosper up apace
And flourish, whilest they grow asunder far,
But on a day, they meet all in one place,
And when they meet, they one another mar;
And they be these, the wood, the weed, the wag.   5
The wood is that which makes the gallow tree,
The weed is that which strings the hangman's bag,
The wag, my pretty knave, betokeneth thee.
Mark well, dear boy, whilest these assemble not,
Green springs the tree, hemp grows, the wag is wild,   10
But when they meet, it makes the timber rot,
It frets the halter, and it chokes the child.
Then bless thee, and beware, and let us pray
We part not with thee at this meeting day.

SAMUEL DANIEL
(1562–1619)

·

FROM DELIA

Beauty, sweet love, is like the morning dew,
Whose short refresh upon the tender green
Cheers for a time, but till the sun doth show,
And straight 'tis gone as it had never been.
Soon doth it fade that makes the fairest flourish,   5
Short is the glory of the blushing rose;
The hue which thou so carefully dost nourish,
Yet which at length thou must be forced to lose,
When thou, surcharged with burthen of thy years,
Shalt bend thy wrinkles homeward to the earth,   10
And that in beauty's lease expired appears
The date of age, the kalends of our death.
But ah! no more, this must not be foretold,
For women grieve to think they must be old.

12. *kalends*   first day of the month in the Roman calendar.

ULYSSES AND THE SIREN

SIREN.   Come, worthy Greek, Ulysses, come
Possess these shores with me;
The winds and seas are troublesome,
And here we may be free.
     Here may we sit, and view their toil   5
That travail in the deep,
And joy the day in mirth the while,
And spend the night in sleep.

ULYSSES.   Fair nymph, if fame or honor were
To be attained with ease,   10
Then would I come and rest me there,
And leave such toils as these.
     But here it dwells, and here must I
With danger seek it forth;
To spend the time luxuriously   15
Becomes not men of worth.

SIREN.   Ulysses, O be not deceived
With that unreal name;
This honor is a thing conceived,
And rests on others' fame.   20
     Begotten only to molest
Our peace, and to beguile
(The best thing of our life) our rest,
And give us up to toil.

ULYSSES.   Delicious nymph, suppose there were   25
Nor honor nor report,
Yet manliness would scorn to wear
The time in idle sport.
     For toil doth give a better touch,
To make us feel our joy;   30
And ease finds tediousness, as much
As labor yields annoy.

SIREN.   Then pleasure likewise seems the shore
Whereto tends all your toil,
Which you forgo to make it more,   35
And perish oft the while.
     Who may disport them diversly,

Find never tedious day,
And ease may have variety,
As well as action may.   40

ULYSSES. But natures of the noblest frame
          These toils and dangers please,
          And they take comfort in the same,
          As much as you in ease.
                And with the thoughts of actions past   45
          Are recreated still;
          When pleasure leaves a touch at last,
          To show that it was ill.

SIREN.   That doth opinion only cause
          That's out of custom bred,   50
          Which makes us many other laws
          Than ever nature did.
                No widows wail for our delights,
          Our sports are without blood;
          The world, we see, by warlike wights,   55
          Receives more hurt than good.

ULYSSES. But yet the state of things require
          These motions of unrest,
          And these great spirits of high desire
          Seem born to turn them best,   60
                To purge the mischiefs that increase
          And all good order mar;
          For oft we see a wicked peace
          To be well changed for war.

SIREN.   Well, well, Ulysses, then I see   65
          I shall not have thee here,
          And therefore I will come to thee,
          And take my fortunes there.
                I must be won that cannot win,
          Yet lost were I not won: 70
          For beauty hath created been
          T'undo, or be undone.

MICHAEL DRAYTON
(*1563–1631*)

·

FROM IDEA

6

How many paltry, foolish, painted things,
That now in coaches trouble every street,
Shall be forgotten, whom no poet sings,
Ere they be well wrapped in their winding-sheet?
Where I to thee eternity shall give,   5
When nothing else remaineth of these days,
And queens hereafter shall be glad to live
Upon the alms of thy superfluous praise.
Virgins and matrons, reading these my rimes,
Shall be so much delighted with thy story   10
That they shall grieve, they lived not in these times,
To have seen thee, their sex's only glory.
So shalt thou fly above the vulgar throng,
Still to survive in my immortal song.

61

Since there's no help, come let us kiss and part;
Nay, I have done; you get no more of me,
And I am glad, yea glad with all my heart,
That thus so cleanly I myself can free;
Shake hands forever, cancel all our vows,   5
And when we meet at any time again,
Be it not seen in either of our brows,
That we one jot of former love retain;
Now at the last gasp of Love's latest breath,
When, his pulse failing, Passion speechless lies,   10
When Faith is kneeling by his bed of death,
And Innocence is closing up his eyes,
Now if thou wouldst, when all have given him over,
From death to life thou mightst him yet recover.

≺☼≻

THOMAS NASHE
(*1567–1601*)

·

A LITANY IN TIME OF PLAGUE

Adieu, farewell, earth's bliss;
This world uncertain is;
Fond are life's lustful joys;
Death proves them all but toys;
None from his darts can fly;   5
I am sick, I must die.
   Lord, have mercy on us.

Rich men, trust not in wealth,
Gold cannot buy you health;
Physic himself must fade.   10
All things to end are made,
The plague full swift goes by;
I am sick, I must die.
   Lord, have mercy on us.

Beauty is but a flower   15
Which wrinkles will devour;
Brightness falls from the air;
Queens have died young and fair;
Dust hath closed Helen's eye.
I am sick, I must die.   20
   Lord, have mercy on us.

Strength stoops unto the grave,
Worms feed on Hector brave;
Swords may not fight with fate,
Earth still holds ope her gate.   25
"Come, come!" the bells do cry.
I am sick, I must die.
   Lord, have mercy on us.

3. *fond*   foolish.

Wit with his wantonness
Tasteth death's bitterness;   30
Hell's executioner
Hath no ears for to hear
What vain art can reply.
I am sick, I must die.
   Lord, have mercy on us.   35

Haste, therefore, each degree,
To welcome destiny;
Heaven is our heritage,
Earth but a player's stage;
Mount we unto the sky.   40
I am sick, I must die.
   Lord, have mercy on us.

THOMAS CAMPION
(1567–1620)
·

I CARE NOT FOR THESE LADIES

I care not for these ladies
That must be wooed and prayed;
Give me kind Amaryllis,
The wanton country maid;
Nature art disdaineth,   5
Her beauty is her own;
Her when we court and kiss,
She cries, forsooth, let go.
But when we come where comfort is,
She never will say no.   10

If I love Amaryllis,
She gives me fruit and flowers,
But if we love these ladies,
We must give golden showers;
Give them gold that sell love,   15
Give me the nut-brown lass,
Who when we court and kiss,
She cries, forsooth, let go.
But when we come where comfort is,
She never will say no.   20

These ladies must have pillows,
And beds by strangers wrought;
Give me a bower of willows,
Of moss and leaves unbought,
And fresh Amaryllis   25
With milk and honey fed,
Who, when we court and kiss,
She cries, forsooth, let go.
But when we come where comfort is,
She never will say no.   30

WHEN THOU MUST HOME TO
SHADES OF UNDERGROUND

When thou must home to shades of underground,
And there arrived, a new admiréd guest,
The beauteous spirits do engirt thee round,
White Iope, blithe Helen, and the rest,
To hear the stories of thy finished love   5
From that smooth tongue whose music hell can move,

Then wilt thou speak of banqueting delights,
Of masques and revels which sweet youth did make,
Of tourneys and great challenges of knights,
And all these triumphs for thy beauty's sake;   10
When thou hast told these honors done to thee,
Then tell, O tell, how thou didst murther me.

FOLLOW THY FAIR SUN,
UNHAPPY SHADOW

Follow thy fair sun, unhappy shadow,
Though thou be black as night,
And she made all of light,
Yet follow thy fair sun, unhappy shadow.

Follow her whose light thy light depriveth,   5
Though here thou liv'st disgraced,
And she in heaven is placed,
Yet follow her whose light the world reviveth.

4. *Iope* daughter of Iphicles, and one of the wives of Theseus.

Follow those pure beams whose beauty burneth,
That so have scorchéd thee,
As thou still black must be,   10
Till her kind beams thy black to brightness turneth.

Follow her while yet her glory shineth:
There comes a luckless night,
That will dim all her light;   15
And this the black unhappy shade divineth.

Follow still since so thy fates ordainéd;
The sun must have his shade,
Till both at once do fade,
The sun still proud, the shadow still disdainéd.   20

RICHARD CORBETT
(1582–1635)

·

TO HIS SON VINCENT CORBETT

What I shall leave thee none can tell,
But all shall say I wish thee well;
I wish thee, Vin, before all wealth,
Both bodily and ghostly health.
Nor too much wealth, nor wit, come to thee;   5
Too much of either may undo thee.
I wish thee learning, not for show,
But truly to instruct and know;
Not such as gentlemen require,
To prate at table, or at fire.   10
I wish thee all thy mother's graces,
Thy father's fortunes, and his places.
I wish thee friends, and one at court,
Not to build up, but to support;
To keep thee, not in doing many   15
Oppressions, but from suffering any.
I wish thee peace in all thy ways,
Nor lazy nor contentious days;
And when thy soul and body part,
As innocent as now thou art.   20

ROBERT HERRICK
(1591–1674)
·

TO MEADOWS

Ye have been fresh and green,
  Ye have been filled with flowers,
And ye the walks have been
  Where maids have spent their hours.

You have beheld, how they   5
  With wicker arks did come
To kiss, and bear away
  The richer cowslips home.

Y'ave heard them sweetly sing,
  And seen them in a round: 10
Each virgin, like a spring,
  With honeysuckles crowned.

But now, we see, none here,
  Whose silv'ry feet did tread,
And with dishevelled hair,   15
  Adorned this smoother mead.

Like unthrifts, having spent
  Your stock, and needy grown,
Y'are left here to lament
  Your poor estates, alone.   20

TO BLOSSOMS

Fair pledges of a fruitful tree,
  Why do ye fall so fast?
  Your date is not so past;
But you may stay yet here a while,
  To blush and gently smile;   5
    And go at last.

What, were ye born to be
  An hour or half's delight;
  And so to bid good-night?

'Twas pity nature brought ye forth   10
    Merely to show your worth,
        And lose you quite.

But you are lovely leaves, where we
    May read how soon things have
        Their end, though ne'er so brave: 15
And after they have shown their pride,
    Like you a while, they glide
        Into the grave.

HENRY KING
(1592-1669)

·

THE EXEQUY
TO HIS MATCHLESS NEVER-TO-BE-FORGOTTEN FRIEND

Accept, thou shrine of my dead saint,
Instead of dirges this complaint;
And for sweet flowers to crown thy hearse,
Receive a strew of weeping verse
From thy grieved friend, whom thou might'st see   5
Quite melted into tears for thee.

    Dear loss! since thy untimely fate,
My task hath been to meditate
On thee, on thee: thou art the book,
The library whereon I look,   10
Though almost blind. For thee (loved clay)
I languish out, not live, the day,
Using no other exercise
But what I practice with mine eyes;
By which wet glasses I found out   15
How lazily time creeps about
To one that mourns; this, only this,
My exercise and business is;
So I compute the weary hours
With sighs dissolvéd into showers.   20

    Nor wonder, if my time go thus
Backward and most preposterous;
Thou hast benighted me; thy set

This eve of blackness did beget,
Who wast my day (though overcast,   25
Before thou had'st thy noontide past),
And I remember must in tears,
Thou scarce had'st seen so many years
As day tells hours. By thy clear sun,
My life and fortune first did run;   30
But thou wilt never more appear
Folded within my hemisphere,
Since both thy light and motion
Like a fled star is fallen and gone,
And 'twixt me and my soul's dear wish   35
An earth now interposéd is,
Which such a strange eclipse doth make
As ne'er was read in almanac.

   I could allow thee, for a time,
To darken me and my sad clime,   40
Were it a month, a year, or ten,
I would thy exile live till then;
And all that space my mirth adjourn,
So thou would'st promise to return;
And putting off thy ashy shroud,   45
At length disperse this sorrow's cloud.

   But woe is me! the longest date
Too narrow is to calculate
These empty hopes; never shall I
Be so much blest as to descry   50
A glimpse of thee, till that day come,
Which shall the earth to cinders doom,
And a fierce fever must calcine
The body of this world, like thine,
My little world! That fit of fire   55
Once off, our bodies shall aspire
To our souls' bliss; then we shall rise,
And view ourselves with clearer eyes
In that calm region, where no night
Can hide us from each other's sight.   60

   Meantime, thou hast her, earth; much good
May my harm do thee. Since it stood
With Heaven's will, I might not call
Her longer mine, I give thee all

53. *calcine*   burn to a powder.

My short-lived right and interest   65
In her, whom living I loved best;
With a most free and bounteous grief
I give thee what I could not keep.
Be kind to her, and prithee look
Thou write into thy doomsday book   70
Each parcel of this rarity
Which in thy casket shrined doth lie;
See that thou make thy reckoning straight,
And yield her back again by weight;
For thou must audit on thy trust   75
Each grain and atom of this dust,
As thou wilt answer Him that lent,
Not gave thee, my dear monument.

    So close the ground, and 'bout her shade
Black curtains draw; my bride is laid.   80

    Sleep on, my love, in thy cold bed,
Never to be disquieted!
My last good-night! Thou wilt not wake,
Till I thy fate shall overtake;
Till age, or grief, or sickness must   85
Marry my body to that dust
It so much loves; and fill the room
My heart keeps empty in thy tomb.
Stay for me there; I will not fail
To meet thee in that hollow vale;   90
And think not much of my delay;
I am already on the way,
And follow thee with all the speed
Desire can make, or sorrows breed.
Each minute is a short degree,   95
And every hour a step towards thee.
At night, when I betake to rest,
Next morn I rise nearer my West
Of life, almost by eight hours sail
Than when sleep breathed his drowsy gale.   100

    Thus from the sun my bottom steers,
And my day's compass downward bears;
Nor labor I to stem the tide,
Through which to thee I swiftly glide.

'Tis true, with shame and grief I yield,   105
Thou, like the van first took'st the field,
And gotten hast the victory,
In thus adventuring to die
Before me, whose more years might crave
A just precedence in the grave.   110
But hark! My pulse, like a soft drum,
Beats my approach, tells thee I come;
And slow howe'er my marches be,
I shall at last sit down by thee.

The thought of this bids me go on,   115
And wait my dissolution
With hope and comfort. Dear (forgive
The crime), I am content to live
Divided, with but half a heart,
Till we shall meet and never part.   120

A CONTEMPLATION UPON FLOWERS

Brave flowers, that I could gallant it like you
    And be as little vain!
You come abroad, and make a harmless show,
    And to your beds of earth again;
You are not proud, you know your birth,   5
For your embroidered garments are from earth.

You do obey your months, and times, but I
    Would have it ever spring;
My fate would know no winter, never die,
    Nor think of such a thing.   10
Oh that I could my bed of earth but view,
And smile, and look as cheerfully as you!

Oh teach me to see death, and not to fear,
    But rather to take truce;
How often have I seen you at a bier,   15
    And there look fresh and spruce.
You fragrant flowers then teach me that my breath
Like yours may sweeten and perfume my death.

A Contemplation upon Flowers usually attributed to Henry King.

THOMAS CAREW
(ca. 1594–1640)

·

SONG: TO MY INCONSTANT MISTRESS

When thou, poor excommunicate
   From all the joys of love, shalt see
The full reward, and glorious fate,
   Which my strong faith shall purchase me,
   Then curse thine own inconstancy.   5

A fairer hand than thine shall cure
   That heart, which thy false oaths did wound;
And to my soul, a soul more pure
   Than thine shall by Love's hand be bound,
   And both with equal glory crowned.   10

Then shalt thou weep, entreat, complain
   To Love, as I did once to thee;
When all thy tears shall be as vain
   As mine were then, for thou shalt be
   Damned for thy false apostasy.   15

INGRATEFUL BEAUTY THREATENED

Know, Celia (since thou art so proud)
   'Twas I that gave thee thy renown;
Thou hadst in the forgotten crowd
   Of common beauties lived unknown,
Had not my verse exhaled thy name,   5
And with it imped the wings of fame.

That killing power is none of thine,
   I gave it to thy voice and eyes;
Thy sweets, thy graces, all are mine;
   Thou art my star, shin'st in my skies;   10
Then dart not from thy borrowed sphere
Lightning on him that fixed thee there.

6. *imped*   from falconry, to repair an injured wing by grafting feathers.

Tempt me with such affrights no more,
   Lest what I made, I uncreate;
Let fools thy mystic forms adore,   15
   I know thee in thy mortal state;
Wise poets, that wrapped truth in tales,
Knew her themselves, through all her veils.

TO A LADY THAT DESIRED
I WOULD LOVE HER

Now you have freely given me leave to love,
   What will you do?
   Shall I your mirth, or passion move
     When I begin to woo;
Will you torment, or scorn, or love me too?   5

Each petty beauty can disdain, and I
     Spite of your hate
   Without your leave can see, and die;
     Dispense a nobler fate,
'Tis easy to destroy, you may create.   10

Then give me leave to love, and love me too,
     Not with design
   To raise, as love's cursed rebels do,
     When puling poets whine,
Fame to their beauty, from their blubbered eyne.   15

Grief is a puddle, and reflects not clear
     Your beauty's rays;
   Joys are pure streams, your eyes appear
     Sullen in sadder lays;
In cheerful numbers they shine bright with praise,   20

Which shall not mention to express you fair,
     Wounds, flames, and darts,
   Storms in your brow, nets in your hair,
     Suborning all your parts,
Or to betray, or torture captive hearts.   25

I'll make your eyes like morning suns appear,
     As mild, and fair;
   Your brow as crystal smooth, and clear,
     And your dishevelled hair
Shall flow like a calm region of the air.   30

Rich nature's store (which is the poet's treasure)
    I'll spend, to dress
   Your beauties, if your mine of pleasure
    In equal thankfulness
You but unlock, so we each other bless.   35

JAMES SHIRLEY
(*1596–1666*)

·

FROM AJAX AND ULYSSES

The glories of our blood and state
  Are shadows, not substantial things,
There is no armor against fate,
  Death lays his icy hand on kings,
     Scepter and crown   5
     Must tumble down,
And in the dust be equal made,
With the poor crooked scythe and spade.

Some men with swords may reap the field,
  And plant fresh laurels where they kill,
But their strong nerves at last must yield,   10
  They tame but one another still;
     Early or late,
     They stoop to fate,
And must give up their murmuring breath,   15
When they pale captives creep to death.

The garlands wither on your brow,
  Then boast no more your mighty deeds,
Upon Death's purple altar now,
  See where the victor-victim bleeds,   20
     Your heads must come
     To the cold tomb;
Only the actions of the just
Smell sweet, and blossom in their dust.

EDMUND WALLER
(*1606–1687*)

·

SONG

 Go, lovely rose!
Tell her that wastes her time and me
 That now she knows,
When I resemble her to thee,
How sweet and fair she seems to be.   5

 Tell her that's young,
And shuns to have her graces spied,
 That hadst thou sprung
In deserts, where no men abide,
Thou must have uncommended died.   10

 Small is the worth
Of beauty from the light retired;
 Bid her come forth,
Suffer herself to be desired,
And not blush so to be admired.   15

 Then die! that she
The common fate of all things rare
 May read in thee;
How small a part of time they share
That are so wondrous sweet and fair!   20

SIR WILLIAM DAVENANT
(*1606–1668*)

·

TO A MISTRESS DYING

LOVER. Your beauty, ripe and calm and fresh
  As eastern summers are,
  Must now, forsaking time and flesh,
  Add light to some small star.

PHILOSOPHER. Whilst she yet lives, were stars decayed,   5
        Their light by hers relief might find;
        But death will lead her to a shade
            Where love is cold and beauty blind.

LOVER. Lovers, whose priests all poets are,
        Think every mistress, when she dies,   10
        Is changed at least into a star:
            And who dares doubt the poets wise?

PHILOSOPHER. But ask not bodies doomed to die
        To what abode they go;
        Since knowledge is but sorrow's spy,   15
            It is not safe to know.

SIR JOHN SUCKLING
(1609–1642)
·

SONG

I prithee spare me, gentle boy,
Press me no more for that slight toy,
That foolish trifle of an heart;
I swear it will not do its part,
Though thou dost thine, employ'st thy power and art.   5

For through long custom it has known
The little secrets, and is grown
Sullen and wise, will have its will!
And, like old hawks, pursues that still
That makes least sport, flies only where't can kill.   10

Some youth that has not made his story,
Will think perchance the pain's the glory;
And mannerly sit out love's feast;
I shall be carving of the best,
Rudely call for the last course 'fore the rest.   15

And, O, when once that course is passed,
How short a time the feast doth last!
Men rise away, and scarce say grace,
Or civilly once thank the face
That did invite, but seek another place.   20

‹ ☼ ›

ABRAHAM COWLEY
(1618–1667)

·

THE SPRING

Though you be absent here, I needs must say
The trees as beauteous are, and flowers as gay,
   As ever they were wont to be;
   Nay the birds' rural music too
   Is as melodious and free,   5
   As if they sung to pleasure you;
I saw a rosebud ope this morn; I'll swear
The blushing morning opened not more fair.

How could it be so fair, and you away?
How could the trees be beauteous, flowers so gay?   10
   Could they remember but last year,
   How you did them, they you delight,
   The sprouting leaves which saw you here,
   And called their fellows to the sight,
Would, looking round for the same sight in vain,   15
Creep back into their silent barks again.

Where'er you walked trees were as reverend made,
As when of old gods dwelt in every shade.
   Is't possible they should not know,
   What loss of honor they sustain,   20
   That thus they smile and flourish now,
   And still their former pride retain?
Dull creatures! 'tis not without cause that she,
Who fled the God of wit, was made a tree.

In ancient times sure they much wiser were,   25
When they rejoiced the Thracian verse to hear;
   In vain did Nature bid them stay,
   When Orpheus had his song begun,
   They called their wond'ring roots away,
   And bad them silent to him run.   30
How would those learned trees have followed you?
You would have drawn them, and their poet, too.

23. *she* Daphne, chased by Apollo, who escaped by being transformed into a laurel tree.

But who can blame them now? for, since you're gone,
They're here the only fair, and shine alone.
    You did their natural rights invade;   35
    Wherever you did walk or sit,
    The thickest boughs could make no shade,
    Although the sun had granted it;
The fairest flowers could please no more, near you,
Than painted flowers, set next to them, could do.   40

Whene'er then you come hither, that shall be
The time, which this to others is, to me.
    The little joys which here are now,
    The name of punishments do bear;
    When by their sight they let us know   45
    How we deprived of greater are.
'Tis you the best of seasons with you bring;
This is for beasts, and that for men, the spring.

RICHARD LOVELACE
(1618–1657)

·

THE GRASSHOPPER
TO MY NOBLE FRIEND, MR. CHARLES COTTON

Oh, thou that swing'st upon the waving hair
    Of some well-filléd oaten beard,
Drunk every night with a delicious tear
    Dropped thee from heav'n, where now th' art reared.

The joys of earth and air are thine entire,   5
    That with thy feet and wings dost hop and fly;
And when thy poppy works thou dost retire
    To thy carved acorn bed to lie.

Up with the day, the sun thou welcom'st then,
    Sport'st in the gilt-plats of his beams,   10
And all these merry days mak'st merry men,
    Thyself, and melancholy streams.

But ah, the sickle! golden ears are cropped;
    Ceres and Bacchus bid goodnight;

10. *plats* plots.

Sharp frosty fingers all your flow'rs have topped,   15
   And what scythes spared, winds shave off quite.

Poor verdant fool! and now green ice! thy joys
   Large and as lasting as thy perch of grass,
Bid us lay in 'gainst winter rain, and poise
   Their floods, with an o'erflowing glass.   20

Thou best of men and friends! we will create
   A genuine summer in each other's breast;
And spite of this cold time and frozen fate
   Thaw us a warm seat to our rest.

Our sacred hearths shall burn eternally   25
   As vestal flames; the North wind, he
Shall strike his frost-stretched wings, dissolve and fly
   This Aetna in epitome.

Dropping December shall come weeping in,
   Bewail th' usurping of his reign;   30
But when in showers of old Greek we begin,
   Shall cry, he hath his crown again!

Night as clear Hesper shall our tapers whip
   From the light casements where we play,
And the dark hag from her black mantle strip,   35
   And stick there everlasting day.

Thus richer than untempted kings are we,
   That asking nothing, nothing need:
Though lord of all what seas embrace; yet he
   That wants himself, is poor indeed.   40

SIR CHARLES SEDLEY
(*1639–1701*)

·

THE INDIFFERENCE

Thanks, fair Urania; to your scorn
I now am free, as I was born,
Of all the pain that I endured
By your late coldness I am cured.

31. *old Greek*   old Greek wine.

In losing me, proud nymph, you lose   5
The humblest slave your beauty knows;
In losing you, I but throw down
A cruel tyrant from her throne.

My ranging love did never find
Such charms of person and of mind;   10
Y'ave beauty, wit, and all things know,
But where you should your love bestow.

I unawares my freedom gave,
And to those tyrants grew a slave;
Would you have kept what you had won,   15
You should have more compassion shown.

Love is a burthen, which two hearts,
When equally they bear their parts,
With pleasure carry; but no one,
Alas, can bear it long alone.   20

I'm not of those who court their pain,
And make an idol of disdain;
My hope in love does ne'er expire,
But it extinguishes desire.

Nor yet of those who ill received,   25
Would have it otherwise believed
And, where their love could not prevail,
Take the vain liberty to rail.

Whoe'er would make his victor less,
Must his own weak defense confess,   30
And while her power he does defame,
He poorly doubles his own shame.

Even that malice does betray,
And speak concern another way;
And all such scorn in men is but   35
The smoke of fires ill put out.

He's still in torment, whom the rage
To detraction does engage;
In love indifference is sure
The only sign of perfect cure.   40

JOHN WILMOT, EARL OF ROCHESTER
(*1647–1680*)

·

LOVE AND LIFE: A SONG

All my past life is mine no more,
  The flying hours are gone:
Like transitory dreams giv'n o'er,
Whose images are kept in store,
  By memory alone.   5

The time that is to come is not;
  How can it then be mine?
The present moment's all my lot,
And that, as fast as it is got,
  Phyllis, is only thine.   10

Then talk not of inconstancy,
  False hearts, and broken vows;
If I, by miracle, can be
This live-long minute true to thee,
  'Tis all that heaven allows.   15

PLAIN DEALING'S DOWNFALL

Long time plain dealing in the haughty town,
Wand'ring about, though in threadbare gown,
At last unanimously was cried down.

When almost starved, she to the country fled,
In hopes, though meanly she should there be fed,   5
And tumble nightly on a pea-straw bed.

But knav'ry knowing her intent, took post,
And rumored her approach through every coast,
Vowing his ruin that should be her host.

Frighted at this, each rustic shut his door,   10
Bid her be gone, and trouble him no more,
For he that entertained her must be poor.

At this grief seized her, grief too great to tell,
When weeping, sighing, fainting, down she fell,
While knavery, laughing, rung her passing bell.　　15

JONATHAN SWIFT
(*1667–1745*)

.

TO THEIR EXCELLENCIES THE LORD JUSTICES OF IRELAND.

THE HUMBLE PETITION OF FRANCES HARRIS,

WHO MUST STARVE, AND DIE A MAID IF IT MISCARRIES.
ANNO. 1700.

Humbly showeth.

That I went to warm myself in Lady Betty's chamber, because I was cold,

And I had in a purse, seven pounds, four shillings, and six pence (besides farthings), in money, and gold;

So, because I had been buying things for my Lady last night,

I was resolved to tell my money, to see if it was right.

Now you must know, because my trunk has a very bad lock,   5

Therefore all the money I have (which, God knows, is a very small stock)

I keep in a pocket tied about my middle, next my smock.

So, when I went to put up my purse, as God would have it, my smock was unripped,

And instead of putting it into my pocket, down it slipped.

Then the bell rung, and I went down to put my Lady to bed,   10

And, God knows, I thought my money was as safe as my maidenhead.

So, when I came up again, I found my pocket feel very light,

But when I searched and missed my purse, Lord! I thought I should have sunk outright:

Lord! Madam, says Mary, how d'ye do? Indeed, says I, never worse;

But pray, Mary, can you tell what I have done with my purse?   15

Lord help me, said Mary, I never stirred out of this place!

Nay, said I, I had it in Lady Betty's chamber, that's a plain case.

So Mary got me to bed, and covered me up warm;

However, she stole away my garters, that I might do myself no harm.

So I tumbled and tossed all night, as you may very well think,   20

But hardly ever set my eyes together, or slept a wink.

So I was a-dreamed, methought, that we went and searched the folks round,

And in a corner of Mrs. Dukes's box, tied in a rag, the money was found.

So, next morning we told Whittle, and he fell a-swearing;

Then my dame Wadgar came, and she, you know, is thick of hearing;   25

Dame, said I, as loud as I could bawl, do you know what a loss I have had?

Nay, said she, my Lord Collway's folks are all very sad,

For my Lord Dromedary comes a Tuesday without fail;

Pugh! said I, but that's not the business that I ail.

Says Cary, says he, I have been a servant this five and twenty years, come spring,   30

And in all the places I lived, I never heard of such a thing.

Yes, says the steward, I remember when I was at my Lady Shrewsbury's,

Such a thing as this happened, just about the time of gooseberries.

So I went to the party suspected, and I found her full of grief;

(Now you must know, of all things in the world, I hate a thief.)   35

However, I was resolved to bring the discourse slyly about;

Mrs. Dukes, said I, here's an ugly accident has happened out;

'Tis not that I value the money three skips of a louse;

But the thing I stand upon, is the credit of the house;

'Tis true, seven pounds, four shillings, and six pence, makes a great hole in my wages,   40

Besides, as they say, service is no inheritance in these ages.

Now, Mrs. Dukes, you know, and everybody understands,

That though 'tis hard to judge, yet money can't go without hands.

The devil take me, said she (blessing herself), if I ever saw't!

So she roared like a Bedlam, as though I had called her all to naught;   45

So you know, what could I say to her any more?

I e'en left her, and came away as wise as I was before.

Well: but then they would have had me gone to the cunning man;

No, said I, 'tis the same thing, the chaplain will be here anon.

So the chaplain came in; now the servants say, he is my sweetheart,   50

Because he's always in my chamber, and I always take his part;

So, as the devil would have it, before I was aware, out I blundered,

Parson, said I, can you cast a nativity, when a body's plundered?

(Now you must know, he hates to be called Parson, like the devil.)

Truly, says he, Mrs. Nab, it might become you to be more civil.   55

If your money be gone, as a learned divine says, d'ye see,

You are no text for my handling, so take that from me.

I was never taken for a conjurer before, I'd have you to know.

48. *cunning man* a man with magical knowledge.

Lord, said I, don't be angry, I'm sure I never thought you so;
You know, I honor the cloth, I design to be a parson's wife,   60
I never took one in your coat for a conjurer in all my life.
With that, he twisted his girdle at me like a rope, as who should
    say,
Now you may go hang yourself for me, and so went away.
Well; I thought I should have swooned; Lord, said I, what shall I
    do?
I have lost my money, and shall lose my true-love too.   65
So, my Lord called me; Harry, said my Lord, don't cry,
I'll give something towards thy loss; and says my Lady, so will I.
Oh but, said I, what if after all, the chaplain won't *come to?*
For that, he said (an't please your Excellencies) I must petition
    you.

The premises tenderly considered, I desire your Excellencies' pro-
    tection,   70
And that I may have a share in next Sunday's collection,
And over and above, that I may have your Excellencies' letter,
With an order for the chaplain aforesaid; or instead of him, a
    better.
And then your poor petitioner, both night and day,
Or the chaplain (for 'tis his trade) as in duty bound, shall ever
    pray.   75

A DESCRIPTION OF THE MORNING

Now hardly here and there an hackney-coach
Appearing, showed the ruddy morn's approach.
Now Betty from her master's bed had flown,
And softly stole to discompose her own.
The slipshod 'prentice from his master's door,   5
Had pared the dirt, and sprinkled round the floor.
Now Moll had whirled her mop with dext'rous airs,
Prepared to scrub the entry and the stairs.
The youth with broomy stumps began to trace
The kennel edge, where wheels had worn the place.   10
The small-coal man was heard with cadence deep,
'Till drowned in shriller notes of chimney sweep,
Duns at his lordship's gate began to meet,
And brickdust Moll had screamed through half a street.
The turnkey now his flock returning sees,   15
Duly let out a-nights to steal for fees.
The watchful bailiffs take their silent stands;
And schoolboys lag with satchels in their hands.

10. *kennel edge* edge of the gutter.

A DESCRIPTION OF A CITY SHOWER

Careful observers may foretell the hour
(By sure prognostics) when to dread a shower:
While rain depends, the pensive cat gives o'er
Her frolics, and pursues her tail no more.
Returning home at night, you'll find the sink   5
Strike your offended sense with double stink.
If you be wise, then go not far to dine;
You'll spend in coach hire more than save in wine.
A coming shower your shooting corns presage,
Old achés throb, your hollow tooth will rage.   10
Saunt'ring in coffeehouse is Dulman seen;
He damns the climate and complains of spleen.

Meanwhile the South, rising with dabbled wings,
A sable cloud athwart the welkin flings,
That swilled more liquor than it could contain,   15
And like a drunkard gives it up again.
Brisk Susan whips her linen from the rope,
While the first drizzling shower is borne aslope:
Such is that sprinkling which some careless quean
Flirts on you from her mop, but not so clean: 20
You fly, invoke the gods; then turning, stop
To rail; she singing, still whirls on her mop.
Not yet the dust had shunned the unequal strife,
But aided by the wind, fought still for life;
And wafted with its foe by violent gust,   25
'Twas doubtful which was rain and which was dust.
Ah! where must needy poet seek for aid,
When dust and rain at once his coat invade?
Sole coat, where dust cemented by the rain
Erects the nap, and leaves a cloudy stain.   30

Now, in contiguous drops the flood comes down,
Threat'ning with deluge this devoted town.
To shops in crowds the daggled females fly,
Pretend to cheapen goods, but nothing buy.
The Templar spruce, while every spout's abroach,   35
Stays till 'tis fair, yet seems to call a coach.
The tucked-up sempstress walks with hasty strides,

3. *depends* hangs down (Latin), im-
pends.
19. *quean* rowdy woman.

34. *cheapen* purchase.
35. *Templar* lawyer living in Inner or
Middle Temple, London.

While streams run down her oiled umbrella's sides.
Here various kinds, by various fortunes led,
Commence acquaintance underneath a shed.   40
Triumphant Tories and desponding Whigs
Forget their feuds, and join to save their wigs.
Boxed in a chair the beau impatient sits,
While spouts run clatt'ring o'er the roof by fits,
And ever and anon with frightful din   45
The leather sounds; he trembles from within.
So when Troy chairmen bore the wooden steed,
Pregnant with Greeks impatient to be freed
(Those bully Greeks, who, as the moderns do,
Instead of paying chairmen, run them through),   50
Laocoön struck the outside with his spear,
And each imprisoned hero quaked for fear.

   Now from all parts the swelling kennels flow,
And bear their trophies with them as they go:
Filths of all hues and odors seem to tell   55
What street they sailed from, by the sight and smell.
They, as each torrent drives with rapid force,
From Smithfield or St. Pulchre's shape their course,
And in huge confluence joined at Snow Hill ridge,
Fall from the Conduit prone to Holborn Bridge.   60
Sweepings from butchers' stalls, dung, guts, and blood,
Drowned puppies, stinking sprats, all drenched in mud,
Dead cats, and turnip tops come tumbling down the flood.

STELLA'S BIRTHDAY
WRITTEN IN THE YEAR 1718

   Stella this day is thirty four
(We shan't dispute a year or more),
However Stella, be not troubled,
Although thy size and years are doubled,
Since first I saw thee at sixteen   5
The brightest virgin of the green.
So little is thy form declin'd,
Made up so largely in thy mind.

     Oh, would it please the gods to *split*
Thy beauty, size, and years, and wit,   10
No age could furnish out a pair

39. *kinds* natural types, genera.

Of nymphs so graceful, wise, and fair
　　With half the luster of your eyes,
With half your wit, your years, and size:
　　And then, before it grew too late,　　　　　15
How should I beg of gentle fate
　　(That either nymph might have her swain)
To split my Worship too in twain.

THE PROGRESS OF BEAUTY

When first Diana leaves her bed
　　Vapors and steams her looks disgrace,
A frouzy dirty colored red
　　Sits on her cloudy wrinkled face.

But, by degrees, when mounted high,　　　　　5
　　Her artificial face appears
Down from her window in the sky,
　　Her spots are gone, her visage clears.

'Twixt earthly females and the moon
　　All parallels exactly run;　　　　　　　　10
If Celia should appear too soon
　　Alas, the nymph would be undone!

To see her from her pillow rise
　　All reeking in a cloudy steam;
Cracked lips, foul teeth, and gummy eyes,　　15
　　Poor Strephon, how would he blaspheme!

The soot or powder which was wont
　　To make her hair look black as jet,
Falls from her tresses on her front
　　A mingled mass of dirt and sweat.　　　　20

Three colors, black, and red, and white,
　　So graceful in their proper place,
Remove them to a different light
　　They form a frightful hideous face,

For instance; when the lily slips　　　　　　25
　　Into the precincts of the rose,
And takes possession of the lips,
　　Leaving the purple to the nose.

So, Celia went entire to bed,
　　All her complexions safe and sound,　　　　30
But when she rose, the black and red
　　Though still in sight, had changed their ground.

The black, which would not be confined,
　　A more inferior station seeks,
Leaving the fiery red behind,　　　　　　35
　　And mingles in her muddy cheeks.

The paint by perspiration cracks,
　　And falls in rivulets of sweat,
On either side you see the tracks,
　　While at her chin the confluents met.　　40

A skillful housewife thus her thumb
　　With spittle while she spins, anoints,
And thus the brown meanders come
　　In trickling streams betwixt her joints.

But Celia can with ease reduce　　　　45
　　By help of pencil, paint, and brush
Each color to its place and use,
　　And teach her cheeks again to blush.

She knows her early self no more,
　　But filled with admiration, stands,　　50
As other painters oft adore
　　The workmanship of their own hands.

Thus, after four important hours
　　Celia's the wonder of her sex;
Say, which among the Heav'nly Pow'rs　　55
　　Could cause such wonderful effects?

Venus, indulgent to her kind,
　　Gave women all their hearts could wish
When first she taught them where to find
　　White lead and Lusitanian dish.　　60

Love with white lead cements his wings,
　　White lead was sent us to repair
Two brightest, brittlest earthly things,
　　A lady's face and chinaware.

She ventures now to lift the sash,   65
    The Window is her proper sphere;
Ah lovely nymph be not too rash,
    Nor let the beaux approach too near.

Take pattern by your sister star,
    Delude at once and bless our sight,   70
When you are seen, be seen from far,
    And chiefly choose to shine by night.

In the Pell-mell when passing by,
    Keep up the glasses of your chair,
Then each transported fop will cry,   75
    "G—d d—m me Jack, she's wondrous fair."

But, art no longer can prevail
    When the materials all are gone,
The best mechanic hand must fail
    Where nothing's left to work upon.   80

Matter, as wise logicians say,
    Cannot without a form subsist;
And form, say I, as well as they,
    Must fail if matter brings no grist.

And this is fair Diana's case;   85
    For, all astrologers maintain,
Each night a bit drops off her face
    When mortals say she's in her wane.

While Partridge wisely shows the cause
    Efficient of the moon's decay,
That cancer with his pois'nous claws   90
    Attacks her in the Milky Way:

But Gadbury in art profound
    From her pale cheeks pretends to show
That swain Endymion is not sound,
    Or else, that Mercury's her foe.   95

But, let the cause be what it will,
    In half a month she looks so thin
That Flamstead can with all his skill
    See but her forehead and her chin.   100

73. *Pell-mell* Pall Mall, a street in London (pronounced as spelled). 93. *Gadbury* an astrologer. 99. *Flamstead* the first astronomer royal.

Yet as she wastes, she grows discreet,
    Till midnight never shows her head;
So rotting Celia strolls the street,
    When sober folks are all a-bed.

For sure if this be luna's fate,   105
    Poor Celia, but of mortal race
In vain expects a longer date
    To the materials of her face.

When Mercury her tresses mows,
    To think of oil and soot, is vain,   110
No painting can restore a nose,
    Nor will her teeth return again.

Two balls of glass may serve for eyes,
    White lead can plaster up a cleft,
But these alas are poor supplies   115
    If neither cheeks nor lips be left.

Ye pow'rs who over Love preside,
    Since mortal beauties drop so soon,
If you would have us well supplied,
    Send us new nymphs with each new moon.   120

STELLA'S BIRTHDAY
MARCH 13, 1726/7

    This day, whate'er the fates decree,
Shall still be kept with joy by me:
This day then, let us not be told
That you are sick, and I grown old,
Nor think on our approaching ills,   5
And talk of spectacles and pills.
Tomorrow will be time enough
To hear such mortifying stuff.
Yet, since from reason may be brought
A better and more pleasing thought,   10
Which can, in spite of all decays,
Support a few remaining days:
From not the gravest of divines,
Accept, for once, some serious lines.

Although we now can form no more 15
Long schemes of life, as heretofore;
Yet you, while time is running fast,
Can look with joy on what is past.

Were future happiness and pain
A mere contrivance of the brain, 20
As atheists argue, to entice
And fit their proselytes for vice
(The only comfort they propose,
To have companions in their woes),
Grant this the case, yet sure 'tis hard 25
That virtue, styled its own reward,
And by all sages understood
To be the chief of human good,
Should acting, die, nor leave behind
Some lasting pleasure in the mind, 30
Which by remembrance will assuage
Grief, sickness, poverty, and age;
And strongly shoot a radiant dart,
To shine through life's declining part.

Say, Stella, feel you no content, 35
Reflecting on a life well spent?
Your skillful hand employed to save
Despairing wretches from the grave;
And then supporting from your store
Those whom you dragged from death before 40
(So Providence on mortals waits,
Preserving what it first creates);
Your generous boldness to defend
An innocent and absent friend;
That courage which can make you just, 45
To merit humbled in the dust;
The detestation you express
For vice in all its glittering dress;
That patience under torturing pain,
Where stubborn stoics would complain. 50

Shall these, like empty shadows, pass,
Or forms reflected from a glass?
Or mere chimeras in the mind,
That fly and leave no marks behind?
Does not the body thrive and grow 55
By food of twenty years ago?

And, had it not been still supplied,
It must a thousand times have died.
Then, who with reason can maintain
That no effects of food remain?   60
And is not virtue in mankind
The nutriment that feeds the mind?
Upheld by each good action past,
And still continued by the last:
Then, who with reason can pretend   65
That all effects of virtue end?

Believe me, Stella, when you show
That true contempt for things below,
Nor prize your life for other ends
Than merely to oblige your friends,   70
Your former actions claim their part,
And join to fortify your heart.
For virtue, in her daily race,
Like Janus, bears a double face,
Looks back with joy where she has gone,   75
And therefore goes with courage on.
She at your sickly couch will wait,
And guide you to a better state.

O then, whatever Heav'n intends,
Take pity on your pitying friends;   80
Nor let your ills affect your mind,
To fancy they can be unkind.
Me, surely me, you ought to spare,
Who gladly would your suff'rings share;
Or give my scrap of life to you,   85
And think it far beneath your due;
You, to whose care so oft I owe
That I'm alive to tell you so.

THE FURNITURE OF A WOMAN'S MIND

A set of phrases learned by rote;
A passion for a Scarlet-Coat;
When at a play to laugh, or cry,
Yet cannot tell the reason why;
Never to hold her tongue a minute,   5
While all she prates has nothing in it.

2. *Scarlet-Coat* soldier.

Whole hours can with a coxcomb sit,
And take his nonsense all for wit:
Her learning mounts to read a song,
But, half the words pronouncing wrong;   10
Has ev'ry repartee in store,
She spoke ten thousand times before.
Can ready compliments supply
On all occasions, cut and dry.
Such hatred to a parson's gown,   15
The sight will put her in a swown.
For conversation well endu'd;
She calls it witty to be rude;
And, placing raillery in railing,
Will tell aloud your greatest failing;   20
Nor makes a scruple to expose
Your bandy leg, or crooked nose.
Can, at her morning tea, run o'er
The scandal of the day before.
Improving hourly in her skill,   25
To cheat and wrangle at quadrille.

      In choosing lace a critic nice,
Knows to a groat the lowest price;
Can in her female clubs dispute
What lining best the silk will suit;   30
What colors each complexion match,
And where with art to place a patch.

      If chance a mouse creeps in her sight,
Can finely counterfeit a fright;
So sweetly screams if it comes near her,   35
She ravishes all hearts to hear her.
Can dext'rously her husband tease,
By taking fits whene'er she please;
By frequent practice learns the trick
At proper seasons to be sick;   40
Thinks nothing gives one airs so pretty;
At once creating love and pity.
If Molly happens to be careless,
And but neglects to warm her hair-lace,
She gets a cold as sure as death;   45
And vows she scarce can fetch her breath.
Admires how modest women can
Be so *robustious* like a man.

26. *quadrille*   card game.

In party, furious to her power;
A bitter Whig, or Tory sour; 50
Her arguments directly tend
Against the side she would defend:
Will prove herself a Tory plain,
From principles the Whigs maintain;
And, to defend the Whiggish cause, 55
Her topics from the Tories draws.

O yes! If any man can find
More virtues in a woman's mind,
Let them be sent to Mrs. Harding;
She'll pay the charges to a farthing. 60
Take notice, she has my commission
To add them in the next edition;
They may out-sell a better thing;
So, Holla Boys; God save the King.

THE DAY OF JUDGMENT

With a whirl of thought oppressed,
I sink from reverie to rest.
An horrid vision seized my head,
I saw the graves give up their dead.
Jove, armed with terrors, burst the skies, 5
And thunder roars and lightning flies.
Amazed, confused, its fate unknown,
The world stands trembling at his throne.
While each pale sinner hangs his head,
Jove, nodding, shook the heavens and said, 10
"Offending race of human kind,
By nature, reason, *learning*, blind;
You who through frailty stepped aside,
And you who never fell—*through pride;*
You who in different sects have shammed, 15
And come to see each other damned;
(So some folks told you, but they knew
No more of Jove's designs than you);
The world's mad business now is o'er,
And I resent these pranks no more. 20
I to such blockheads set my wit!
I damn such fools!—Go, go, you're bit."

59. *Harding*   a printer.   22. *bit*   taken in.
15. *shammed*   tricked.

ALEXANDER POPE
(1688–1744)

·

THE RAPE OF THE LOCK
AN HEROI-COMICAL POEM

Nolueram, Belinda, tuos violare capillos;
sed juvat hoc precibus me tribuisse tuis.
—MARTIAL

TO MRS. ARABELLA FERMOR

Canto I

What dire offense from am'rous causes springs,
What mighty contests rise from trivial things,
I sing—This verse to Caryll, Muse! is due:
This, even Belinda may vouchsafe to view:
Slight is the subject, but not so the praise,   5
If she inspire, and he approve my lays.
  Say what strange motive, Goddess! could compel
A well-bred lord to assault a gentle belle?
Oh, say what stranger cause, yet unexplored,
Could make a gentle belle reject a lord?   10
In tasks so bold can little men engage,
And in soft bosoms dwells such mighty rage?
  Sol through white curtains shot a tim'rous ray,
And oped those eyes that must eclipse the day;
Now lapdogs give themselves the rousing shake,   15
And sleepless lovers just at twelve awake.
Thrice rung the bell, the slipper knocked the ground,
And the pressed watch returned a silver sound.
Belinda still her downy pillow pressed,
Her guardian Sylph prolonged the balmy rest.   20
'Twas he had summoned to her silent bed
The Morning Dream that hovered o'er her head.
A youth more glitt'ring than a birthnight beau
(That even in slumber caused her cheek to glow)
Seemed to her ear his winning lips to lay,   25

Nolueram . . . tuis I was sorry, Belinda, to injure your locks, but I am pleased to have made this offering in answer to your prayers.
Mrs. Arabella Fermor the "Belinda" of the poem; "Mrs." for present-day "Miss."
3. *Caryll* friend of Pope and of Miss Fermor, who suggested that the poet "write a poem to make a jest of" the "stealing of Miss Belle Fermor's hair" (Pope).

And thus in whispers said, or seemed to say:
  "Fairest of mortals, thou distinguished care
Of thousand bright inhabitants of air!
If e'er one vision touched thy infant thought,
Of all the nurse and all the priest have taught,   30
Of airy elves by moonlight shadows seen,
The silver token, and the circled green,
Or virgins visited by angel powers,
With golden crowns and wreaths of heavenly flowers,
Hear and believe! thy own importance know,   35
Nor bound thy narrow views to things below.
Some secret truths, from learned pride concealed,
To maids alone and children are revealed:
What though no credit doubting wits may give?
The fair and innocent shall still believe.   40
Know, then, unnumbered spirits round thee fly,
The light militia of the lower sky:
These, though unseen, are ever on the wing,
Hang o'er the box, and hover round the Ring.
Think what an equipage thou hast in air,   45
And view with scorn two pages and a chair.
As now your own, our beings were of old,
And once enclosed in woman's beauteous mold;
Thence, by a soft transition, we repair
From earthly vehicles to these of air.   50
Think not, when woman's transient breath is fled,
That all her vanities at once are dead:
Succeeding vanities she still regards,
And though she plays no more, o'erlooks the cards.
Her joy in gilded chariots, when alive,   55
And love of ombre, after death survive.
For when the Fair in all their pride expire,
To their first elements their souls retire:
The sprites of fiery termagants in flame
Mount up, and take a Salamander's name.   60
Soft yielding minds to water glide away,
And sip, with Nymphs, their elemental tea.
The graver prude sinks downward to a Gnome,
In search of mischief still on earth to roam.
The light coquettes in Sylphs aloft repair,   65
And sport and flutter in the fields of air.
  "Know further yet; whoever fair and chaste
Rejects mankind, is by some Sylph embraced:

44. *Ring* in Hyde Park, where people   56. *ombre* a card game.
of fashion went to drive.

For spirits, freed from mortal laws, with ease
Assume what sexes and what shapes they please.   70
What guards the purity of melting maids,
In courtly balls, and midnight masquerades,
Safe from the treacherous friend, the daring spark,
The glance by day, the whisper in the dark,
When kind occasion prompts their warm desires,   75
When music softens, and when dancing fires?
'Tis but their Sylph, the wise Celestials know,
Though Honor is the word with men below.
    "Some nymphs there are, too conscious of their face,
For life predestined to the Gnomes' embrace.   80
These swell their prospects and exalt their pride,
When offers are disdained, and love denied.
Then gay ideas crowd the vacant brain,
While peers, and dukes, and all their sweeping train,
And garters, stars, and coronets appear,   85
And in soft sounds, 'your Grace' salutes their ear.
'Tis these that early taint the female soul,
Instruct the eyes of young coquettes to roll,
Teach infant cheeks a bidden blush to know,
And little hearts to flutter at a beau.   90
    "Oft, when the world imagine women stray,
The Sylphs through mystic mazes guide their way,
Through all the giddy circle they pursue,
And old impertinence expel by new.
What tender maid but must a victim fall   95
To one man's treat, but for another's ball?
When Florio speaks what virgin could withstand,
If gentle Damon did not squeeze her hand?
With varying vanities, from every part,
They shift the moving toyshop of their heart;   100
Where wigs with wigs, with sword-knots sword-knots strive,
Beaux banish beaux, and coaches coaches drive.
This erring mortals levity may call;
Oh, blind to truth! the Sylphs contrive it all.
    "Of these am I, who thy protection claim,   105
A watchful sprite, and Ariel is my name.
Late, as I ranged the crystal wilds of air,
In the clear mirror of thy ruling star
I saw, alas! some dread event impend,
Ere to the main this morning sun descend,   110
But Heaven reveals not what, or how, or where:
Warned by the Sylph, O pious maid, beware!

94. *impertinence* trifle.

This to disclose is all thy guardian can.
Beware of all, but most beware of Man!"
    He said; when Shock, who thought she slept too long,   115
Leaped up, and waked his mistress with his tongue.
'Twas then Belinda! if report say true,
Thy eyes first opened on a billet-doux;
Wounds, charms, and ardors were no sooner read,
But all the vision vanished from thy head.   120
    And now, unveiled, the toilet stands displayed,
Each silver vase in mystic order laid.
First, robed in white, the nymph intent adores,
With head uncovered, the cosmetic powers.
A heavenly image in the glass appears;   125
To that she bends, to that her eyes she rears.
Th' inferior priestess, at her altar's side,
Trembling begins the sacred rites of Pride.
Unnumbered treasures ope at once, and here
The various off'rings of the world appear;   130
From each she nicely culls with curious toil,
And decks the goddess with the glitt'ring spoil.
This casket India's glowing gems unlocks,
And all Arabia breathes from yonder box.
The tortoise here and elephant unite,   135
Transformed to combs, the speckled and the white.
Here files of pins extend their shining rows,
Puffs, powders, patches, Bibles, billet-doux.
Now awful Beauty puts on all its arms,
The fair each moment rises in her charms,   140
Repairs her smiles, awakens every grace,
And calls forth all the wonders of her face;
Sees by degrees a purer blush arise,
And keener lightnings quicken in her eyes.
The busy Sylphs surround their darling care,   145
These set the head, and those divide the hair,
Some fold the sleeve, whilst others plait the gown;
And Betty's praised for labors not her own.

Canto II

    Not with more glories, in th' ethereal plain,
The sun first rises o'er the purpled main,
Than, issuing forth, the rival of his beams
Launched on the bosom of the silver Thames.
Fair nymphs and well-dressed youths around her shone,   5

But ev'ry eye was fixed on her alone.
On her white breast a sparkling cross she wore,
Which Jews might kiss, and infidels adore.
Her lively looks a sprightly mind disclose,
Quick as her eyes, and as unfixed as those: 10
Favors to none, to all she smiles extends;
Oft she rejects, but never once offends.
Bright as the sun, her eyes the gazers strike,
And, like the sun, they shine on all alike.
Yet graceful ease, and sweetness void of pride,   15
Might hide her faults, if belles had faults to hide:
If to her share some female errors fall,
Look on her face, and you'll forget 'em all.
    This nymph, to the destruction of mankind,
Nourished two locks which graceful hung behind   20
In equal curls, and well conspired to deck
With shining ringlets the smooth iv'ry neck.
Love in these labyrinths his slaves detains,
And mighty hearts are held in slender chains.
With hairy springes we the birds betray,   25
Slight lines of hair surprise the finny prey,
Fair tresses man's imperial race ensnare,
And beauty draws us with a single hair.
    The adventurous Baron the bright locks admired,
He saw, he wished, and to the prize aspired.   30
Resolved to win, he meditates the way,
By force to ravish, or by fraud betray;
For when success a lover's toil attends,
Few ask if fraud or force attained his ends.
    For this, ere Phoebus rose, he had implored   35
Propitious Heaven, and ev'ry power adored,
But chiefly Love—to Love an altar built,
Of twelve vast French romances, neatly gilt.
There lay three garters, half a pair of gloves,
And all the trophies of his former loves.   40
With tender billet-doux he lights the pyre,
And breathes three am'rous sighs to raise the fire.
Then prostrate falls, and begs with ardent eyes
Soon to obtain, and long possess the prize:
The powers gave ear, and granted half his prayer,   45
The rest the winds dispersed in empty air.
    But now secure the painted vessel glides,
The sunbeams trembling on the floating tides,
While melting music steals upon the sky,

25. *springes*   snares.

And softened sounds along the waters die.   50
Smooth flow the waves, the zephyrs gently play,
Belinda smiled, and all the world was gay.
All but the Sylph—with careful thoughts oppressed,
The impending woe sat heavy on his breast.
He summons straight his denizens of air;   55
The lucid squadrons round the sails repair:
Soft o'er the shrouds aërial whispers breathe
That seemed but zephyrs to the train beneath.
Some to the sun their insect-wings unfold,
Waft on the breeze, or sink in clouds of gold.   60
Transparent forms too fine for mortal sight,
Their fluid bodies half dissolved in light,
Loose to the wind their airy garments flew,
Thin glitt'ring textures of the filmy dew,
Dipped in the richest tincture of the skies,   65
Where light disports in ever-mingling dyes,
While ev'ry beam new transient colors flings,
Colors that change whene'er they wave their wings.
Amid the circle, on the gilded mast,
Superior by the head, was Ariel placed;   70
His purple pinions opening to the sun,
He raised his azure wand, and thus begun:
    "Ye Sylphs and Sylphids, to your chief give ear!
Fays, Fairies, Genii, Elves, and Daemons, hear!
Ye know the spheres and various tasks assigned   75
By laws eternal to the aërial kind.
Some in the fields of purest ether play,
And bask and whiten in the blaze of day.
Some guide the course of wandering orbs on high,
Or roll the planets through the boundless sky.   80
Some less refined, beneath the moon's pale light
Pursue the stars that shoot athwart the night,
Or suck the mists in grosser air below,
Or dip their pinions in the painted bow,
Or brew fierce tempests on the wintry main,   85
Or o'er the glebe distill the kindly rain.
Others on earth o'er human race preside,
Watch all their ways, and all their actions guide:
Of these the chief the care of nations own,
And guard with arms divine the British Throne.   90
    "Our humbler province is to tend the Fair,
Not a less pleasing, though less glorious care:
To save the powder from too rude a gale,
Nor let the imprisoned essences exhale,

To draw fresh colors from the vernal flowers,   95
To steal from rainbows e'er they drop in showers
A brighter wash; to curl their waving hairs,
Assist their blushes, and inspire their airs;
Nay oft, in dreams invention we bestow,
To change a flounce, or add a furbelow.   100
    "This day black omens threat the brightest fair,
That e'er deserved a watchful spirit's care;
Some dire disaster, or by force or slight,
But what, or where, the Fates have wrapped in night:
Whether the nymph shall break Diana's law,   105
Or some frail china jar receive a flaw,
Or stain her honor or her new brocade,
Forget her prayers, or miss a masquerade,
Or lose her heart, or necklace, at a ball;
Or whether Heaven has doomed that Shock must fall.   110
Haste, then, ye spirits! to your charge repair:
The flutt'ring fan be Zephyretta's care;
The drops to thee, Brillante, we consign;
And, Momentilla, let the watch be thine;
Do thou, Crispissa, tend her favorite Lock;   115
Ariel himself shall be the guard of Shock.
    "To fifty chosen Sylphs, of special note,
We trust th' important charge, the petticoat;
Oft have we known that sevenfold fence to fail,
Though stiff with hoops, and armed with ribs of whale.   120
Form a strong line about the silver bound,
And guard the wide circumference around.
    "Whatever spirit, careless of his charge,
His post neglects, or leaves the Fair at large,
Shall feel sharp vengeance soon o'ertake his sins,   125
Be stopped in vials, or transfixed with pins,
Or plunged in lakes of bitter washes lie,
Or wedged whole ages in a bodkin's eye;
Gums and pomatums shall his flight restrain,
While clogged he beats his silken wings in vain,   130
Or alum styptics with contracting power
Shrink his thin essence like a riveled flower:
Or, as Ixion fixed, the wretch shall feel
The giddy motion of the whirling mill,
In fumes of burning chocolate shall glow,   135
And tremble at the sea that froths below!"
    He spoke; the spirits from the sails descend;

113. *drops* diamond ear rings.   fold shield of a Homeric hero.
119. *sevenfold fence* like the seven-   132. *riveled* wrinkled by shrinking.

Some, orb in orb, around the nymph extend;
Some thread the mazy ringlets of her hair;
Some hang up the pendants of her ear;   140
With beating hearts the dire event they wait,
Anxious, and trembling for the birth of Fate.

Canto III

Close by those meads, forever crowned with flowers,
Where Thames with pride surveys his rising towers,
There stands a structure of majestic frame,
Which from the neighboring Hampton takes its name.
Here Britain's statesmen oft the fall foredoom   5
Of foreign tyrants and of nymphs at home;
Here thou, great Anna! whom three realms obey,
Dost sometimes counsel take—and sometimes tea.
Hither the heroes and the nymphs resort,
To taste awhile the pleasures of a court;   10
In various talk the instructive hours they passed,
Who gave the ball, or paid the visit last;
One speaks the glory of the British Queen,
And one describes a charming Indian screen;
A third interprets motions, looks, and eyes;   15
At every word a reputation dies.
Snuff, or the fan, supply each pause of chat,
With singing, laughing, ogling, and all that.
Meanwhile, declining from the noon of day,
The sun obliquely shoots his burning ray;   20
The hungry judges soon the sentence sign,
And wretches hang that jurymen may dine;
The merchant from th' Exchange returns in peace,
And the long labors of the toilet cease.
Belinda now, whom thirst of fame invites,   25
Burns to encounter two adventurous knights,
At ombre singly to decide their doom,
And swells her breast with conquests yet to come.
Straight the three bands prepare in arms to join,
Each band the number of the sacred nine.   30
Soon as she spreads her hand, the aërial guard
Descend, and sit on each important card:
First Ariel perched upon a Matadore,
Then each, according to the rank they bore;
For Sylphs, yet mindful of their ancient race,   35

3. *structure* Hampton Court Palace.

Are, as when women, wondrous fond of place.
   Behold, four Kings in majesty revered,
With hoary whiskers and a forky beard;
And four fair Queens whose hands sustain a flower,
Th' expressive emblem of their softer power;   40
Four Knaves in garbs succinct, a trusty band,
Caps on their heads, and halberts in their hand;
And parti-colored troops, a shining train,
Draw forth to combat on the velvet plain.
   The skillful nymph reviews her force with care;   45
"Let Spades be trumps!" she said, and trumps they were.
   Now move to war her sable Matadores,
In show like leaders of the swarthy Moors.
Spadillio first, unconquerable lord!
Led off two captive trumps, and swept the board.   50
As many more Manillio forced to yield,
And marched a victor from the verdant field.
Him Basto followed, but his fate more hard
Gained but one trump and one plebeian card.
With his broad saber next, a chief in years,   55
The hoary Majesty of Spades appears,
Puts forth one manly leg, to sight revealed,
The rest his many-colored robe concealed.
The rebel Knave, who dares his prince engage,
Proves the just victim of his royal rage.   60
Even mighty Pam, that kings and queens o'erthrew
And mowed down armies in the fights of loo,
Sad chance of war! now destitute of aid,
Falls undistinguished by the victor Spade.
   Thus far both armies to Belinda yield;   65
Now to the Baron fate inclines the field.
His warlike amazon her host invades,
The imperial consort of the crown of Spades.
The Club's black tyrant first her victim died,
Spite of his haughty mien and barbarous pride.   70
What boots the regal circle on his head,
His giant limbs, in state unwieldy spread?
That long behind he trails his pompous robe,
And of all monarchs only grasps the globe?
   The Baron now his Diamonds pours apace;   75
Th' embroidered King who shows but half his face,
And his refulgent Queen, with powers combined
Of broken troops an easy conquest find.
Clubs, Diamonds, Hearts, in wild disorder seen,
With throngs promiscuous strew the level green.   80

Thus when dispersed a routed army runs,
Of Asia's troops, and Afric's sable sons,
With like confusion different nations fly,
Of various habit, and of various dye,
The pierced battalions disunited fall   85
In heaps on heaps; one fate o'erwhelms them all.
   The Knave of Diamonds tries his wily arts,
And wins (oh shameful chance!) the Queen of Hearts.
At this, the blood the virgin's cheek forsook,
A livid paleness spreads o'er all her look;   90
She sees, and trembles at the approaching ill,
Just in the jaws of ruin, and Codille,
And now (as oft in some distempered state)
On one nice trick depends the gen'ral fate.
An Ace of Hearts steps forth: the King unseen   95
Lurked in her hand, and mourned his captive Queen.
He springs to vengeance with an eager pace,
And falls like thunder on the prostrate Ace.
The nymph exulting fills with shouts the sky,
The walls, the woods, and long canals reply.   100
   O thoughtless mortals! ever blind to fate,
Too soon dejected, and too soon elate:
Sudden these honors shall be snatched away,
And cursed forever this victorious day.
   For lo! the board with cups and spoons is crowned,   105
The berries crackle, and the mill turns round;
On shining altars of Japan they raise
The silver lamp; the fiery spirits blaze:
From silver spouts the grateful liquors glide,
While China's earth receives the smoking tide.   110
At once they gratify their scent and taste,
And frequent cups prolong the rich repast.
Straight hover round the fair her airy band;
Some, as she sipped, the fuming liquor fanned,
Some o'er her lap their careful plumes displayed,   115
Trembling, and conscious of the rich brocade.
Coffee (which makes the politician wise,
And see through all things with his half-shut eyes)
Sent up in vapors to the Baron's brain
New stratagems, the radiant Lock to gain.   120
Ah, cease, rash youth! desist ere 'tis too late,
Fear the just Gods, and think of Scylla's fate!
Changed to a bird, and sent to flit in air,

107. *altars of Japan* lacquered tables.   Nisus, by plucking the purple hair on
122. *Scylla* Scylla betrayed her father,   which his life depended.

She dearly pays for Nisus' injured hair!
But when to mischief mortals bend their will,   125
How soon they find fit instruments of ill!
Just then, Clarissa drew with tempting grace
A two-edged weapon from her shining case;
So ladies in romance assist their knight,
Present the spear, and arm him for the fight.   130
He takes the gift with rev'rence, and extends
The little engine on his fingers' ends;
This just behind Belinda's neck he spread,
As o'er the fragrant steams she bends her head.
Swift to the Lock a thousand sprites repair,   135
A thousand wings, by turns, blow back the hair,
And thrice they twitched the diamond in her ear,
Thrice she looked back, and thrice the foe drew near.
Just in that instant, anxious Ariel sought
The close recesses of the virgin's thought;   140
As on the nosegay in her breast reclined,
He watched th' ideas rising in her mind,
Sudden he viewed, in spite of all her art,
An earthly lover lurking at her heart.
Amazed, confused, he found his power expired,   145
Resigned to fate, and with a sigh retired.
The Peer now spreads the glitt'ring forfex wide,
T'inclose the Lock; now joins it, to divide.
Ev'n then, before the fatal engine closed,
A wretched Sylph too fondly interposed;   150
Fate urged the shears, and cut the Sylph in twain
(But airy substance soon unites again);
The meeting points the sacred hair dissever
From the fair head, forever, and forever!
Then flashed the living lightning from her eyes,   155
And screams of horror rend th' affrighted skies.
Not louder shrieks to pitying Heav'n are cast,
When husbands or when lapdogs breathe their last;
Or when rich china vessels fall'n from high,
In glitt'ring dust and painted fragments lie!   160
"Let wreaths of triumph now my temples twine,"
The victor cried, "the glorious prize is mine!
While fish in streams, or birds delight in air,
Or in a coach and six the British Fair,
As long as *Atalantis* shall be read,   165
Or the small pillow grace a lady's bed,
While visits shall be paid on solemn days,
When num'rous wax-lights in bright order blaze,

While nymphs take treats, or assignations give,
So long my honor, name, and praise shall live!   170
    What Time would spare, from Steel receives its date,
And monuments, like men, submit to fate!
Steel could the labor of the Gods destroy,
And strike to dust th' imperial towers of Troy;
Steel could the works of mortal pride confound,   175
And hew triumphal arches to the ground.
What wonder then, fair nymph! thy hairs should feel,
The conqu'ring force of unresisted Steel?"

Canto IV

    But anxious cares the pensive nymph oppressed,
And secret passions labored in her breast.
Not youthful kings in battle seized alive,
Not scornful virgins who their charms survive,
Not ardent lovers robbed of all their bliss,   5
Not ancient ladies when refused a kiss,
Not tyrants fierce that unrepenting die,
Not Cynthia when her manteau's pinned awry,
E'er felt such rage, resentment, and despair,
As thou, sad virgin! for thy ravished hair.   10
    For, that sad moment, when the Sylphs withdrew
And Ariel weeping from Belinda flew,
Umbriel, a dusky, melancholy sprite
As ever sullied the fair face of light,
Down to the central earth, his proper scene,   15
Repaired to search the gloomy Cave of Spleen.
    Swift on his sooty pinions flits the Gnome,
And in a vapor reached the dismal dome.
No cheerful breeze this sullen region knows,
The dreaded east is all the wind that blows.   20
Here in a grotto, sheltered close from air,
And screened in shades from day's detested glare,
She sighs forever on her pensive bed,
Pain at her side, and Megrim at her head.
    Two handmaids wait the throne: alike in place,   25
But diff'ring far in figure and in face.
Here stood Ill-Nature like an ancient maid,
Her wrinkled form in black and white arrayed;
With store of prayers for mornings, nights, and noons,

16. *Spleen*   or "the vapors," a fashion-   24. *Megrim*   migraine headache.
able illness.

Her hand is filled; her bosom with lampoons.   30
   There Affectation, with a sickly mien,
Shows in her cheek the roses of eighteen,
Practiced to lisp, and hang the head aside,
Faints into airs, and languishes with pride,
On the rich quilt sinks with becoming woe,   35
Wrapped in a gown, for sickness and for show.
The fair ones feel such maladies as these,
When each new nightdress gives a new disease.
   A constant vapor o'er the palace flies,
Strange phantoms rising as the mists arise;   40
Dreadful as hermit's dreams in haunted shades,
Or bright as visions of expiring maids.
Now glaring fiends, and snakes on rolling spires,
Pale specters, gaping tombs, and purple fires;
Now lakes of liquid gold, Elysian scenes,   45
And crystal domes, and angels in machines.
   Unnumbered throngs on every side are seen
Of bodies changed to various forms by Spleen.
Here living teapots stand, one arm held out,
One bent; the handle this, and that the spout: 50
A pipkin there, like Homer's tripod, walks;
Here sighs a jar, and there a goose pie talks;
Men prove with child, as powerful fancy works,
And maids, turned bottles, call aloud for corks.
   Safe passed the Gnome through this fantastic band,   55
A branch of healing spleenwort in his hand.
Then thus addressed the Power: "Hail, wayward Queen!
Who rule the sex to fifty from fifteen,
Parent of vapors and of female wit,
Who give the hysteric or poetic fit,   60
On various tempers act by various ways,
Make some take physic, others scribble plays;
Who cause the proud their visits to delay,
And send the godly in a pet to pray.
A nymph there is that all your power disdains,   65
And thousands more in equal mirth maintains.
But oh! if e'er thy Gnome could spoil a grace,
Or raise a pimple on a beauteous face,
Like citron-waters matrons' cheeks inflame,
Or change complexions at a losing game;   70
If e'er with airy horns I planted heads,
Or rumpled petticoats, or tumbled beds,
Or caused suspicion when no soul was rude,
Or discomposed the headdress of a prude,

Or e'er to costive lapdog gave disease,   75
Which not the tears of brightest eyes could ease,
Hear me, and touch Belinda with chagrin:
That single act gives half the world the spleen."
    The Goddess with a discontented air
Seems to reject him, though she grants his prayer.   80
A wondrous bag with both her hands she binds,
Like that where once Ulysses held the winds;
There she collects the force of female lungs,
Sighs, sobs, and passions, and the war of tongues.
A vial next she fills with fainting fears,   85
Soft sorrows, melting griefs, and flowing tears.
The Gnome rejoicing bears her gifts away,
Spreads his black wings, and slowly mounts to day.
    Sunk in Thalestris' arms the nymph he found,
Her eyes dejected and her hair unbound.   90
Full o'er their heads the swelling bag he rent,
And all the Furies issued at the vent.
Belinda burns with more than mortal ire,
And fierce Thalestris fans the rising fire.
"O wretched maid!" she spread her hands, and cried   95
(While Hampton's echoes, "Wretched maid!" replied),
"Was it for this you took such constant care
The bodkin, comb, and essence to prepare?
For this your locks in paper durance bound,
For this with torturing irons wreathed around?   100
For this with fillets strained your tender head,
And bravely bore the double loads of lead?
Gods! shall the ravisher display your hair,
While the fops envy, and the ladies stare!
Honor forbid! at whose unrivaled shrine   105
Ease, pleasure, virtue, all, our sex resign.
Methinks already I your tears survey,
Already hear the horrid things they say,
Already see you a degraded toast,
And all your honor in a whisper lost!   110
How shall I, then, your helpless fame defend?
'Twill then be infamy to seem your friend!
And shall this prize, th' inestimable prize,
Exposed through crystal to the gazing eyes,
And heightened by the diamond's circling rays,   115
On that rapacious hand forever blaze?
Sooner shall grass in Hyde Park Circus grow,

---

109. *toast* a woman who is often   117. *Circus* the Ring, Canto I, line
"toasted" for her charms.   44.

And wits take lodgings in the sound of Bow;
Sooner let earth, air, sea, to chaos fall,
Men, monkeys, lapdogs, parrots, perish all!"   120
   She said; then raging to Sir Plume repairs,
And bids her beau demand the precious hairs
(Sir Plume of amber snuffbox justly vain,
And the nice conduct of a clouded cane).
With earnest eyes, and round unthinking face,   125
He first the snuffbox opened, then the case,
And thus broke out—"My Lord, why, what the devil!
Z——ds! damn the lock! 'fore Gad, you must be civil!
Plague on't! 'tis past a jest—nay prithee, pox!
Give her the hair"—he spoke, and rapped his box.   130
   "It grieves me much," replied the Peer again,
"Who speaks so well should ever speak in vain.
But by this Lock, this sacred Lock I swear
(Which never more shall join its parted hair;
Which never more its honors shall renew,   135
Clipped from the lovely head where late it grew),
That while my nostrils draw the vital air,
This hand, which won it, shall forever wear."
He spoke, and speaking, in proud triumph spread
The long-contended honors of her head.   140
   But Umbriel, hateful Gnome, forbears not so;
He breaks the vial whence the sorrows flow.
Then see! the nymph in beauteous grief appears,
Her eyes half languishing, half drowned in tears;
On her heaved bosom hung her drooping head,   145
Which, with a sigh, she raised, and thus she said:
   "Forever cursed be this detested day,
Which snatched my best, my fav'rite curl away!
Happy! ah, ten times happy had I been,
If Hampton Court these eyes had never seen!   150
Yet am not I the first mistaken maid,
By love of courts to num'rous ills betrayed.
Oh, had I rather unadmired remained
In some lone isle, or distant northern land;
Where the gilt chariot never marks the way,   155
Where none learn ombre, none e'er taste bohea!
There kept my charms concealed from mortal eye,
Like roses that in deserts bloom and die.
What moved my mind with youthful lords to roam?
Oh, had I stayed, and said my prayers at home!   160
'Twas this the morning omens seemed to tell;

156. *bohea* a kind of tea.

Thrice from my trembling hand the patch box fell;
The tottering china shook without a wind,
Nay, Poll sat mute, and Shock was most unkind!
A Sylph too warned me of the threats of fate,   165
In mystic visions, now believed too late!
See the poor remnants of these slighted hairs!
My hands shall rend what ev'n thy rapine spares.
These in two sable ringlets taught to break,
Once gave new beauties to the snowy neck.   170
The sister lock now sits uncouth, alone,
And in its fellow's fate foresees its own;
Uncurled it hangs, the fatal shears demands,
And tempts once more thy sacrilegious hands.
Oh, hadst thou, cruel! been content to seize   175
Hairs less in sight, or any hairs but these!"

Canto V

    She said: the pitying audience melt in tears.
But Fate and Jove had stopped the Baron's ears.
In vain Thalestris with reproach assails,
For who can move when fair Belinda fails?
Not half so fixed the Trojan could remain,   5
While Anna begged and Dido raged in vain.
Then grave Clarissa graceful waved her fan;
Silence ensued, and thus the nymph began:
    "Say why are beauties praised and honored most,
The wise man's passion, and the vain man's toast?   10
Why decked with all that land and sea afford,
Why angels called, and angel-like adored?
Why round our coaches crowd the white-gloved beaux,
Why bows the side box from its inmost rows?
How vain are all these glories, all our pains,   15
Unless good sense preserve what beauty gains;
That men may say, when we the front box grace,
'Behold the first in virtue as in face!'
Oh! if to dance all night, and dress all day,
Charmed the smallpox, or chased old age away,   20
Who would not scorn what housewife's cares produce,
Or who would learn one earthly thing of use?
To patch, nay ogle, might become a saint,
Nor could it sure be such a sin to paint.
But since, alas! frail beauty must decay,   25
Curled or uncurled, since locks will turn to gray;

Since painted, or not painted, all shall fade,
And she who scorns a man must die a maid;
What then remains but well our power to use,
And keep good humor still whate'er we lose?   30
And trust me, dear! good humor can prevail
When airs, and flights, and screams, and scolding fail.
Beauties in vain their pretty eyes may roll;
Charms strike the sight, but merit wins the soul."
     So spoke the dame, but no applause ensued;   35
Belinda frowned, Thalestris called her prude.
"To arms, to arms!" the fierce virago cries,
And swift as lightning to the combat flies.
All side in parties, and begin the attack;
Fans clap, silks rustle, and tough whalebones crack;   40
Heroes' and heroines' shouts confus'dly rise,
And bass and treble voices strike the skies.
No common weapons in their hands are found,
Like Gods they fight, nor dread a mortal wound.
     So when bold Homer makes the Gods engage,   45
And heavenly breasts with human passions rage;
'Gainst Pallas, Mars; Latona, Hermes arms;
And all Olympus rings with loud alarms:
Jove's thunder roars, heav'n trembles all around,
Blue Neptune storms, the bellowing deeps resound: 50
Earth shakes her nodding towers, the ground gives way,
And the pale ghosts start at the flash of day!
     Triumphant Umbriel on a sconce's height
Clapped his glad wings, and sat to view the fight:
Propped on the bodkin spears, the sprites survey   55
The growing combat, or assist the fray.
     While through the press enraged Thalestris flies,
And scatters death around from both her eyes,
A beau and witling perished in the throng,
One died in metaphor, and one in song.   60
"O cruel nymph! a living death I bear,"
Cried Dapperwit, and sunk beside his chair.
A mournful glance Sir Fopling upwards cast,
"Those eyes are made so killing"—was his last.
Thus on Maeander's flowery margin lies   65
Th' expiring swan, and as he sings he dies.
     When bold Sir Plume had drawn Clarissa down,
Chloe stepped in, and killed him with a frown;
She smiled to see the doughty hero slain,
But, at her smile, the beau revived again.   70
     Now Jove suspends his golden scales in air,
Weighs the men's wits against the lady's hair;

The doubtful beam long nods from side to side;
At length the wits mount up, the hairs subside.
  See, fierce Belinda on the Baron flies,   75
With more than usual lightning in her eyes;
Nor feared the chief the unequal fight to try,
Who sought no more than on his foe to die.
But this bold lord with manly strength endued,
She with one finger and a thumb subdued: 80
Just where the breath of life his nostrils drew,
A charge of snuff the wily virgin threw;
The Gnomes direct, to every atom just,
The pungent grains of titillating dust.
Sudden, with starting tears each eye o'erflows,   85
And the high dome re-echoes to his nose.
  "Now meet thy fate," incensed Belinda cried,
And drew a deadly bodkin from her side.
(The same, his ancient personage to deck,
Her great-great-grandsire wore about his neck,   90
In three seal rings; which after, melted down,
Formed a vast buckle for his widow's gown:
Her infant grandame's whistle next it grew,
The bells she jingled, and the whistle blew;
Then in a bodkin graced her mother's hairs,   95
Which long she wore, and now Belinda wears.)
  "Boast not my fall," he cried, "insulting foe!
Thou by some other shalt be laid as low.
Nor think to die dejects my lofty mind:
All that I dread is leaving you behind!   100
Rather than so, ah, let me still survive,
And burn in Cupid's flames—but burn alive."
  "Restore the Lock!" she cries; and all around
"Restore the Lock!" the vaulted roofs rebound.
Not fierce Othello in so loud a strain   105
Roared for the handkerchief that caused his pain.
But see how oft ambitious aims are crossed,
And chiefs contend till all the prize is lost!
The lock, obtained with guilt, and kept with pain,
In every place is sought, but sought in vain: 110
With such a prize no mortal must be blessed,
So Heaven decrees! with Heaven who can contest?
  Some thought it mounted to the lunar sphere,
Since all things lost on earth are treasured there.
There heroes' wits are kept in ponderous vases,   115
And beaux' in snuffboxes and tweezer cases.
There broken vows and deathbed alms are found,
And lovers' hearts with ends of riband bound,

The courtier's promises, and sick man's prayers,
The smiles of harlots, and the tears of heirs,   120
Cages for gnats, and chains to yoke a flea,
Dried butterflies, and tomes of casuistry.
   But trust the Muse—she saw it upward rise,
Though marked by none but quick, poetic eyes
(So Rome's great founder to the heavens withdrew,   125
To Proculus alone confessed in view);
A sudden star, it shot through liquid air,
And drew behind a radiant trail of hair.
Not Berenice's locks first rose so bright,
The heavens bespangling with disheveled light.   130
The Sylphs behold it kindling as it flies,
And pleased pursue its progress through the skies.
   This the beau monde shall from the Mall survey,
And hail with music its propitious ray.
This the blest lover shall for Venus take,   135
And send up vows from Rosamonda's Lake.
This Partridge soon shall view in cloudless skies,
When next he looks through Galileo's eyes;
And hence the egregious wizard shall foredoom
The fate of Louis, and the fall of Rome.   140
   Then cease, bright nymph! to mourn thy ravished hair,
Which adds new glory to the shining sphere!
Not all the tresses that fair head can boast,
Shall draw such envy as the Lock you lost.
For, after all the murders of your eye,   145
When, after millions slain, yourself shall die:
When those fair suns shall set, as set they must,
And all those tresses shall be laid in dust,
This Lock the Muse shall consecrate to fame,
And 'midst the stars inscribe Belinda's name.   150

EPISTLE TO MISS BLOUNT, ON HER LEAVING THE TOWN, AFTER THE CORONATION

   As some fond virgin, whom her mother's care
Drags from the town to wholesome country air,
Just when she learns to roll a melting eye,
And hear a spark, yet think no danger nigh;

129. *Berenice* heroine of a poem by
the Greek poet Callimachus. Her hair
too became a star.
136. *Lake* in Hyde Park.

137. *Partridge* "a ridiculous star-
gazer" (Pope), who every year gave out
false prophecies.

From the dear man unwilling she must sever,   5
Yet takes one kiss before she parts forever:
Thus from the world fair Zephalinda flew,
Saw others happy, and with sighs withdrew;
Not that their pleasures caused her discontent;
She sighed not that they stayed, but that she went.   10
   She went to plain-work, and to purling brooks,
Old-fashioned halls, dull aunts, and croaking rooks:
She went from opera, park, assembly, play,
To morning walks, and prayers three hours a day;
To part her time 'twixt reading and bohea,   15
To muse, and spill her solitary tea,
Or o'er cold coffee trifle with the spoon,
Count the slow clock, and dine exact at noon;
Divert her eyes with pictures in the fire,
Hum half a tune, tell stories to the squire;   20
Up to her godly garret after seven,
There starve and pray, for that's the way to heaven.
   Some squire, perhaps, you take delight to rack,
Whose game is whist, whose treat a toast in sack;
Who visits with a gun, presents you birds,   25
Then gives a smacking buss, and cries—"No words!"
Or with his hound comes hollowing from the stable,
Makes love with nods and knees beneath a table;
Whose laughs are hearty, though his jests are coarse,
And loves you best of all things—but his horse.   30
   In some fair evening, on your elbow laid,
You dream of triumphs in the rural shade;
In pensive thought recall the fancied scene,
See coronations rise on every green:
Before you pass the imaginary sights   35
Of lords and earls and dukes and gartered knights,
While the spread fan o'ershades your closing eyes;
Then give one flirt, and all the vision flies.
Thus vanish scepters, coronets, and balls,
And leave you in lone woods, or empty walls!   40
   So when your slave, at some dear idle time
(Not plagued with headaches or the want of rhyme)
Stands in the streets, abstracted from the crew,
And while he seems to study, thinks of you;
Just when his fancy points your sprightly eyes,   45
Or sees the blush of soft Parthenia rise,
Gay pats my shoulder, and you vanish quite;
Streets, chairs, and coxcombs rush upon my sight;

48. *chairs* sedan-chairs.

Vexed to be still in town, I knit my brow,
Look sour, and hum a tune—as you may now. 50

TO A LADY

OF THE CHARACTERS OF WOMEN

Nothing so true as what you once let fall,
"Most women have no characters at all."
Matter too soft a lasting mark to bear,
And best distinguished by black, brown, or fair.
    How many pictures of one nymph we view, 5
All how unlike each other, all how true!
Arcadia's Countess, here, in ermined pride,
Is, there, Pastora by a fountain side.
Here Fannia, leering on her own good man,
And there, a naked Leda with a swan. 10
Let then the fair one beautifully cry,
In Magdalen's loose hair and lifted eye,
Or dressed in smiles of sweet Cecilia shine,
With simp'ring angels, palms, and harps divine;
Whether the charmer sinner it, or saint it, 15
If Folly grow romantic, I must paint it.
    Come then, the colors and the ground prepare!
Dip in the rainbow, trick her off in air;
Choose a firm cloud, before it fall, and in it
Catch, ere she change, the Cynthia of this minute. 20
    Rufa, whose eye quick-glancing o'er the park,
Attracts each light gay meteor of a spark,
Agrees as ill with Rufa studying Locke,
As Sappho's diamonds with her dirty smock;
Or Sappho at her toilet's greasy task, 25
With Sappho fragrant at an evening masque:
So morning insects that in muck begun,
Shine, buzz, and flyblow in the setting sun.
    How soft is Silia! fearful to offend;
The frail one's advocate, the weak one's friend: 30
To her, Calista proved her conduct nice;
And good Simplicius asks of her advice.
Sudden, she storms! She raves! You tip the wink,
But spare your censure; Silia does not drink.
All eyes may see from what the change arose, 35

Lady Martha Blount, Pope's friend for many years.
7. *Countess* Countess of Pembroke, sister of Sir Philip Sidney, author of *Arcadia,* a pastoral tale.
31. *Calista* a nymph made pregnant by Zeus.

All eyes may see—a pimple on her nose.
   Papillia, wedded to her doting spark,
Sighs for the shades—"How charming is a park!"
A park is purchased, but the fair he sees
All bathed in tears—"Oh, odious, odious trees!"   40
   Ladies, like variegated tulips, show;
'Tis to their changes half their charms we owe;
Their happy spots the nice admirer take,
Fine by defect, and delicately weak.
'Twas thus Calypso once each heart alarmed,   45
Awed without virtue, without beauty charmed;
Her tongue bewitched as oddly as her eyes,
Less wit than mimic, more a wit than wise;
Strange graces still, and stranger flights she had,
Was just not ugly, and was just not mad;   50
Yet ne'er so sure our passion to create,
As when she touched the brink of all we hate.
   Narcissa's nature, tolerably mild,
To make a wash, would hardly stew a child;
Has ev'n been proved to grant a lover's prayer,   55
And paid a tradesman once to make him stare;
Gave alms at Easter, in a Christian trim,
And made a widow happy, for a whim.
Why then declare good nature is her scorn,
When 'tis by that alone she can be borne?   60
Why pique all mortals, yet affect a name?
A fool to pleasure, yet a slave to fame:
Now deep in Taylor and the Book of Martyrs,
Now drinking citron with his Grace and Chartres;
Now conscience chills her, and now passion burns;   65
And atheism and religion take their turns;
A very heathen in the carnal part,
Yet still a sad, good Christian at her heart.
   See sin in state, majestically drunk;
Proud as a peeress, prouder as a punk;   70
Chaste to her husband, frank to all beside,
A teeming mistress, but a barren bride.
What then? let blood and body bear the fault,
Her head's untouched, that noble seat of thought:
Such this day's doctrine—in another fit   75
She sins with poets through pure love of wit.

---

37. *Papillia* from Latin for a butter-fly.
63. *Taylor* a cleric, author of *Holy Living and Dying.*

64. *Grace* Duke of Wharton, brilliant and erratic statesman; *Chartres* . "a man infamous for all manner of vices" (Pope).

What has not fired her bosom or her brain?
Caesar and Tallboy, Charles and Charlemagne.
As Helluo, late dictator of the feast,
The nose of hautgout, and the tip of taste,   80
Critiqued your wine, and analysed your meat,
Yet on plain pudding deigned at home to eat;
So Philomedé, lecturing all mankind
On the soft passion, and the taste refined,
Th' address, the delicacy—stoops at once,   85
And makes her hearty meal upon a dunce.

    Flavia's a wit, has too much sense to pray;
To toast our wants and wishes, is her way;
Nor asks of God, but of her stars, to give
The mighty blessing, "while we live, to live."   90
Then all for death, that opiate of the soul!
Lucretia's dagger, Rosamonda's bowl.
Say, what can cause such impotence of mind?
A spark too fickle, or a spouse too kind.
Wise wretch! with pleasures too refined to please;   95
With too much spirit to be e'er at ease;
With too much quickness ever to be taught;
With too much thinking to have common thought:
You purchase pain with all that joy can give,
And die of nothing but a rage to live.   100

    Turn then from wits; and look on Simo's mate,
No ass so meek, no ass so obstinate.
Or her, that owns her faults, but never mends,
Because she's honest, and the best of friends.
Or her, whose life the church and scandal share,   105
For ever in a passion, or a prayer.
Or her, who laughs at Hell, but (like her Grace)
Cries, "Ah! how charming, if there's no such place!"
Or who in sweet vicissitude appears
Of mirth and opium, ratafie and tears,   110
The daily anodyne, and nightly draught,
To kill those foes to fair ones, time and thought.
Woman and fool are two hard things to hit;
For true no-meaning puzzles more than wit.

    But what are these to great Atossa's mind?   115
Scarce once herself, by turns all womankind!
Who, with herself, or others, from her birth

---

78. *Tallboy* a booby lover in a popular comedy.
79. *Helluo* glutton.
110. *ratafie* a kind of cherry brandy.

115. *Atossa* sister of Cambyses, the king with a terrible temper; certain details in the portrait fit the Duchess of Buckinghamshire.

Finds all her life one warfare upon earth:
Shines, in exposing knaves, and painting fools,
Yet is, whate'er she hates and ridicules.   120
No thought advances, but her eddy brain
Whisks it about, and down it goes again.
Full sixty years the world has been her trade,
The wisest fool much time has ever made.
From loveless youth to unrespected age,   125
No passion gratified except her rage.
So much the fury still outran the wit,
The pleasure missed her, and the scandal hit.
Who breaks with her, provokes revenge from Hell,
But he's a bolder man who dares be well;   130
Her every turn with violence pursued,
Nor more a storm her hate than gratitude:
To that each passion turns, or soon or late;
Love, if it makes her yield, must make her hate:
Superiors? death! and equals? what a curse!   135
But an inferior not dependent? worse.
Offend her, and she knows not to forgive;
Oblige her, and she'll hate you while you live:
But die, and she'll adore you—then the bust
And temple rise—then fall again to dust.   140
Last night, her Lord was all that's good and great;
A knave this morning, and his will a cheat.
Strange! by the means defeated of the ends,
By spirit robbed of power, by warmth of friends,
By wealth of follow'rs! without one distress   145
Sick of herself through very selfishness!
Atossa, cursed with ev'ry granted prayer,
Childless with all her children, wants an heir.
To heirs unknown descends th' unguarded store,
Or wanders, Heav'n-directed, to the poor.   150
    Pictures like these, dear Madam, to design,
Asks no firm hand, and no unerring line;
Some wand'ring touches, some reflected light,
Some flying stroke alone can hit 'em right:
For how should equal colors do the knack?   155
Chameleons who can paint in white and black?
    "Yet Chloe sure was formed without a spot"—
Nature in her then erred not, but forgot.
"With every pleasing, every prudent part,
Say, what can Chloe want?"—She wants a heart.   160
She speaks, behaves, and acts just as she ought;
But never, never, reached one gen'rous thought.

Virtue she finds too painful an endeavor,
Content to dwell in decencies forever.
So very reasonable, so unmoved,   165
As never yet to love, or to be loved.
She, while her lover pants upon her breast,
Can mark the figures on an Indian chest;
And when she sees her friend in deep despair,
Observes how much a chintz exceeds mohair.   170
Forbid it Heav'n, a favor or a debt
She e'er should cancel—but she may forget.
Safe is your secret still in Chloe's ear;
But none of Chloe's shall you ever hear.
Of all her dears she never slandered one,   175
But cares not if a thousand are undone.
Would Chloe know if you're alive or dead?
She bids her footman put it in her head.
Chloe is prudent—would you too be wise?
Then never break your heart when Chloe dies.   180
   One certain portrait may (I grant) be seen,
Which Heav'n has varnished out, and made a Queen:
The same for ever! and described by all
With truth and goodness, as with crown and ball.
Poets heap virtues, painters gems at will,   185
And show their zeal, and hide their want of skill.
'Tis well—but, artists! who can paint or write,
To draw the naked is your true delight.
That robe of quality so struts and swells,
None see what parts of nature it conceals.   190
Th' exactest traits of body or of mind,
We owe to models of an humble kind.
If Queensbury to strip there's no compelling,
'Tis from a handmaid we must take a Helen.
From peer or bishop 'tis no easy thing   195
To draw the man who loves his God, or king:
Alas! I copy (or my draught would fail)
From honest Máhomet, or plain Parson Hale.
   But grant, in public men sometimes are shown,
A woman's seen in private life alone: 200
Our bolder talents in full light displayed;
Your virtues open fairest in the shade.
Bred to disguise, in public 'tis you hide;
There, none distinguish twixt your shame or pride,
Weakness or delicacy; all so nice,   205
That each may seem a virtue, or a vice.

193. *Queensbury* Duchess of Queensbury, noted for her beauty.

In men, we various ruling passions find;
In women, two almost divide the kind;
Those, only fixed, they first or last obey,
The love of pleasure, and the love of sway.   210
    That, nature gives; and where the lesson taught
Is but to please, can pleasure seem a fault?
Experience, this; by man's oppression curst,
They seek the second not to lose the first.
    Men, some to business, some to pleasure take;   215
But every woman is at heart a rake:
Men, some to quiet, some to public strife;
But ev'ry lady would be queen for life.
    Yet mark the fate of a whole sex of queens!
Power all their end, but beauty all the means: 220
In youth they conquer, with so wild a rage,
As leaves them scarce a subject in their age:
For foreign glory, foreign joy, they roam;
No thought of peace or happiness at home.
But wisdom's triumph is well-timed retreat,   225
As hard a science to the fair as great!
Beauties, like tyrants, old and friendless grown,
Yet hate repose, and dread to be alone,
Worn out in public, weary ev'ry eye,
Nor leave one sigh behind them when they die.   230
    Pleasures the sex, as children birds, pursue,
Still out of reach, yet never out of view;
Sure, if they catch, to spoil the toy at most,
To covet flying, and regret when lost:
At last, to follies youth could scarce defend,   235
'Tis half their age's prudence to pretend;
Ashamed to own they gave delight before,
Reduced to feign it, when they give no more:
As hags hold sabbaths, less for joy than spite,
So these their merry, miserable night;   240
Still round and round the ghosts of beauty glide,
And haunt the places where their honor died.
    See how the world its veterans rewards!
A youth of frolics, an old age of cards;
Fair to no purpose, artful to no end,   245
Young without lovers, old without a friend;
A fop their passion, but their prize a sot;
Alive, ridiculous, and dead, forgot!
    Ah! Friend! to dazzle let the vain design;
To raise the thought, and touch the heart be thine!   250

240. *night*   night when they are "at home" to visitors.

That charm shall grow, while what fatigues the Ring,
Flaunts and goes down, an unregarded thing:
So when the sun's broad beam has tired the sight,
All mild ascends the moon's more sober light,
Serene in virgin modesty she shines,   255
And unobserved the glaring orb declines.
    Oh! blest with temper, whose unclouded ray
Can make tomorrow cheerful as today;
She, who can love a sister's charms, or hear
Sighs for a daughter with unwounded ear;   260
She, who ne'er answers till a husband cools,
Or, if she rules him, never shows she rules;
Charms by accepting, by submitting sways,
Yet has her humor most, when she obeys;
Lets fops or fortune fly which way they will;   265
Disdains all loss of tickets, or codille;
Spleen, vapors, or smallpox, above them all,
And mistress of herself, though China fall.
    And yet, believe me, good as well as ill,
Woman's at best a contradiction still.   270
Heav'n, when it strives to polish all it can
Its last best work, but forms a softer man;
Picks from each sex, to make its fav'rite blest,
Your love of pleasure, our desire of rest:
Blends, in exception to all gen'ral rules,   275
Your taste of follies, with our scorn of fools:
Reserve with frankness, art with truth allied,
Courage with softness, modesty with pride;
Fixed principles, with fancy ever new;
Shakes all together, and produces—you.   280
    Be this a woman's fame: with this unblest,
Toasts live a scorn, and queens may die a jest.
This Phoebus promised (I forget the year)
When those blue eyes first opened on the sphere;
Ascendant Phoebus watched that hour with care,   285
Averted half your parents' simple prayer;
And gave you beauty, but denied the pelf
That buys your sex a tyrant o'er itself.
The gen'rous God, who wit and gold refines,
And ripens spirits as he ripens mines,   290
Kept dross for duchesses, the world shall know it,
To you gave sense, good humor, and a poet.

266. *tickets* lottery tickets; *codille* term in card game of ombre.
289. *gen'rous God* Phoebus, as god of poetry (or "Wit"), and as sun god (the sun was supposed to produce gold).

TO RICHARD BOYLE, EARL OF BURLINGTON

OF THE USE OF RICHES

'Tis strange, the miser should his cares employ
To gain those riches he can ne'er enjoy:
Is it less strange, the prodigal should waste
His wealth, to purchase what he ne'er can taste?
Not for himself he sees, or hears, or eats; 5
Artists must choose his pictures, music, meats:
He buys for Topham, drawings and designs,
For Pembroke, statues, dirty gods, and coins;
Rare monkish manuscripts for Hearne alone,
And books for Mead, and butterflies for Sloane. 10
Think we all these are for himself! no more
Than his fine wife, alas! or finer whore.
    For what has Virro painted, built, and planted?
Only to show, how many tastes he wanted.
What brought Sir Visto's ill got wealth to waste? 15
Some Daemon whispered, "Visto! have a taste."
Heaven visits with a taste the wealthy fool,
And needs no rod but Ripley with a rule.
See! sportive fate, to punish awkward pride,
Bids Bubo build, and sends him such a guide: 20
A standing sermon, at each year's expense,
That never coxcomb reached magnificence!
    You show us, Rome was glorious, not profuse,
And pompous buildings once were things of use.
Yet shall (my Lord) your just, your noble rules 25
Fill half the land with imitating fools;
Who random drawings from your sheets shall take,
And of one beauty many blunders make;
Load some vain church with old theatric state,
Turn arcs of triumph to a garden gate; 30
Reverse your ornaments, and hang them all
On some patched dog-hole eked with ends of wall;
Then clap four slices of pilaster on't,
That, laced with bits of rustic, makes a front.

Burlington enthusiastic promoter of classical architecture in the style of the English architect Inigo Jones and of the Venetian Andrea Palladio, whose designs he published (lines 23–27).
7. *Topham* a famous collector, like the other men named in lines 8–10.

18. *Ripley* a carpenter who practiced architecture "without any genius in the art" (Pope).
20. *Bubo* Latin for "owl."
34. *rustic* masonry with blocks cut to make the joints conspicuous.

Shall call the winds through long arcades to roar,   35
Proud to catch cold at a Venetian door;
Conscious they act a true Palladian part,
And, if they starve, they starve by rules of art.
　　Oft have you hinted to your brother peer,
A certain truth, which many buy too dear: 40
Something there is more needful than expense,
And something previous ev'n to taste—'tis sense:
Good sense, which only is the gift of Heav'n,
And though no science, fairly worth the sev'n:
A light, which in yourself you must perceive;   45
Jones and Le Nôtre have it not to give.
　　To build, to plant, whatever you intend,
To rear the column, or the arch to bend,
To swell the terrace, or to sink the grot;
In all, let Nature never be forgot.   50
But treat the Goddess like a modest fair,
Nor overdress, nor leave her wholly bare;
Let not each beauty everywhere be spied,
Where half the skill is decently to hide.
He gains all points, who pleasingly confounds,   55
Surprises, varies, and conceals the bounds.
　　Consult the genius of the place in all;
That tells the waters or to rise, or fall;
Or helps th' ambitious hill the heavens to scale,
Or scoops in circling theatres the vale;   60
Calls in the country, catches opening glades,
Joins willing woods, and varies shades from shades;
Now breaks, or now directs, th' intending lines;
Paints as you plant, and, as you work, designs.
　　Still follow sense, of every art the soul,   65
Parts answ'ring parts shall slide into a whole,
Spontaneous beauties all around advance,
Start ev'n from difficulty, strike from chance;
Nature shall join you; time shall make it grow
A work to wonder at—perhaps a STOWE.   70
　　Without it, proud Versailles! thy glory falls;
And Nero's terraces desert their walls:
The vast parterres a thousand hands shall make,
Lo! COBHAM comes, and floats them with a lake:
Or cut wide views through mountains to the plain,   75
You'll wish your hill or sheltered seat again.

---

46. *Le Nôtre* French designer of gardens in the formal style, as at Versailles
(line 71).

70. *Stowe* house of Viscount Cobham,
with gardens in the more natural landscape style admired by Pope.

Ev'n in an ornament its place remark,
Nor in an Hermitage set Dr. Clarke.
    Behold Villario's ten years' toil complete;
His quincunx darkens, his espaliers meet;   80
The wood supports the plain, the parts unite,
And strength of shade contends with strength of light;
A waving glow the bloomy beds display,
Blushing in bright diversities of day,
With silver-quiv'ring rills meandered o'er—   85
Enjoy them, you! Villario can no more;
Tired of the scene parterres and fountains yield,
He finds at last he better likes a field.
    Through his young woods, how pleased Sabinus strayed,
Or sat delighted in the thick'ning shade,   90
With annual joy the redd'ning shoots to greet,
Or see the stretching branches long to meet!
His son's fine taste an op'ner vista loves,
Foe to the dryads of his father's groves;
One boundless green, or flourished carpet views,   95
With all the mournful family of yews;
The thriving plants ignoble broomsticks made,
Now sweep those alleys they were born to shade.
    At Timon's villa let us pass a day,
Where all cry out, "What sums are thrown away!"   100
So proud, so grand; of that stupendous air,
Soft and agreeable come never there.
Greatness, with Timon, dwells in such a draught
As brings all Brobdingnag before your thought.
To compass this, his building is a town,   105
His pond an ocean, his parterre a down:
Who but must laugh, the master when he sees,
A puny insect, shiv'ring at a breeze!
Lo, what huge heaps of littleness around!
The whole, a labored quarry above ground.   110
Two cupids squirt before: a lake behind
Improves the keenness of the northern wind.
His gardens next your admiration call,
On ev'ry side you look, behold the wall!
No pleasing intricacies intervene,   115
No artful wildness to perplex the scene;
Grove nods at grove, each alley has a brother,
And half the platform just reflects the other.

---

78. *Clarke* Samuel Clarke, philosopher; *Hermitage* an ornamental structure, where the Queen set Clarke's bust.

80. *quincunx* four trees planted to form a square, with a fifth in the center.

The suff'ring eye inverted Nature sees,
Trees cut to statues, statues thick as trees;   120
With here a fountain, never to be played;
And there a summerhouse, that knows no shade;
Here Amphitrite sails through myrtle bowers;
There gladiators fight, or die in flowers;
Unwatered see the drooping sea-horse mourn,   125
And swallows roost in Nilus' dusty urn.
      My Lord advances with majestic mien,
Smit with the mighty pleasure, to be seen:
But soft—by regular approach—not yet—
First through the length of yon hot terrace sweat;   130
And when up ten steep slopes you've dragged your thighs,
Just at his study door he'll bless your eyes.
      His study! with what authors is it stored?
In books, not authors, curious is my Lord;
To all their dated backs he turns you round: 135
These Aldus printed, those Du Sueil has bound.
Lo, some are vellum, and the rest as good
For all his Lordship knows, but they are wood.
For Locke or Milton 'tis in vain to look,
These shelves admit not any modern book.   140
      And now the chapel's silver bell you hear,
That summons you to all the pride of prayer:
Light quirks of music, broken and uneven,
Make the soul dance upon a jig to Heaven.
On painted ceilings you devoutly stare,   145
Where sprawl the saints of Verrio or Laguerre,
On gilded clouds in fair expansion lie,
And bring all Paradise before your eye.
To rest, the cushion and soft dean invite,
Who never mentions Hell to ears polite.   150
      But hark! the chiming clocks to dinner call;
A hundred footsteps scrape the marble hall:
The rich buffet well-colored serpents grace,
And gaping Tritons spew to wash your face.
Is this a dinner? this a genial room?   155
No, 'tis a temple, and a hecatomb.
A solemn sacrifice, performed in state,
You drink by measure, and to minutes eat.
So quick retires each flying course, you'd swear
Sancho's dread Doctor and his wand were there.   160
Between each act the trembling salvers ring,

---

146. *Laguerre*   Verrio   and   Laguerre,
painters of ceilings in English palaces
and country houses.
155. *genial*   festive, for a feast.

160. *Doctor*   in *Don Quixote* (Part II,
ch. 47), a doctor who whisks the food
away before Sancho can eat it.

From soup to sweet wine, and God bless the King.
In plenty starving, tantalized in state,
And complaisantly helped to all I hate,
Treated, caressed, and tired, I take my leave,   165
Sick of his civil pride from morn to eve;
I curse such lavish cost, and little skill,
And swear no day was ever passed so ill.
    Yet hence the poor are clothed, the hungry fed;
Health to himself, and to his infants bread   170
The lab'rer bears: what his hard heart denies,
His charitable vanity supplies.
    Another age shall see the golden ear
Embrown the Slope, and nod on the parterre,
Deep harvests bury all his pride has planned,   175
And laughing Ceres reassume the land.
    Who then shall grace, or who improve the soil?
Who plants like BATHURST, or who builds like BOYLE.
'Tis use alone that sanctifies expense,
And splendor borrows all her rays from sense.   180
    His father's acres who enjoys in peace,
Or makes his neighbors glad, if he increase:
Whose cheerful tenants bless their yearly toil,
Yet to their lord owe more than to the soil;
Whose ample lawns are not ashamed to feed   185
The milky heifer and deserving steed;
Whose rising forests, not for pride or show,
But future buildings, future navies, grow:
Let his plantations stretch from down to down,
First shade a country, and then raise a town.   190
    You too proceed! make falling arts your care,
Erect new wonders, and the old repair;
Jones and Palladio to themselves restore,
And be whate'er Vitruvius was before:
Till kings call forth th' ideas of your mind,   195
(Proud to accomplish what such hands designed,)
Bid harbors open, public ways extend,
Bid temples, worthier of the God, ascend;
Bid the broad arch the dangerous flood contain,
The mole projected break the roaring main;   200
Back to his bounds their subject sea command,
And roll obedient rivers through the land:
These honors, peace to happy Britain brings,
These are imperial works, and worthy kings.

178. *Bathurst* Allen, Lord Bathurst, famed for the landscape gardening of his country houses.   194. *Vitruvius* a Roman writer on architecture.

EPITAPH. INTENDED FOR SIR ISAAC NEWTON, IN WESTMINSTER ABBEY ·

Nature, and Nature's laws, lay hid in night,
God said, "Let Newton be!" And all was light.

EPITAPH. ON MRS. CORBET, WHO DIED OF A CANCER IN HER BREAST

Here rests a woman, good without pretense,
Blest with plain reason and with sober sense;
No conquests she, but o'er herself desired,
No arts essayed, but not to be admired.
Passion and pride were to her soul unknown,   5
Convinced that virtue only is our own.
So unaffected, so composed a mind,
So firm yet soft, so strong yet so refined,
Heav'n, as its purest gold, by tortures tried;
The saint sustained it, but the woman died.   10

SAMUEL JOHNSON
(*1709–1784*)

·

THE VANITY OF HUMAN WISHES
THE TENTH SATIRE OF JUVENAL, IMITATED

Let observation with extensive view,
Survey mankind, from China to Peru;
Remark each anxious toil, each eager strife,
And watch the busy scenes of crowded life;
Then say how hope and fear, desire and hate,   5
O'erspread with snares the clouded maze of fate,
Where wav'ring man, betrayed by vent'rous pride,
To tread the dreary paths without a guide,
As treach'rous phantoms in the mist delude,
Shuns fancied ills, or chases airy good;   10
How rarely reason guides the stubborn choice,
Rules the bold hand, or prompts the suppliant voice;
How nations sink, by darling schemes oppressed,
When vengeance listens to the fool's request.
Fate wings with ev'ry wish th' afflictive dart,   15
Each gift of nature, and each grace of art,
With fatal heat impetuous courage glows,
With fatal sweetness elocution flows,
Impeachment stops the speaker's pow'rful breath,
And restless fire precipitates on death.   20
   But scarce observed, the knowing and the bold
Fall in the gen'ral massacre of gold;
Wide-wasting pest! that rages unconfined,
And crowds with crimes the records of mankind;
For gold his sword the hireling ruffian draws,   25
For gold the hireling judge distorts the laws;
Wealth heaped on wealth, nor truth nor safety buys,
The dangers gather as the treasures rise.
   Let hist'ry tell where rival kings command,
And dubious title shakes the madded land,   30
When statutes glean the refuse of the sword,
How much more safe the vassal than the lord;
Low skulks the hind beneath the rage of pow'r,
And leaves the wealthy traitor in the Tow'r,
Untouched his cottage, and his slumbers sound,   35
Though confiscation's vultures hover round.

The needy traveler, serene and gay,
Walks the wild heath, and sings his toil away.
Does envy seize thee? crush th' upbraiding joy,
Increase his riches and his peace destroy;   40
Now fears in dire vicissitude invade,
The rustling brake alarms, and quiv'ring shade,
Nor light nor darkness bring his pain relief,
One shows the plunder, and one hides the thief.

    Yet still one gen'ral cry the skies assails,   45
And gain and grandeur load the tainted gales;
Few know the toiling statesman's fear or care,
Th' insidious rival and the gaping heir.

    Once more, Democritus, arise on earth,
With cheerful wisdom and instructive mirth,   50
See motley life in modern trappings dressed,
And feed with varied fools th' eternal jest:
Thou who couldst laugh where want enchained caprice,
Toil crushed conceit, and man was of a piece;
Where wealth unloved without a mourner died,   55
And scarce a sycophant was fed by pride;
Where ne'er was known the form of mock debate,
Or seen a new-made mayor's unwieldy state;
Where change of fav'rites made no change of laws,
And senates heard before they judged a cause;   60
How wouldst thou shake at Britain's modish tribe,
Dart the quick taunt, and edge the piercing gibe?
Attentive truth and nature to descry,
And pierce each scene with philosophic eye.
To thee were solemn toys or empty show,   65
The robes of pleasure and the veils of woe:
All aid the farce, and all thy mirth maintain,
Whose joys are causeless, or whose griefs are vain.

    Such was the scorn that filled the sage's mind,
Renewed at ev'ry glance on humankind;   70
How just that scorn ere yet thy voice declare,
Search every state, and canvass ev'ry prayer.

    Unnumbered suppliants crowd Preferment's gate,
Athirst for wealth, and burning to be great;
Delusive Fortune hears th' incessant call,   75
They mount, they shine, evaporate, and fall.
On ev'ry stage the foes of peace attend,
Hate dogs their flight, and insult mocks their end.
Love ends with hope, the sinking statesman's door

49. *Democritus* Greek philosopher, an
atomist, who believed that the aim of
life is happiness achieved through inner
tranquillity.

Pours in the morning worshiper no more;   80
For growing names the weekly scribbler lies,
To growing wealth the dedicator flies,
From every room descends the painted face,
That hung the bright Palladium of the place,
And smoked in kitchens, or in auctions sold,   85
To better features yields the frame of gold;
For now no more we trace in ev'ry line
Heroic worth, benevolence divine:
The form distorted justifies the fall,
And detestation rids th' indignant wall.   90
     But will not Britain hear the last appeal,
Sign her foes' doom, or guard her fav'rites' zeal?
Through Freedom's sons no more remonstrance rings,
Degrading nobles and controlling kings;
Our supple tribes repress their patriot throats,   95
And ask no questions but the price of votes;
With weekly libels and septennial ale,
Their wish is full to riot and to rail.
     In full-blown dignity, see Wolsey stand,
Law in his voice, and fortune in his hand: 100
To him the church, the realm, their pow'rs consign,
Through him the rays of regal bounty shine,
Turn'd by his nod the stream of honor flows,
His smile alone security bestows:
Still to new heights his restless wishes tow'r,   105
Claim leads to claim, and pow'r advances pow'r;
Till conquest unresisted ceased to please,
And rights submitted, left him none to seize.
At length his sov'reign frowns—the train of state
Mark the keen glance, and watch the sign to hate.   110
Where'er he turns he meets a stranger's eye,
His suppliants scorn him, and his followers fly;
At once is lost the pride of aweful state,
The golden canopy, the glitt'ring plate,
The regal palace, the luxurious board,   115
The liv'ried army, and the menial lord.
With age, with cares, with maladies oppressed,
He seeks the refuge of monastic rest.
Grief aids disease, remembered folly stings,
And his last sighs reproach the faith of kings.   120
     Speak thou, whose thoughts at humble peace repine,

97. *septennial* referring to elections of
Parliament every seven years.
99. *Wolsey* Cardinal Wolsey, who after
gaining immense power under Henry
VIII, was tried for treason and put to
death.

Shall Wolsey's wealth, with Wolsey's end be thine?
Or liv'st thou now, with safer pride content,
The wisest justice on the banks of Trent?
For why did Wolsey near the steeps of fate,   125
On weak foundations raise th' enormous weight?
Why but to sink beneath misfortune's blow,
With louder ruin to the gulfs below?
    What gave great Villiers to th' assassin's knife,
And fixed disease on Harley's closing life?   130
What murdered Wentworth, and what exiled Hyde,
By kings protected, and to kings allied?
What but their wish indulged in courts to shine,
And pow'r too great to keep, or to resign?
    When first the college rolls receive his name,   135
The young enthusiast quits his ease for fame;
Through all his veins the fever of renown
Burns from the strong contagion of the gown;
O'er Bodley's dome his future labors spread,
And Bacon's mansion trembles o'er his head.   140
Are these thy views? proceed, illustrious youth,
And virtue guard thee to the throne of Truth!
Yet should thy soul indulge the gen'rous heat,
Till captive Science yields her last retreat;
Should Reason guide thee with her brightest ray,   145
And pour on misty Doubt resistless day;
Should no false Kindness lure to loose delight,
Nor Praise relax, nor Difficulty fright;
Should tempting Novelty thy cell refrain,
And Sloth effuse her opiate fumes in vain;   150
Should Beauty blunt on fops her fatal dart,
Nor claim the triumph of a lettered heart;
Should no Disease thy torpid veins invade,
Nor Melancholy's phantoms haunt thy shade;
Yet hope not life from grief or danger free,   155
Nor think the doom of man reversed for thee:
Deign on the passing world to turn thine eyes,
And pause awhile from letters, to be wise;
    There mark what ills the scholar's life assail,

129. *Villiers* George Villiers, first
Duke of Buckingham, assassinated in
1628 because of his failure in conduct-
ing a military expedition.
130. *Harley* Robert Harley, Earl of
Oxford, minister under Queen Anne,
impeached for treason.
131. *Wentworth* friend of Charles I,
condemned to death; *Hyde* Edward
Hyde, Earl of Clarendon, Lord Chancel-
lor under Charles II, impeached and
exiled.
139. *Bodley* Bodleian Library at Oxford.
140. *Bacon* Roger Bacon, thirteenth-
century philosopher, supposedly lived at
Oxford in a cell over Folly Bridge. It
was said that if anyone greater than
Bacon passed beneath the cell, the
bridge would fall upon him.

Toil, envy, want, the patron, and the jail.   160
See nations slowly wise, and meanly just,
To buried merit raise the tardy bust.
If dreams yet flatter, once again attend,
Hear Lydiat's life, and Galileo's end.
    Nor deem, when learning her last prize bestows,   165
The glitt'ring eminence exempt from foes;
See when the vulgar 'scape, despised or awed,
Rebellion's vengeful talons seize on Laud.
From meaner minds, though smaller fines content,
The plundered palace or sequestered rent;   170
Marked out by dangerous parts he meets the shock,
And fatal Learning leads him to the block:
Around his tomb let Art and Genius weep,
But hear his death, ye blockheads, hear and sleep.
    The festal blazes, the triumphal show,   175
The ravished standard, and the captive foe,
The senate's thanks, the gazette's pompous tale,
With force resistless o'er the brave prevail.
Such bribes the rapid Greek o'er Asia whirled,
For such the steady Romans shook the world;   180
For such in distant lands the Britons shine,
And stain with blood the Danube or the Rhine;
This pow'r has praise, that virtue scarce can warm,
Till fame supplies the universal charm.
Yet Reason frowns on War's unequal game,   185
Where wasted nations raise a single name,
And mortgaged states their grandsires' wreaths regret,
From age to age in everlasting debt;
Wreaths which at last the dear-bought right convey
To rust on medals, or on stones decay.   190
    On what foundation stands the warrior's pride,
How just his hopes let Swedish Charles decide;
A frame of adamant, a soul of fire,
No dangers fright him, and no labors tire;
O'er love, o'er fear, extends his wide domain,   195
Unconquered lord of pleasure and of pain;
No joys to him pacific scepters yield,
War sounds the trump, he rushes to the field;
Behold surrounding kings their pow'r combine,
And one capitulate, and one resign;   200
Peace courts his hand, but spreads her charms in vain;

164. *Lydiat* a divine, persecuted in the 1640's for his royalist sympathies. 179. *Greek* Alexander the Great. 192. *Charles* Charles XII of Sweden, defeated by the Russians at Pultowa, 1709.

"Think nothing gained," he cries, " 'till nought remain,
On Moscow's walls till Gothic standards fly,
And all be mine beneath the polar sky."
The march begins in military state,   205
And nations on his eye suspended wait;
Stern Famine guards the solitary coast,
And Winter barricades the realms of Frost;
He comes, not want and cold his course delay;—
Hide, blushing Glory, hide Pultowa's day: 210
The vanquished hero leaves his broken bands,
And shows his miseries in distant lands;
Condemned a needy supplicant to wait,
While ladies interpose, and slaves debate.
But did not Chance at length her error mend?   215
Did no subverted empire mark his end?
Did rival monarchs give the fatal wound?
Or hostile millions press him to the ground?
His fall was destined to a barren strand,
A petty fortress, and a dubious hand;   220
He left the name, at which the world grew pale,
To point a moral, or adorn a tale.
     All times their scenes of pompous woes afford,
From Persia's tyrant to Bavaria's lord.
In gay hostility, and barb'rous pride,   225
With half mankind embattled at his side,
Great Xerxes comes to seize the certain prey,
And starves exhausted regions in his way;
Attendant Flatt'ry counts his myriads o'er,
Till counted myriads sooth his pride no more;   230
Fresh praise is tried till madness fires his mind,
The waves he lashes, and enchains the wind;
New pow'rs are claimed, new pow'rs are still bestowed,
Till rude resistance lops the spreading god;
The daring Greeks deride the martial show,   235
And heap their valleys with the gaudy foe;
Th' insulted sea with humbler thoughts he gains,
A single skiff to speed his flight remains;
Th' incumbered oar scarce leaves the dreaded coast
Through purple billows and a floating host.   240
     The bold Bavarian, in a luckless hour,

---

224. *Persia's tyrant* Xerxes, who attempted to conquer Greece, was defeated at Salamis, 480 B.C. He actually had the sea "lashed"; and he bridged the Hellespont. *Bavaria's lord* Charles Albert, Elector of Bavaria, asserted his claim to the title of Holy Roman Emperor (*Caesarean pow'r,* line 242) in opposition to Maria Theresa (*the queen,* line 246), and so started the War of the Austrian Succession, 1740–1748.

Tries the dread summits of Caesarean pow'r,
With unexpected legions bursts away,
And sees defenseless realms receive his sway;
Short sway! fair Austria spreads her mournful charms,   245
The queen, the beauty, sets the world in arms;
From hill to hill the beacons rousing blaze
Spreads wide the hope of plunder and of praise;
The fierce Croatian, and the wild Hussar,
And all the sons of ravage crowd the war;   250
The baffled prince in honor's flatt'ring bloom
Of hasty greatness finds the fatal doom,
His foes derision, and his subjects blame,
And steals to death from anguish and from shame.

Enlarge my life with multitude of days,   255
In health, in sickness, thus the suppliant prays;
Hides from himself his state, and shuns to know,
That life protracted is protracted woe.
Time hovers o'er, impatient to destroy,
And shuts up all the passages of joy: 260
In vain their gifts the bounteous seasons pour,
The fruit autumnal, and the vernal flow'r,
With listless eyes the dotard views the store,
He views, and wonders that they please no more;
Now pall the tasteless meats, and joyless wines,   265
And Luxury with sighs her slave resigns.
Approach, ye minstrels, try the soothing strain,
Diffuse the tuneful lenitives of pain:
No sounds alas would touch th' impervious ear,
Though dancing mountains witnessed Orpheus near;   270
Nor lute nor lyre his feeble pow'rs attend,
Nor sweeter music of a virtuous friend,
But everlasting dictates crowd his tongue,
Perversely grave, or positively wrong.
The still returning tale, and ling'ring jest,   275
Perplex the fawning niece and pampered guest,
While growing hopes scarce awe the gath'ring sneer,
And scarce a legacy can bribe to hear;
The watchful guests still hint the last offence,
The daughter's petulance, the son's expence,   280
Improve his heady rage with treach'rous skill,
And mold his passions till they make his will.

Unnumbered maladies his joints invade,
Lay siege to life and press the dire blockade;
But unextinguished avarice still remains,   285
And dreaded losses aggravate his pains;

He turns, with anxious heart and crippled hands,
His bonds of debt, and mortgages of lands;
Or views his coffers with suspicious eyes,
Unlocks his gold, and counts it till he dies.   290
    But grant, the virtues of a temp'rate prime
Bless with an age exempt from scorn or crime;
An age that melts with unperceived decay,
And glides in modest innocence away;
Whose peaceful day Benevolence endears,   295
Whose night congratulating Conscience cheers;
The gen'ral fav'rite as the gen'ral friend:
Such age there is, and who shall wish its end?
    Yet ev'n on this her load Misfortune flings,
To press the weary minutes' flagging wings: 300
New sorrow rises as the day returns,
A sister sickens, or a daughter mourns.
Now kindred Merit fills the sable bier,
Now lacerated Friendship claims a tear.
Year chases year, decay pursues decay,   305
Still drops some joy from with'ring life away;
New forms arise, and diff'rent views engage,
Superfluous lags the vet'ran on the stage,
Till pitying Nature signs the last release,
And bids afflicted worth retire to peace.   310
    But few there are whom hours like these await,
Who set unclouded in the gulfs of fate.
From Lydia's monarch should the search descend,
By Solon cautioned to regard his end,
In life's last scene what prodigies surprise,   315
Fears of the brave, and follies of the wise?
From Marlb'rough's eyes the streams of dotage flow,
And Swift expires a driv'ler and a show.
    The teeming mother, anxious for her race,
Begs for each birth the fortune of a face: 320
Yet Vane could tell what ills from beauty spring;
And Sedley cursed the form that pleased a king.
Ye nymphs of rosy lips and radiant eyes,
Whom pleasure keeps too busy to be wise,
Whom joys with soft varieties invite,   325
By day the frolic, and the dance by night,
Who frown with vanity, who smile with art,

313. *monarch* Croesus, who was warned by Solon, wise man of Greece, to consider no man happy until he had seen "his end."
321. *Vane* Anne Vane, mistress of Frederick, Prince of Wales, who cast her off.
322. *Sedley* Catherine Sedley, mistress of the Duke of York (later James II), who abandoned her.

And ask the latest fashion of the heart,
What care, what rules your heedless charms shall save,
Each nymph your rival, and each youth your slave?   330
Against your fame with fondness hate combines,
The rival batters, and the lover mines.
With distant voice neglected Virtue calls,
Less heard and less, the faint remonstrance falls;
Tired with contempt, she quits the slipp'ry reign,   335
And Pride and Prudence take her seat in vain.
In crowd at once, where none the pass defend,
The harmless Freedom, and the private Friend.
The guardians yield, by force superior plied;
By Int'rest, Prudence; and by Flatt'ry, Pride.   340
Now beauty falls betrayed, despised, distressed,
And hissing Infamy proclaims the rest.
    Where then shall Hope and Fear their objects find?
Must dull Suspense corrupt the stagnant mind?
Must helpless man, in ignorance sedate,   345
Roll darkling down the torrent of his fate?
Must no dislike alarm, no wishes rise,
No cries attempt the mercies of the skies?
Enquirer, cease, petitions yet remain,
Which heav'n may hear, nor deem religion vain.   350
Still raise for good the supplicating voice,
But leave to heav'n the measure and the choice,
Safe in his pow'r, whose eyes discern afar
The secret ambush of a specious prayer.
Implore his aid, in his decisions rest,   355
Secure whate'er he gives, he gives the best.
Yet when the sense of sacred presence fires,
And strong devotion to the skies aspires,
Pour forth thy fervors for a healthful mind,
Obedient passions, and a will resigned;   360
For love, which scarce collective man can fill;
For patience sov'reign o'er transmuted ill;
For faith, that panting for a happier seat,
Counts death kind Nature's signal of retreat:
These goods for man the laws of heav'n ordain,   365
These goods he grants, who grants the pow'r to gain;
With these celestial wisdom calms the mind,
And makes the happiness she does not find.

ON THE DEATH OF MR. ROBERT LEVET

Condemned to hope's delusive mine,
  As on we toil from day to day,
By sudden blasts, or slow decline,
  Our social comforts drop away.

Well tried through many a varying year,   5
  See Levet to the grave descend;
Officious, innocent, sincere,
  Of ev'ry friendless name the friend.

Yet still he fills affection's eye,
  Obscurely wise, and coarsely kind;   10
Nor, lettered arrogance, deny
  Thy praise to merit unrefined.

When fainting nature called for aid,
  And hov'ring death prepared the blow,
His vig'rous remedy displayed   15
  The power of art without the show.

In misery's darkest cavern known,
  His useful care was ever nigh,
Where hopeless anguish poured his groan,
  And lonely want retired to die.   20

No summons mocked by chill delay,
  No petty gain disdained by pride,
The modest wants of ev'ry day
  The toil of ev'ry day supplied.

His virtues walked their narrow round,   25
  Nor made a pause, nor left a void;
And sure th' Eternal Master found
  The single talent well employed.

The busy day, the peaceful night,
  Unfelt, uncounted, glided by;   30
His frame was firm, his powers were bright,
  Though now his eightieth year was nigh.

6. *Levet* doctor, "an obscure practicer in physic" (Boswell), who lived in Johnson's lodgings many years.

Then with no throbbing fiery pain,
　No cold gradations of decay,
Death broke at once the vital chain,　　　　　35
　And freed his soul the nearest way.

WILLIAM COWPER
(*1731–1800*)

·

THE SHRUBBERY
WRITTEN IN A TIME OF AFFLICTION

Oh, happy shades to me unblest!
   Friendly to peace, but not to me!
How ill the scene that offers rest,
   And heart that cannot rest, agree!

This glassy stream, that spreading pine,   5
   Those alders quiv'ring to the breeze,
Might soothe a soul less hurt than mine,
   And please, if anything could please,

But fixed unalterable care
   Foregoes not what she feels within,   10
Shows the same sadness everywhere,
   And slights the season and the scene.

For all that pleased in wood or lawn,
   While peace possessed these silent bowers,
Her animating smile withdrawn,   15
   Has lost its beauties and its powers.

The saint or moralist should tread
   This moss-grown alley, musing slow;
They seek, like me, the secret shade,
   But not, like me, to nourish woe!   20

Me fruitful scenes and prospects waste
   Alike admonish not to roam;
These tell me of enjoyments past,
   And those of sorrows yet to come.

ON THE LOSS OF THE ROYAL GEORGE
WRITTEN WHEN THE NEWS ARRIVED, BY DESIRE OF
LADY AUSTEN, WHO WANTED WORDS

To the March in Scipio

Toll for the brave,
The brave that are no more!
    All sunk beneath the wave,
Fast by their native shore!
    Eight hundred of the brave,   5
Whose courage well was tried,
    Had made the vessel heel,
And laid her on her side.
    A land breeze shook the shrouds,
And she was overset;   10
    Down went the Royal George,
With all her crew complete.

Toll for the brave!
Brave Kempenfelt is gone;
    His last sea fight is fought;   15
His work of glory done.
    It was not in the battle;
No tempest gave the shock;
    She sprang no fatal leak;
She ran upon no rock.   20
    His sword was in its sheath;
His fingers held the pen,
    When Kempenfelt went down
With twice four hundred men.

Weigh the vessel up,   25
Once dreaded by our foes!
    And mingle with our cup
The tear that England owes.
    Her timbers yet are sound,
And she may float again,   30
    Full charged with England's thunder,
And plough the distant main.
    But Kempenfelt is gone,
His victories are o'er;
    And he and his eight hundred   35
Shall plough the wave no more.

LIGHT SHINING OUT OF DARKNESS

God moves in a mysterious way,
  His wonders to perform;
He plants his footsteps in the sea,
  And rides upon the storm.

Deep in unfathomable mines   5
  Of never failing skill,
He treasures up his bright designs,
  And works his sovereign will.

Ye fearful saints fresh courage take;
  The clouds ye so much dread   10
Are big with mercy, and shall break
  In blessings on your head.

Judge not the Lord by feeble sense,
  But trust him for his grace;
Behind a frowning providence,   15
  He hides a smiling face.

His purposes will ripen fast,
  Unfolding every hour;
The bud may have a bitter taste,
  But sweet will be the flower.   20

Blind unbelief is sure to err,
  And scan his work in vain;
God is his own interpreter,
  And he will make it plain.

EPITAPH ON A HARE

Here lies, whom hound did ne'er pursue,
  Nor swifter greyhound follow,
Whose foot ne'er tainted morning dew,
  Nor ear heard huntsman's halloo;

Old Tiney, surliest of his kind,   5
  Who, nursed with tender care,
And to domestic bounds confined,
  Was still a wild jack hare.

Though duly from my hand he took
   His pittance every night;   10
He did it with a jealous look,
   And, when he could, would bite.

His diet was of wheaten bread
   And milk, and oats, and straw;
Thistles, or lettuces instead,   15
   With sand to scour his maw.

On twigs of hawthorn he regaled,
   On pippins' russet peel;
And, when his juicy salads failed,
   Sliced carrot pleased him well.   20

A Turkey carpet was his lawn,
   Whereon he loved to bound,
To skip and gambol like a fawn,
   And swing his rump around.

His frisking was at evening hours,   25
   For then he lost his fear;
But most before approaching showers,
   Or when a storm drew near.

Eight years and five round rolling moons
   He thus saw steal away,
Dozing out all his idle noons,   30
   And every night at play.

I kept him for his humor's sake,
   For he would oft beguile
My heart of thoughts that made it ache,   35
   And force me to a smile.

But now beneath this walnut shade
   He finds his long last home,
And waits, in snug concealment laid,
   Till gentler Puss shall come.   40

He, still more aged, feels the shocks,
   From which no care can save,
And, partner once of Tiney's box,
   Must soon partake his grave.

40. *Puss*   another pet hare.

THE POPLAR-FIELD

The poplars are felled, farewell to the shade,
And the whispering sound of the cool colonnade,
The winds play no longer and sing in the leaves,
Nor Ouse on his bosom their image receives.

Twelve years had elapsed since I last took a view   5
Of my favorite field and the bank where they grew;
And now in the grass behold they are laid,
And the tree is my seat that once lent me a shade.

The blackbird has fled to another retreat,
Where the hazels afford him a screen from the heat,   10
And the scene where his melody charmed me before
Resounds with his sweet-flowing ditty no more.

My fugitive years are all hasting away,
And I must ere long lie as lowly as they,
With a turf on my breast, and a stone at my head,   15
Ere another such grove shall arise in its stead.

'Tis a sight to engage me, if anything can,
To muse on the perishing pleasures of man;
Though his life be a dream, his enjoyments, I see,
Have a being less durable even than he.   20

THE CASTAWAY

Obscurest night involved the sky,
   Th' Atlantic billows roared,
When such a destined wretch as I,
   Washed headlong from on board,
Of friends, of hope, of all bereft,   5
His floating home forever left.

No braver chief could Albion boast
   Than he with whom he went,
Nor ever ship left Albion's coast,
   With warmer wishes sent.   10
He loved them both, but both in vain,
Nor him beheld, nor her again.

4. *Ouse*   a river.

Not long beneath the whelming brine,
    Expert to swim, he lay;
Nor soon he felt his strength decline,   15
    Or courage die away;
But waged with death a lasting strife,
Supported by despair of life.

He shouted; nor his friends had failed
    To check the vessel's course,
But so the furious blast prevailed,   20
    That, pitiless perforce,
They left their outcast mate behind,
And scudded still before the wind.

Some succor yet they could afford;   25
    And, such as storms allow,
The cask, the coop, the floated cord,
    Delayed not to bestow.
But he (they knew) nor ship, nor shore,
Whate'er they gave, should visit more.   30

Nor, cruel as it seemed, could he
    Their haste himself condemn,
Aware that flight, in such a sea,
    Alone could rescue them;
Yet bitter felt it still to die   35
Deserted, and his friends so nigh.

He long survives, who lives an hour
    In ocean, self-upheld;
And so long he, with unspent power,
    His destiny repelled;   40
And ever, as the minutes flew,
Entreated help, or cried, "Adieu!"

At length, his transient respite past,
    His comrades, who before
Had heard his voice in every blast,   45
    Could catch the sound no more.
For then, by toil subdued, he drank
The stifling wave, and then he sank.

27. *coop*   barrel (thrown out as a life preserver).

No poet wept him; but the page
    Of narrative sincere,   50
That tells his name, his worth, his age,
    Is wet with Anson's tear.
And tears by bards or heroes shed
Alike immortalize the dead.

I therefore purpose not, or dream,   55
    Descanting on his fate,
To give the melancholy theme
    A more enduring date:
But misery still delights to trace
Its semblance in another's case.   60

No voice divine the storm allayed,
    No light propitious shone,
When, snatched from all effectual aid,
    We perished, each alone;
But I beneath a rougher sea,   65
And whelmed in deeper gulfs than he.

50. *narrative* *A Voyage Round the World* by George Anson: Anson, leader of a naval expedition, tells the story on which this poem is based.

WILLIAM BLAKE
(*1757–1827*)

·

FROM SONGS OF INNOCENCE
INTRODUCTION

Piping down the valleys wild,
Piping songs of pleasant glee,
On a cloud I saw a child,
And he laughing said to me:

"Pipe a song about a Lamb!"   5
So I piped with merry cheer.
"Piper, pipe that song again";
So I piped: he wept to hear.

"Drop thy pipe, thy happy pipe;
Sing thy songs of happy cheer":   10
So I sung the same again,
While he wept with joy to hear.

"Piper, sit thee down and write
In a book that all may read."
So he vanished from my sight,   15
And I plucked a hollow reed,

And I made a rural pen,
And I stained the water clear,
And I wrote my happy songs
Every child may joy to hear.   20

THE ECHOING GREEN

The Sun does arise,
And make happy the skies;
The merry bells ring
To welcome the Spring;
The skylark and thrush,   5
The birds of the bush,
Sing louder around

To the bells' cheerful sound,
While our sports shall be seen
On the Echoing Green.   10

Old John, with white hair,
Does laugh away care,
Sitting under the oak,
Among the old folk.
They laugh at our play,   15
And soon they all say:
"Such, such were the joys
When we all, girls and boys,
In our youth time were seen
On the Echoing Green."   20

Till the little ones, weary,
No more can be merry;
The sun does descend,
And our sports have an end.
Round the laps of their mothers   25
Many sisters and brothers,
Like birds in their nest,
Are ready for rest,
And sport no more seen
On the darkening Green.   30

THE LAMB

Little Lamb, who made thee?
  Dost thou know who made thee?
Gave thee life, and bid thee feed,
By the stream and o'er the mead;
Gave thee clothing of delight,   5
Softest clothing, woolly, bright;
Gave thee such a tender voice,
Making all the vales rejoice?
  Little Lamb, who made thee?
  Dost thou know who made thee?   10

  Little Lamb, I'll tell thee,
  Little Lamb, I'll tell thee:
He is calléd by thy name,
For He calls Himself a Lamb.
He is meek, and He is mild;   15

He became a little child.
I a child, and thou a lamb,
We are calléd by His name.
   Little Lamb, God bless thee!
   Little Lamb, God bless thee!   20

THE CHIMNEY SWEEPER

When my mother died I was very young,
And my father sold me while yet my tongue
Could scarcely cry " 'weep! 'weep! 'weep! 'weep!"
So your chimneys I sweep, and in soot I sleep.

There's little Tom Dacre, who cried when his head,   5
That curled like a lamb's back, was shaved: so I said,
"Hush, Tom! never mind it, for when your head's bare
You know that the soot cannot spoil your white hair."

And so he was quiet, and that very night
As Tom was a-sleeping, he had such a sight!   10
That thousands of sweepers, Dick, Joe, Ned, and Jack,
Were all of them locked up in coffins of black.

And by came an Angel who had a bright key,
And he opened the coffins and set them all free;
Then down a green plain leaping, laughing, they run,   15
And wash in a river, and shine in the Sun.

Then naked and white, all their bags left behind,
They rise upon clouds and sport in the wind;
And the Angel told Tom, if he'd be a good boy,
He'd have God for his father, and never want joy.   20

And so Tom awoke; and we rose in the dark,
And got with our bags and our brushes to work.
Though the morning was cold, Tom was happy and warm;
So if all do their duty they need not fear harm.

       · · ·

FROM SONGS OF EXPERIENCE

INTRODUCTION

Hear the voice of the Bard!
Who Present, Past, and Future sees;
Whose ears have heard

The Holy Word
That walked among the ancient trees,   5

Calling the lapséd Soul,
And weeping in the evening dew;
That might control
The starry pole,
And fallen, fallen light renew!   10

"O Earth, O Earth, return!
Arise from out the dewy grass;
Night is worn,
And the morn
Rises from the slumberous mass.   15

"Turn away no more;
Why wilt thou turn away?
The starry floor,
The wat'ry shore,
Is given thee till the break of day."   20

THE CHIMNEY SWEEPER

A little black thing among the snow,
Crying " 'weep! 'weep!" in notes of woe!
"Where are thy father and mother? say?"
"They are both gone up to the church to pray.

"Because I was happy upon the heath,   5
And smiled among the winter's snow,
They clothéd me in the clothes of death,
And taught me to sing the notes of woe.

"And because I am happy and dance and sing,
They think they have done me no injury,   10
And are gone to praise God and his Priest and King,
Who make up a heaven of our misery."

THE SICK ROSE

O Rose, thou art sick!
The invisible worm
That flies in the night,
In the howling storm,

Has found out thy bed   5
Of crimson joy,
And his dark secret love
Does thy life destroy.

THE TIGER

Tiger, tiger, burning bright
In the forests of the night,
What immortal hand or eye
Could frame thy fearful symmetry?

In what distant deeps or skies   5
Burnt the fire of thine eyes?
On what wings dare he aspire?
What the hand dare seize the fire?

And what shoulder, and what art,
Could twist the sinews of thy heart?   10
And when thy heart began to beat,
What dread hand and what dread feet?

What the hammer? What the chain?
In what furnace was thy brain?
What the anvil? What dread grasp   15
Dare its deadly terrors clasp?

When the stars threw down their spears,
And watered heaven with their tears,
Did He smile His work to see?
Did He who made the lamb make thee?   20

Tiger, tiger, burning bright
In the forests of the night,
What immortal hand or eye
Dare frame thy fearful symmetry?

7. *aspire*   fly upward.   against God's rule.
17. *stars*   the angels who had rebelled

LONDON

I wander through each chartered street,
Near where the chartered Thames does flow,
And mark in every face I meet
Marks of weakness, marks of woe.

In every cry of every man,   5
In every infant's cry of fear,
In every voice, in every ban,
The mind-forged manacles I hear.

How the chimney-sweeper's cry
Every black'ning church appalls;   10
And the hapless soldier's sigh
Runs in blood down palace walls.

But most through midnight streets I hear
How the youthful harlot's curse
Blasts the new born infant's tear,   15
And blights with plagues the marriage hearse.

INFANT SORROW

My mother groaned! my father wept.
Into the dangerous world I leapt:
Helpless, naked, piping loud:
Like a fiend hid in a cloud.

Struggling in my father's hands,   5
Striving against my swaddling bands,
Bound and weary I thought best
To sulk upon my mother's breast.

A POISON TREE

I was angry with my friend:
I told my wrath, my wrath did end.
I was angry with my foe:
I told it not, my wrath did grow.

And I watered it in fears,   5
Night and morning with my tears;
And I sunnéd it with smiles,
And with soft deceitful wiles.

1. *chartered*   mapped (also, established by proper authorities).

And it grew both day and night,
Till it bore an apple bright;   10
And my foe beheld it shine,
And he knew that it was mine,

And into my garden stole
When the night had veiled the pole:
In the morning glad I see   15
My foe outstretched beneath the tree.

WILLIAM WORDSWORTH

(*1770–1850*)

·

LINES

COMPOSED A FEW MILES ABOVE TINTERN ABBEY
ON REVISITING THE BANKS OF THE WYE
DURING A TOUR. JULY 13, 1798

Five years have passed; five summers, with the length
Of five long winters! and again I hear
These waters, rolling from their mountain-springs
With a soft inland murmur.—Once again
Do I behold these steep and lofty cliffs,   5
That on a wild secluded scene impress
Thoughts of more deep seclusion; and connect
The landscape with the quiet of the sky.
The day is come when I again repose
Here, under this dark sycamore, and view   10
These plots of cottage-ground, these orchard-tufts,
Which at this season, with their unripe fruits,
Are clad in one green hue, and lose themselves
'Mid groves and copses. Once again I see
These hedgerows, hardly hedgerows, little lines   15
Of sportive wood run wild: these pastoral farms,
Green to the very door; and wreaths of smoke
Sent up, in silence, from among the trees!
With some uncertain notice, as might seem
Of vagrant dwellers in the houseless woods,   20
Or of some hermit's cave, where by his fire
The hermit sits alone.

              These beauteous forms,
Through a long absence, have not been to me
As is a landscape to a blind man's eye;
But oft, in lonely rooms, and 'mid the din   25
Of towns and cities, I have owed to them
In hours of weariness, sensations sweet,
Felt in the blood, and felt along the heart;
And passing even into my purer mind,
With tranquil restoration—feelings too   30
Of unremembered pleasure: such, perhaps,
As have no slight or trivial influence

On that best portion of a good man's life,
His little, nameless, unremembered acts
Of kindness and of love. Nor less, I trust,   35
To them I may have owed another gift,
Of aspect more sublime; that blessèd mood
In which the burthen of the mystery,
In which the heavy and the weary weight
Of all this unintelligible world,   40
Is lightened—that serene and blessèd mood,
In which the affections gently lead us on—
Until, the breath of this corporeal frame
And even the motion of our human blood
Almost suspended, we are laid asleep   45
In body, and become a living soul;
While with an eye made quiet by the power
Of harmony, and the deep power of joy,
We see into the life of things.

               If this
Be but a vain belief, yet, oh! how oft—   50
In darkness and amid the many shapes
Of joyless daylight; when the fretful stir
Unprofitable, and the fever of the world,
Have hung upon the beatings of my heart—
How oft, in spirit, have I turned to thee,   55
O sylvan Wye! thou wanderer through the woods,
How often has my spirit turned to thee!

   And now, with gleams of half-extinguished thought,
With many recognitions dim and faint,
And somewhat of a sad perplexity,   60
The picture of the mind revives again;
While here I stand, not only with the sense
Of present pleasure, but with pleasing thoughts
That in this moment there is life and food
For future years. And so I dare to hope,   65
Though changed, no doubt, from what I was when first
I came among these hills; when like a roe
I bounded o'er the mountains, by the sides
Of the deep rivers, and the lonely streams,
Wherever nature led: more like a man   70
Flying from something that he dreads than one
Who sought the thing he loved. For nature then
(The coarser pleasures of my boyish days,
And their glad animal movements all gone by)

To me was all in all.—I cannot paint   75
What then I was. The sounding cataract
Haunted me like a passion; the tall rock,
The mountain, and the deep and gloomy wood,
Their colors and their forms, were then to me
An appetite; a feeling and a love,   80
That had no need of a remoter charm,
By thought supplied, nor any interest
Unborrowed from the eye.—That time is past,
And all its aching joys are now no more,
And all its dizzy raptures. Not for this   85
Faint I, nor mourn nor murmur; other gifts
Have followed; for such loss, I would believe,
Abundant recompense. For I have learned
To look on nature, not as in the hour
Of thoughtless youth; but hearing oftentimes   90
The still, sad music of humanity,
Nor harsh nor grating, though of ample power
To chasten and subdue. And I have felt
A presence that disturbs me with the joy
Of elevated thoughts; a sense sublime   95
Of something far more deeply interfused,
Whose dwelling is the light of setting suns,
And the round ocean and the living air,
And the blue sky, and in the mind of man:
A motion and a spirit, that impels   100
All thinking things, all objects of all thought,
And rolls through all things. Therefore am I still
A lover of the meadows and the woods
And mountains; and of all that we behold
From this green earth; of all the mighty world   105
Of eye, and ear—both what they half create,
And what perceive; well pleased to recognize
In nature and the language of the sense
The anchor of my purest thoughts, the nurse,
The guide, the guardian of my heart, and soul   110
Of all my moral being.

                Nor perchance,
If I were not thus taught, should I the more
Suffer my genial spirits to decay:
For thou art with me here upon the banks
Of this fair river; thou my dearest friend,   115
My dear, dear friend; and in thy voice I catch

The language of my former heart, and read
My former pleasures in the shooting lights
Of thy wild eyes. Oh! yet a little while
May I behold in thee what I was once,   120
My dear, dear sister! and this prayer I make,
Knowing that Nature never did betray
The heart that loved her; 'tis her privilege,
Through all the years of this our life, to lead
From joy to joy: for she can so inform   125
The mind that is within us, so impress
With quietness and beauty, and so feed
With lofty thoughts, that neither evil tongues,
Rash judgments, nor the sneers of selfish men,
Nor greetings where no kindness is, nor all   130
The dreary intercourse of daily life,
Shall e'er prevail against us, or disturb
Our cheerful faith, that all which we behold
Is full of blessings. Therefore let the moon
Shine on thee in thy solitary walk;   135
And let the misty mountain winds be free
To blow against thee: and, in after years,
When these wild ecstasies shall be matured
Into a sober pleasure; when thy mind
Shall be a mansion for all lovely forms,   140
Thy memory be as a dwelling place
For all sweet sounds and harmonies; oh! then,
If solitude, or fear, or pain, or grief
Should be thy portion, with what healing thoughts
Of tender joy wilt thou remember me,   145
And these my exhortations! Nor, perchance—
If I should be where I no more can hear
Thy voice, nor catch from thy wild eyes these gleams
Of past existence—wilt thou then forget
That on the banks of this delightful stream   150
We stood together; and that I, so long
A worshiper of Nature, hither came
Unwearied in that service; rather say
With warmer love—oh! with far deeper zeal
Of holier love. Nor wilt thou then forget,   155
That after many wanderings, many years
Of absence, these steep woods and lofty cliffs,
And this green pastoral landscape, were to me
More dear, both for themselves and for thy sake!

THERE WAS A BOY

There was a boy; ye knew him well, ye cliffs
And islands of Winander!—many a time,
At evening, when the earliest stars began
To move along the edges of the hills,
Rising or setting, would he stand alone,   5
Beneath the trees, or by the glimmering lake;
And there, with fingers interwoven, both hands
Pressed closely palm to palm and to his mouth
Uplifted, he, as through an instrument,
Blew mimic hootings to the silent owls,   10
That they might answer him.—And they would shout
Across the watery vale, and shout again,
Responsive to his call,—with quivering peals,
And long halloos, and screams, and echoes loud
Redoubled and redoubled; concourse wild   15
Of jocund din! And, when there came a pause
Of silence such as baffled his best skill:
Then, sometimes, in that silence, while he hung
Listening, a gentle shock of mild surprise
Has carried far into his heart the voice   20
Of mountain-torrents; or the visible scene
Would enter unawares into his mind
With all its solemn imagery, its rocks,
Its woods, and that uncertain heaven received
Into the bosom of the steady lake.   25

    This boy was taken from his mates, and died
In childhood, ere he was full twelve years old.
Pre-eminent in beauty is the vale
Where he was born and bred: the church-yard hangs
Upon a slope above the village-school;   30
And, through that church-yard when my way has led
On summer evenings, I believe, that there
A long half hour together I have stood
Mute—looking at the grave in which he lies!

A SLUMBER DID MY SPIRIT SEAL

A slumber did my spirit seal;
    I had no human fears:
She seemed a thing that could not feel
    The touch of earthly years.

No motion has she now, no force;   5
  She neither hears nor sees;
Rolled round in earth's diurnal course,
  With rocks, and stones, and trees.

TO A BUTTERFLY

I've watched you now a full half hour,
Self-poised upon that yellow flower;
And, little butterfly! indeed
I know not if you sleep or feed.
How motionless!—not frozen seas   5
More motionless! and then
What joy awaits you, when the breeze
Hath found you out among the trees,
And calls you forth again!

This plot of orchard-ground is ours;   10
My trees they are, my sister's flowers;
Here rest your wings when they are weary;
Here lodge as in a sanctuary!
Come often to us, fear no wrong;
Sit near us on the bough!   15
We'll talk of sunshine and of song,
And summer days, when we were young;
Sweet childish days, that were as long
As twenty days are now.

COMPOSED UPON
WESTMINSTER BRIDGE,
SEPTEMBER 3, 1802

Earth has not anything to show more fair:
Dull would he be of soul who could pass by
A sight so touching in its majesty:
This city now doth, like a garment, wear
The beauty of the morning; silent, bare,   5
Ships, towers, domes, theaters, and temples lie
Open unto the fields, and to the sky;
All bright and glittering in the smokeless air.
Never did sun more beautifully steep
In his first splendor, valley, rock, or hill;   10
Ne'er saw I, never felt, a calm so deep!

The river glideth at his own sweet will:
Dear God! the very houses seem asleep;
And all that mighty heart is lying still!

IT IS A BEAUTEOUS EVENING

It is a beauteous evening, calm and free,
The holy time is quiet as a nun
Breathless with adoration; the broad sun
Is sinking down in its tranquility;
The gentleness of heaven broods o'er the sea: 5
Listen! the mighty Being is awake,
And doth with his eternal motion make
A sound like thunder—everlastingly.
Dear child! dear girl! that walkest with me here,
If thou appear untouched by solemn thought,   10
Thy nature is not therefore less divine:
Thou liest in Abraham's bosom all the year,
And worship'st at the Temple's inner shrine,
God being with thee when we know it not.

THE SOLITARY REAPER

Behold her, single in the field,
Yon solitary Highland lass!
Reaping and singing by herself;
Stop here, or gently pass!
Alone she cuts and binds the grain,   5
And sings a melancholy strain;
O listen! for the vale profound
Is overflowing with the sound.

No nightingale did ever chaunt
More welcome notes to weary bands   10
Of travelers in some shady haunt,
Among Arabian sands:
A voice so thrilling ne'er was heard
In springtime from the cuckoo-bird,
Breaking the silence of the seas   15
Among the farthest Hebrides.

Will no one tell me what she sings?—
Perhaps the plaintive numbers flow

12. *Abraham's bosom*   in *Luke*, xvi.22, the place where the souls were to rest after death.

For old, unhappy, far-off things,
And battles long ago: 20
Or is it some more humble lay,
Familiar matter of today?
Some natural sorrow, loss, or pain,
That has been, and may be again?

Whate'er the theme, the maiden sang   25
As if her song could have no ending;
I saw her singing at her work,
And o'er the sickle bending:—
I listened, motionless and still;
And, as I mounted up the hill,   30
The music in my heart I bore,
Long after it was heard no more.

I WANDERED LONELY AS A CLOUD

I wandered lonely as a cloud
That floats on high o'er vales and hills,
When all at once I saw a crowd,
A host, of golden daffodils;
Beside the lake, beneath the trees,   5
Fluttering and dancing in the breeze.

Continuous as the stars that shine
And twinkle on the milky way,
They stretched in never-ending line
Along the margin of a bay: 10
Ten thousand saw I at a glance,
Tossing their heads in sprightly dance.

The waves beside them danced; but they
Outdid the sparkling waves in glee:
A poet could not but be gay,   15
In such a jocund company:
I gazed—and gazed—but little thought
What wealth the show to me had brought:

For oft, when on my couch I lie
In vacant or in pensive mood,   20
They flash upon that inward eye
Which is the bliss of solitude;
And then my heart with pleasure fills,
And dances with the daffodils.

THE SMALL CELANDINE

There is a flower, the lesser celandine,
That shrinks, like many more, from cold and rain;
And, the first moment that the sun may shine,
Bright as the sun himself, 'tis out again!

When hailstones have been falling, swarm on swarm,   5
Or blasts the green field and the trees distressed,
Oft have I seen it muffled up from harm,
In close self-shelter, like a thing at rest.

But lately, one rough day, this flower I passed
And recognized it, though an altered form,   10
Now standing forth an offering to the blast,
And buffeted at will by rain and storm.

I stopped, and said with inly-muttered voice,
"It doth not love the shower, nor seek the cold:
This neither is its courage nor its choice,   15
But its necessity in being old.

"The sunshine may not cheer it, nor the dew;
It cannot help itself in its decay;
Stiff in its members, withered, changed of hue."
And, in my spleen, I smiled that it was grey.   20

To be a prodigal's favorite—then, worse truth,
A miser's pensioner—behold our lot!
O man, that from thy fair and shining youth
Age might but take the things youth needed not!

COMPOSED BY THE SIDE OF
GRASMERE LAKE

Clouds, lingering yet, extend in solid bars
Through the grey west; and lo! these waters, steeled
By breezeless air to smoothest polish, yield
A vivid repetition of the stars;
Jove, Venus, and the ruddy crest of Mars   5
Amid his fellows beauteously revealed
At happy distance from earth's groaning field,
Where ruthless mortals wage incessant wars.

Is it a mirror?—or the nether sphere
Opening to view the abyss in which she feeds   10
Her own calm fires?—But list! a voice is near;
Great Pan himself low-whispering through the reeds,
"Be thankful, thou; for, if unholy deeds
Ravage the world, tranquillity is here!"

SURPRISED BY JOY

Surprised by joy—impatient as the wind
I turned to share the transport—Oh! with whom
But thee, deep buried in the silent tomb,
That spot which no vicissitude can find?
Love, faithful love, recalled thee to my mind—   5
But how could I forget thee? Through what power,
Even for the least division of an hour,
Have I been so beguiled as to be blind
To my most grievous loss!—That thought's return
Was the worst pang that sorrow ever bore,   10
Save one, one only, when I stood forlorn,
Knowing my heart's best treasure was no more;
That neither present time, nor years unborn
Could to my sight that heavenly face restore.

MUTABILITY

From low to high doth dissolution climb,
And sink from high to low, along a scale
Of awful notes, whose concord shall not fail;
A musical but melancholy chime,
Which they can hear who meddle not with crime,   5
Nor avarice, nor over-anxious care.
Truth fails not; but her outward forms that bear
The longest date do melt like frosty rime,
That in the morning whitened hill and plain
And is no more; drop like the tower sublime   10
Of yesterday, which royally did wear
His crown of weeds, but could not even sustain
Some casual shout that broke the silent air,
Or the unimaginable touch of Time.

COMPOSED AMONG THE RUINS OF A CASTLE IN NORTH WALES

Through shattered galleries, 'mid roofless halls,
Wandering with timid footsteps oft betrayed,
The stranger sighs, nor scruples to upbraid
Old Time, though he, gentlest among the thralls
Of destiny, upon these wounds hath laid   5
His lenient touches, soft as light that falls,
From the wan moon, upon the towers and walls,
Light deepening the profoundest sleep of shade.
Relic of kings! Wreck of forgotten wars,
To winds abandoned and the prying stars,   10
Time *loves* thee! at his call the seasons twine
Luxuriant wreaths around thy forehead hoar;
And, though past pomp no changes can restore,
A soothing recompense, his gift, is thine!

TO ——, IN HER SEVENTIETH YEAR

Such age how beautiful! O lady bright,
Whose mortal lineaments seem all refined
By favoring Nature and a saintly mind
To something purer and more exquisite
Than flesh and blood; whene'er thou meet'st my sight,   5
When I behold thy blanched unwithered cheek,
Thy temples fringed with locks of gleaming white,
And head that droops because the soul is meek,
Thee with the welcome snowdrop I compare;
That child of winter, prompting thoughts that climb   10
From desolation toward the genial prime;
Or with the moon conquering earth's misty air,
And filling more and more with crystal light
As pensive evening deepens into night.

JOHN KEATS
(1795–1821)

·

ON FIRST LOOKING INTO CHAPMAN'S HOMER

Much have I traveled in the realms of gold,
And many goodly states and kingdoms seen;
Round many western islands have I been
Which bards in fealty to Apollo hold.
Oft of one wide expanse had I been told   5
That deep-browed Homer ruled as his demesne;
Yet did I never breathe its pure serene
Till I heard Chapman speak out loud and bold:
Then felt I like some watcher of the skies
When a new planet swims into his ken;   10
Or like stout Cortez when with eagle eyes
He stared at the Pacific—and all his men
Looked at each other with a wild surmise—
Silent, upon a peak in Darien.

ON THE GRASSHOPPER AND CRICKET

The poetry of earth is never dead:
When all the birds are faint with the hot sun,
And hide in cooling trees, a voice will run
From hedge to hedge about the new-mown mead;
That is the Grasshopper's—he takes the lead   5
In summer luxury,—he has never done
With his delights; for when tired out with fun
He rests at ease beneath some pleasant weed.
The poetry of earth is ceasing never:
On a lone winter evening, when the frost   10
Has wrought a silence, from the stove there shrills
The Cricket's song, in warmth increasing ever,
And seems to one in drowsiness half lost,
The Grasshopper's among some grassy hills.

Chapman George Chapman, Eliza-
bethan translator of the *Iliad*.   11. *Cortez* really Balboa.
          14. *Darien* Panama.

AFTER DARK VAPORS

After dark vapors have oppressed our plains
For a long dreary season, comes a day
Born of the gentle South, and clears away
From the sick heavens all unseemly stains.
The anxious month, relievéd of its pains, 5
Takes as a long-lost right the feel of May;
The eyelids with the passing coolness play
Like rose leaves with the drip of summer rains.
The calmest thoughts come round us; as of leaves
Budding—fruit ripening in stillness—autumn suns 10
Smiling at eve upon the quiet sheaves—
Sweet Sappho's cheek—a smiling infant's breath—
The gradual sand that through an hour-glass runs—
A woodland rivulet—a poet's death.

ON THE SEA

It keeps eternal whisperings around
Desolate shores, and with its mighty swell
Gluts twice ten thousand caverns, till the spell
Of Hecate leaves them their old shadowy sound.
Often 'tis in such gentle temper found, 5
That scarcely will the very smallest shell
Be moved for days from where it sometimes fell,
When last the winds of Heaven were unbound.
Oh ye! who have your eyeballs vexed and tired,
Feast them upon the wideness of the sea; 10
Oh ye! whose ears are dinned with uproar rude,
Or fed too much with cloying melody—
Sit ye near some old cavern's mouth, and brood
Until ye start, as if the sea-nymphs quired!

WHEN I HAVE FEARS

When I have fears that I may cease to be
Before my pen has gleaned my teeming brain,
Before high-piléd books, in charact'ry,

4. *Hecate* the moon-goddess drawing
the tides; also the underworld goddess
of witchcraft.

3. *charact'ry* writing.

Hold like rich garners the full-ripened grain;
When I behold, upon the night's starred face,   5
Huge cloudy symbols of a high romance,
And think that I may never live to trace
Their shadows, with the magic hand of chance;
And when I feel, fair creature of an hour,
That I shall never look upon thee more,   10
Never have relish in the faery power
Of unreflecting love!—then on the shore
Of the wide world I stand alone, and think
Till Love and Fame to nothingness do sink.

TO HOMER

Standing aloof in giant ignorance,
Of thee I hear and of the Cyclades,
As one who sits ashore and longs perchance
To visit dolphin-coral in deep seas.
So thou wast blind!—but then the veil was rent;   5
For Jove uncurtained Heaven to let thee live,
And Neptune made for thee a spumy tent,
And Pan made sing for thee his forest-hive;
Aye, on the shores of darkness there is light,
And precipices show untrodden green;   10
There is a budding morrow in midnight;
There is a triple sight in blindness keen;
Such seeing hads't thou, as it once befell
To Dian, Queen of Earth, and Heaven, and Hell.

ON VISITING THE TOMB OF BURNS

The town, the churchyard, and the setting sun,
The clouds, the trees, the rounded hills all seem,
Though beautiful, cold—strange—as in a dream,
I dreaméd long ago, now new begun.
The short-lived, paly summer is but won   5
From winter's ague, for one hour's gleam;
Though sapphire-warm, their stars do never beam:
All is cold Beauty; pain is never done:
For who has mind to relish, Minos-wise,

2. *Cyclades* Aegean islands.
14. *Dian* in her triple role as huntress on earth, goddess of the Moon, and queen of Hell.

Burns Robert Burns, eighteenth-century Scottish poet.
9. *Minos* one of the judges in the underworld.

The Real of Beauty, free from that dead hue   10
Sickly imagination and sick pride
Cast wan upon it? Burns! with honor due
I oft have honored thee. Great shadow, hide
Thy face; I sin against thy native skies.

BRIGHT STAR

Bright star, would I were steadfast as thou art—
Not in lone splendor hung aloft the night
And watching, with eternal lids apart,
Like nature's patient, sleepless Eremite,
The moving waters at their priestlike task   5
Of pure ablution round earth's human shores,
Or gazing on the new soft fallen mask
Of snow upon the mountains and the moors—
No—yet still steadfast, still unchangeable,
Pillowed upon my fair love's ripening breast,   10
To feel forever its soft fall and swell,
Awake forever in a sweet unrest,
Still, still to hear her tender-taken breath,
And so live ever—or else swoon to death.

TO SLEEP

O soft embalmer of the still midnight,
Shutting, with careful fingers and benign,
Our gloom-pleased eyes, embowered from the light,
Enshaded in forgetfulness divine;
O soothest Sleep! if so it please thee, close,   5
In midst of this thine hymn my willing eyes,
Or wait the amen, ere thy poppy throws
Around my bed its lulling charities;
Then save me, or the passéd day will shine
Upon my pillow, breeding many woes;   10
Save me from curious conscience, that still lords
Its strength for darkness, burrowing like a mole;
Turn the key deftly in the oiléd wards,
And seal the hushéd casket of my soul.

4. *Eremite*   hermit.

ODE TO A NIGHTINGALE

My heart aches, and a drowsy numbness pains
    My sense, as though of hemlock I had drunk,
Or emptied some dull opiate to the drains
    One minute past, and Lethe-wards had sunk:
'Tis not through envy of thy happy lot,   5
    But being too happy in thine happiness—
        That thou, light-wingéd Dryad of the trees,
           In some melodious plot
    Of beechen green, and shadows numberless,
        Singest of summer in full-throated ease.   10

O, for a draught of vintage! that hath been
    Cooled a long age in the deep-delvéd earth,
Tasting of Flora and the country green,
    Dance, and Provençal song, and sunburnt mirth!
O for a beaker full of the warm South,   15
    Full of the true, the blushful Hippocrene,
        With beaded bubbles winking at the brim,
           And purple-stainéd mouth;
    That I might drink, and leave the world unseen,
        And with thee fade away into the forest dim: 20

Fade far away, dissolve, and quite forget
    What thou among the leaves hast never known,
The weariness, the fever, and the fret
    Here, where men sit and hear each other groan;
Where palsy shakes a few, sad, last gray hairs,   25
    Where youth grows pale, and specter-thin, and dies;
        Where but to think is to be full of sorrow
           And leaden-eyed despairs,
    Where Beauty cannot keep her lustrous eyes,
        Or new Love pine at them beyond tomorrow.   30

Away! away! for I will fly to thee,
    Not charioted by Bacchus and his pards,
But on the viewless wings of Poesy,
    Though the dull brain perplexes and retards:
Already with thee! tender is the night,   35

4. *Lethe* river of forgetfulness in Hades.
7. *Dryad* wood nymph.
13. *Flora* goddess of flowers.

16. *Hippocrene* fountain of the Muses on Mt. Helicon.
32. *Bacchus* god of wine whose chariot is drawn by leopards (*pards*).

And haply the Queen-Moon is on her throne,
   Clustered around by all her starry Fays;
      But here there is no light,
Save what from heaven is with the breezes blown
   Through verdurous glooms and winding mossy ways.   40

I cannot see what flowers are at my feet,
   Nor what soft incense hangs upon the boughs,
But, in embalmèd darkness, guess each sweet
   Wherewith the seasonable month endows
The grass, the thicket, and the fruit tree wild;   45
   White hawthorn, and the pastoral eglantine;
      Fast fading violets covered up in leaves;
        And mid-May's eldest child,
The coming musk-rose, full of dewy wine,
   The murmurous haunt of flies on summer eves.   50

Darkling I listen; and, for many a time
   I have been been half in love with easeful Death,
Called him soft names in many a musèd rhyme,
   To take into the air my quiet breath;
Now more than ever seems it rich to die,   55
   To cease upon the midnight with no pain,
      While thou art pouring forth thy soul abroad
        In such an ecstasy!
   Still wouldst thou sing, and I have ears in vain—
      To thy high requiem become a sod.   60

Thou was not born for death, immortal Bird!
   No hungry generations tread thee down;
The voice I hear this passing night was heard
   In ancient days by emperor and clown:
Perhaps the selfsame song that found a path   65
   Through the sad heart of Ruth, when, sick for home,
      She stood in tears amid the alien corn;
        The same that ofttimes hath
   Charmed magic casements, opening on the foam
      Of perilous seas, in faery lands forlorn.   70

Forlorn! the very word is like a bell
   To toll me back from thee to my sole self!
Adieu! the fancy cannot cheat so well

51. *Darkling* in darkness.
66. *Ruth* Biblical figure who left her native land to live with Naomi, her mother-in-law.

As she is famed to do, deceiving elf.
Adieu! adieu! thy plaintive anthem fades   75
    Past the near meadows, over the still stream,
        Up the hill side; and now 'tis buried deep
            In the next valley-glades:
    Was it a vision, or a waking dream?
        Fled is that music:—Do I wake or sleep?   80

ODE ON A GRECIAN URN

Thou still unravished bride of quietness,
    Thou foster-child of silence and slow time,
Sylvan historian, who canst thus express
    A flowery tale more sweetly than our rhyme:
What leaf-fringed legend haunts about thy shape   5
    Of deities or mortals, or of both,
        In Tempe or the dales of Arcady?
What men or gods are these? What maidens loath?
    What mad pursuit? What struggle to escape?
        What pipes and timbrels? What wild ecstasy?   10

Heard melodies are sweet, but those unheard
    Are sweeter; therefore, ye soft pipes, play on;
Not to the sensual ear, but, more endeared,
    Pipe to the spirit ditties of no tone:
Fair youth, beneath the trees, thou canst not leave   15
    Thy song, nor ever can those trees be bare;
        Bold lover, never, never canst thou kiss,
Though winning near the goal—yet, do not grieve;
    She cannot fade, though thou hast not thy bliss,
        Forever wilt thou love, and she be fair!   20

Ah, happy, happy boughs! that cannot shed
    Your leaves, nor ever bid the spring adieu;
And, happy melodist, unwearièd,
    Forever piping songs forever new;
More happy love! more happy, happy love!   25
    Forever warm and still to be enjoyed,
        Forever panting, and forever young;
All breathing human passion far above,
    That leaves a heart high-sorrowful and cloyed,
        A burning forehead, and a parching tongue.   30

7. *Tempe . . . Arcady*   traditional scenes of Greek pastoral poetry

Who are these coming to the sacrifice?
　　To what green altar, O mysterious priest,
Lead'st thou that heifer lowing at the skies,
　　　And all her silken flanks with garlands dressed?
What little town by river or sea shore,　　　　　　　　　35
　　Or mountain-built with peaceful citadel,
　　　Is emptied of this folk, this pious morn?
And, little town, thy streets forevermore
　　Will silent be; and not a soul to tell
　　　Why thou art desolate, can e'er return.　　　　　　40

O Attic shape! Fair attitude! with brede
　　Of marble men and maidens overwrought,
With forest branches and the trodden weed;
　　Thou, silent form, dost tease us out of thought
As doth eternity: Cold Pastoral!　　　　　　　　　　　45
　　When old age shall this generation waste,
　　　Thou shalt remain, in midst of other woe
Than ours, a friend to man, to whom thou say'st,
　　"Beauty is truth, truth beauty,"—that is all
　　　Ye know on earth, and all ye need to know.　　　　50

ODE ON MELANCHOLY

No, no, go not to Lethe, neither twist
　　Wolfsbane, tight-rooted, for its poisonous wine;
Nor suffer thy pale forehead to be kissed
　　By nightshade, ruby grape of Proserpine;
Make not your rosary of yew-berries,　　　　　　　　　5
　　Nor let the beetle, nor the death-moth be
　　　Your mournful Psyche, nor the downy owl
A partner in your sorrow's mysteries;
　　For shade to shade will come too drowsily,
　　　And drown the wakeful anguish of the soul.　　　　10

But when the melancholy fit shall fall
　　Sudden from heaven like a weeping cloud,
That fosters the droop-headed flowers all,
　　And hides the green hill in an April shroud;

---

41. *brede* embroidery.

4. *Proserpine* goddess of the under-world.

7. *Psyche* the soul, sometimes repre-sented as a butterfly rising from the mouth of someone who has just died.

Then glut thy sorrow on a morning rose,   15
   Or on the rainbow of the salt sand-wave,
      Or on the wealth of globéd peonies;
Or if thy mistress some rich anger shows,
   Imprison her soft hand, and let her rave,
      And feed deep, deep upon her peerless eyes.   20

She dwells with Beauty—Beauty that must die;
   And Joy, whose hand is ever at his lips
Bidding adieu; and aching Pleasure nigh,
   Turning to poison while the bee-mouth sips:
Aye, in the very temple of Delight   25
   Veiled Melancholy has her sov'reign shrine,
      Though seen of none save him whose strenuous tongue
Can burst Joy's grape against his palate fine;
   His soul shall taste the sadness of her might,
      And be among her cloudy trophies hung.   30

TO AUTUMN

Season of mists and mellow fruitfulness,
   Close bosom-friend of the maturing sun;
Conspiring with him how to load and bless
   With fruit the vines that round the thatch-eves run;
To bend with apples the mossed cottage-trees,   5
   And fill all fruit with ripeness to the core;
      To swell the gourd, and plump the hazel shells
With a sweet kernel; to set budding more,
   And still more, later flowers for the bees,
      Until they think warm days will never cease,   10
      For Summer has o'er-brimmed their clammy cells.

Who hath not seen thee oft amid thy store?
   Sometimes whoever seeks abroad may find
Thee sitting careless on a granary floor,
   Thy hair soft-lifted by the winnowing wind;   15
Or on a half-reaped furrow sound asleep,
   Drowsed with the fume of poppies, while thy hook
      Spares the next swath and all its twinéd flowers:
And sometimes like a gleaner thou dost keep
   Steady thy laden head across a brook;   20
   Or by a cider-press, with patient look,
      Thou watchest the last oozings hours by hours.

Where are the songs of Spring? Aye, where are they?
 Think not of them, thou hast thy music too—
While barréd clouds bloom the soft-dying day,   25
 And touch the stubble-plains with rosy hue;
Then in a wailful choir the small gnats mourn
 Among the river sallows, borne aloft
  Or sinking as the light wind lives or dies;
And full-grown lambs loud bleat from hilly bourn;   30
 Hedge crickets sing; and now with treble soft
 The redbreast whistles from a garden croft;
  And gathering swallows twitter in the skies.

ALFRED, LORD TENNYSON
(1809–1892)

·

ULYSSES

It little profits that an idle king,
By this still hearth, among these barren crags,
Matched with an aged wife, I mete and dole
Unequal laws unto a savage race,
That hoard, and sleep, and feed, and know not me.   5
I cannot rest from travel; I will drink
Life to the lees; all times I have enjoyed
Greatly, have suffered greatly, both with those
That loved me, and alone; on shore, and when
Through scudding drifts the rainy Hyades   10
Vexed the dim sea: I am become a name;
For always roaming with a hungry heart
Much have I seen and known; cities of men
And manners, climates, councils, governments,
Myself not least, but honored of them all;   15
And drunk delight of battle with my peers,
Far on the ringing plains of windy Troy.
I am a part of all that I have met;
Yet all experience is an arch wherethrough
Gleams that untraveled world, whose margin fades   20
Forever and forever when I move.
How dull it is to pause, to make an end,
To rust unburnished, not to shine in use!
As though to breathe were life. Life piled on life
Were all too little, and of one to me   25
Little remains; but every hour is saved
From thàt eternal silence, something more,
A bringer of new things; and vile it were
For some three suns to store and hoard myself,
And this gray spirit yearning in desire   30
To follow knowledge like a sinking star,
Beyond the utmost bound of human thought.
This is my son, mine own Telemachus
To whom I leave the scepter and the isle—
Well-loved of me, discerning to fulfill   35

10. *Hyades*   nymphs.

This labor, by slow prudence to make mild
A rugged people, and through soft degrees
Subdue them to the useful and the good.
Most blameless is he, centered in the sphere
Of common duties, decent not to fail   40
In offices of tenderness, and pay
Meet adoration to my household gods,
When I am gone. He works his work, I mine.
    There lies the port; the vessel puffs her sail;
There gloom the dark broad seas. My mariners,   45
Souls that have toiled, and wrought, and thought with me—
That ever with a frolic welcome took
The thunder and the sunshine, and opposed
Free hearts, free foreheads—you and I are old;
Old age hath yet his honor and his toil;   50
Death closes all; but something ere the end,
Some work of noble note, may yet be done,
Not unbecoming men that strove with gods.
The lights begin to twinkle from the rocks;
The long day wanes; the slow moon climbs; the deep   55
Moans round with many voices. Come, my friends,
'Tis not too late to seek a newer world.
Push off, and sitting well in order smite
The sounding furrows; for my purpose holds
To sail beyond the sunset, and the baths   60
Of all the western stars, until I die.
It may be that the gulfs will wash us down;
It may be we shall touch the Happy Isles,
And see the great Achilles, whom we knew.
Though much is taken, much abides; and though   65
We are not now that strength which in old days
Moved earth and heaven, that which we are, we are;
One equal temper of heroic hearts,
Made weak by time and fate, but strong in will
To strive, to seek, to find, and not to yield.   70

TITHONUS

The woods decay, the woods decay and fall,
The vapors weep their burthen to the ground,
Man comes and tills the field and lies beneath,

Tithonus Trojan prince, loved by Aurora who secured him immortality but forgot to ask for eternal youth. As he grew older and weaker he prayed to Aurora to remove him from the world, and she changed him into a grasshopper.

And after many a summer dies the swan.
Me only cruel immortality   5
Consumes; I wither slowly in thine arms,
Here at the quiet limit of the world,
A white-haired shadow roaming like a dream
The ever-silent spaces of the East,
Far-folded mists, and gleaming halls of morn.   10
   Alas! for this gray shadow, once a man—
So glorious in his beauty and thy choice,
Who madest him thy chosen, that he seemed
To his great heart none other than a God!
I asked thee, "Give me immortality."   15
Then didst thou grant mine asking with a smile,
Like wealthy men who care not how they give.
But thy strong Hours indignant worked their wills,
And beat me down and marred and wasted me,
And though they could not end me, left me maimed   20
To dwell in presence of immortal youth,
Immortal age beside immortal youth,
And all I was, in ashes. Can thy love,
Thy beauty, make amends, though even now,
Close over us, the silver star, thy guide,   25
Shines in those tremulous eyes that fill with tears
To hear me? Let me go: take back thy gift:
Why should a man desire in any way
To vary from the kindly race of men,
Or pass beyond the goal of ordinance   30
Where all should pause, as is most meet for all?
   A soft air fans the cloud apart; there comes
A glimpse of that dark world where I was born.
Once more the old mysterious glimmer steals
From thy pure brows, and from thy shoulders pure,   35
And bosom beating with a heart renewed.
Thy cheek begins to redden through the gloom,
Thy sweet eyes brighten slowly close to mine,
Ere yet they blind the stars, and the wild team
Which love thee, yearning for thy yoke, arise,   40
And shake the darkness from their loosened manes,
And beat the twilight into flakes of fire.
   Lo! ever thus thou growest beautiful
In silence, then before thine answer given
Departest, and thy tears are on my cheek.   45
   Why wilt thou ever scare me with thy tears,
And make me tremble lest a saying learnt,
In days far off, on that dark earth, be true?

"The Gods themselves cannot recall their gifts."
Ay me! ay me! with what another heart   50
In days far off, and with what other eyes
I used to watch—if I be he that watched—
The lucid outline forming round thee; saw
The dim curls kindle into sunny rings;
Changed with thy mystic change, and felt my blood   55
Glow with the glow that slowly crimsoned all
Thy presence and thy portals, while I lay,
Mouth, forehead, eyelids, growing dewy-warm
With kisses balmier than half-opening buds
Of April, and could hear the lips that kissed   60
Whispering I knew not what of wild and sweet,
Like that strange song I heard Apollo sing,
While Ilion like a mist rose into towers.
    Yet hold me not forever in thine East:
How can my nature longer mix with thine?   65
Coldly thy rosy shadows bathe me, cold
Are all thy lights, and cold my wrinkled feet
Upon thy glimmering thresholds, when the steam
Floats up from those dim fields about the homes
Of happy men that have the power to die,   70
And grassy barrows of the happier dead.
Release me, and restore me to the ground;
Thou seest all things, thou wilt see my grave:
Thou wilt renew thy beauty morn by morn;
I earth in earth forget these empty courts,   75
And thee returning on thy silver wheels.

FROM **THE PRINCESS**

TEARS, IDLE TEARS

Tears, idle tears, I know not what they mean,
Tears from the depth of some divine despair
Rise in the heart, and gather to the eyes,
In looking on the happy autumn-fields,
And thinking of the days that are no more.   5

Fresh as the first beam glittering on a sail,
That brings our friends up from the underworld,
Sad as the last which reddens over one
That sinks with all we love below the verge;
So sad, so fresh, the days that are no more.   10

Ah, sad and strange as in dark summer dawns
The earliest pipe of half-awakened birds
To dying ears, when unto dying eyes
The casement slowly grows a glimmering square;
So sad, so strange, the days that are no more. 15

Dear as remembered kisses after death,
And sweet as those by hopeless fancy feigned
On lips that are for others; deep as love,
Deep as first love, and wild with all regret;
O death in life, the days that are no more! 20

NOW SLEEPS THE CRIMSON PETAL

Now sleeps the crimson petal, now the white;
Nor waves the cypress in the palace walk;
Nor winks the gold fin in the porphyry font;
The firefly wakens; waken thou with me.

Now droops the milk-white peacock like a ghost, 5
And like a ghost she glimmers on to me.

Now lies the earth all Danaë to the stars,
And all thy heart lies open unto me.

Now slides the silent meteor on, and leaves
A shining furrow, as thy thoughts in me. 10

Now folds the lily all her sweetness up,
And slips into the bosom of the lake;
So fold thyself, my dearest, thou, and slip
Into my bosom and be lost in me.

FROM IN MEMORIAM A.H.H.

2.

Old Yew, which graspest at the stones
That name the underlying dead,
Thy fibers net the dreamless head,
Thy roots are wrapped about the bones.

---

7. *Danaë* princess visited by Zeus in a golden shower.

In Memoriam A.H.H. in memory of the poet's friend Arthur Henry Hallam, who died in 1833.

The seasons bring the flower again,   5
    And bring the firstling to the flock;
    And in the dusk of thee, the clock
Beats out the little lives of men.

O, not for thee the glow, the bloom,
    Who changest not in any gale,   10
    Nor branding summer suns avail
To touch thy thousand years of gloom;

And gazing on thee, sullen tree,
    Sick for thy stubborn hardihood,
    I seem to fail from out my blood   15
And grow incorporate into thee.

7.

Dark house, by which once more I stand
    Here in the long unlovely street,
    Doors, where my heart was used to beat
So quickly, waiting for a hand,

A hand that can be clasped no more—   5
    Behold me, for I cannot sleep,
    And like a guilty thing I creep
At earliest morning to the door.

He is not here; but far away
    The noise of life begins again,   10
    And ghastly through the drizzling rain
On the bald street breaks the blank day.

DEMETER AND PERSEPHONE
(IN ENNA)

Faint as a climate-changing bird that flies
All night across the darkness, and at dawn
Falls on the threshold of her native land,
And can no more, thou camest, O my child,
Led upward by the god of ghosts and dreams,   5
Who laid thee at Eleusis, dazed and dumb

Persephone daughter of Demeter, god- spend part of each year on earth.
dess of the Earth, was abducted by the *5. god of ghosts and dreams* Hermes,
god of the underworld but allowed to also referred to in line 90.

With passing through at once from state to state,
Until I brought thee hither, that the day,
When here thy hands let fall the gathered flower,
Might break through clouded memories once again   10
On thy lost self. A sudden nightingale
Saw thee, and flashed into a frolic of song
And welcome; and a gleam as of the moon,
When first she peers along the tremulous deep,
Fled wavering o'er thy face, and chased away   15
That shadow of a likeness to the king
Of shadows, thy dark mate. Persephone!
Queen of the dead no more—my child! Thine eyes
Again were human-godlike, and the sun
Burst from a swimming fleece of winter gray,   20
And robed thee in his day from head to feet—
"Mother!" and I was folded in thine arms.

    Child, those imperial, disimpassioned eyes
Awed even me at first, thy mother—eyes
That oft had seen the serpent-wanded power   25
Draw downward into Hades with his drift
Of flickering spectres, lighted from below
By the red race of fiery Phlegethon;
But when before have gods or men beheld
The life that had descended re-arise,   30
And lighted from above him by the sun?
So mighty was the mother's childless cry,
A cry that rang through Hades, Earth, and Heaven!

    So in this pleasant vale we stand again,
The field of Enna, now once more ablaze   35
With flowers that brighten as thy footstep falls,
All flowers—but for one black blur of earth
Left by that closing chasm, through which the car
Of dark Aïdoneus rising rapt thee hence.
And here, my child, though folded in thine arms,   40
I feel the deathless heart of motherhood
Within me shudder, lest the naked glebe
Should yawn once more into the gulf, and thence
The shrilly whinnyings of the team of hell,
Ascending, pierce the glad and songful air,   45
And all at once their arched necks, midnight-maned,
Jet upward through the midday blossom. No!

28. *Phlegethon* a river in the underworld.
39. *Aïdoneus* (Dis) Pluto, god of the underworld.

For, see, thy foot has touched it; all the space
Of blank earth-baldness clothes itself afresh,
And breaks into the crocus-purple hour   50
That saw thee vanish.

                    Child, when thou wert gone,
I envied human wives, and nested birds,
Yea, the cubbed lioness; went in search of thee
Through many a palace, many a cot, and gave
Thy breast to ailing infants in the night,   55
And set the mother waking in amaze
To find her sick one whole; and forth again
Among the wail of midnight winds, and cried,
"Where is my loved one? Wherefore do ye wail?"
And out from all the night an answer shrilled,   60
"We know not, and we know not why we wail."
I climbed on all the cliffs of all the seas,
And asked the waves that moan about the world,
"Where? do ye make your moaning for my child?"
And round from all the world the voices came,   65
"We know not, and we know not why we moan."
"Where?" and I stared from every eagle-peak,
I thridded the black heart of all the woods,
I peered through tomb and cave, and in the storms
Of autumn swept across the city, and heard   70
The murmur of their temples chanting me,
Me, me, the desolate mother! "Where?"—and turned,
And fled by many a waste, forlorn of man,
And grieved for man through all my grief for thee,—
The jungle rooted in his shattered hearth,   75
The serpent coiled about his broken shaft,
The scorpion crawling over naked skulls;—
I saw the tiger in the ruined fane
Spring from his fallen god, but trace of thee
I saw not; and far on, and, following out   80
A league of labyrinthine darkness, came
On three gray heads beneath a gleaming rift.
"Where?" and I heard one voice from all the three,
"We know not, for we spin the lives of men,
And not of gods, and know not why we spin!   85
There is a fate beyond us." Nothing knew.

    Last as the likeness of a dying man,
Without his knowledge, from him flits to warn

82. *three gray heads*   the Fates.

A far-off friendship that he comes no more,
So he, the god of dreams, who heard my cry,   90
Drew from thyself the likeness of thyself
Without thy knowledge, and thy shadow passed
Before me, crying, "The bright one in the highest
Is brother of the dark one in the lowest,
And bright and dark have sworn that I, the child   95
Of thee, the great Earth-Mother, thee, the power
That lifts her buried life from gloom to bloom,
Should be forever and forevermore
The bride of darkness."

                              So the shadow wailed.
Then I, Earth-Goddess, cursed the gods of heaven.   100
I would not mingle with their feasts; to me
Their nectar smacked of hemlock on the lips,
Their rich ambrosia tasted aconite.
The man, that only lives and loves an hour,
Seemed nobler than their hard eternities.   105
My quick tears killed the flower, my ravings hushed
The bird, and lost in utter grief I failed
To send my life through olive-yard and vine
And golden-grain, my gift to helpless man.
Rain-rotten died the wheat, the barley-spears   110
Were hollow-husked, the leaf fell, and the sun,
Pale at my grief, drew down before his time
Sickening, and Aetna kept her winter snow.

   Then he, the brother of this darkness, he
Who still is highest, glancing from his height   115
On earth a fruitless fallow, when he missed
The wonted steam of sacrifice, the praise
And prayer of men, decreed that thou shouldst dwell
For nine white moons of each whole year with me,
Three dark ones in the shadow with thy king.   120

   Once more the reaper in the gleam of dawn
Will see me by the landmark far away,
Blessing his field, or seated in the dusk
Of even, by the lonely threshing-floor,
Rejoicing in the harvest and the grange.   125

   Yet I, Earth-Goddess, am but ill-content
With them who still are highest. Those gray heads,

114. *the brother of this darkness* Zeus.

What meant they by their "Fate beyond the Fates"
But younger kindlier gods to bear us down,
As we bore down the gods before us? gods,   130
To quench, not hurl the thunderbolt, to stay,
Not spread the plague, the famine; gods indeed,
To send the noon into the night and break
The sunless halls of Hades into Heaven?
Till thy dark lord accept and love the sun,   135
And all the shadow die into the light,
When thou shalt dwell the whole bright year with me,
And souls of men, who grew beyond their race,
And made themselves as gods against the fear
Of death and Hell; and thou that hast from men,   140
As Queen of Death, that worship which is fear,
Henceforth, as having risen from out the dead,
Shalt ever send thy life along with mine
From buried grain through springing blade, and bless
Their garnered autumn also, reap with me,   145
Earth-mother, in the harvest hymns of Earth
The worship which is love, and see no more
The stone, the wheel, the dimly-glimmering lawns
Of that Elysium, all the hateful fires
Of torment, and the shadowy warrior glide   150
Along the silent field of Asphodel.

148. *the stone, the wheel*   referring to the torments suffered in the underworld
by Sisyphus and Ixion.

‑<※>‑

WALT WHITMAN
(1819–1892)

·

OUT OF THE CRADLE
ENDLESSLY ROCKING

Out of the cradle endlessly rocking,
Out of the mocking-bird's throat, the musical shuttle,
Out of the Ninth-month midnight,
Over the sterile sands and the fields beyond, where the child leaving
    his bed wandered alone, bareheaded, barefoot,
Down from the showered halo,   5
Up from the mystic play of shadows twining and twisting as if they
    were alive,
Out from the patches of briers and blackberries,
From the memories of the bird that chanted to me,
From your memories, sad brother, from the fitful risings and fall-
    ings I heard,
From under that yellow half-moon late-risen and swollen as if with
    tears,   10
From those beginning notes of yearning and love there in the mist,
From the thousand responses of my heart never to cease,
From the myriad thence-aroused words,
From the word stronger and more delicious than any,
From such as now they start the scene revisiting,   15
As a flock, twittering, rising, or overhead passing,
Borne hither, ere all eludes me, hurriedly,
A man, yet by these tears a little boy again,
Throwing myself on the sand, confronting the waves,
I, chanter of pains and joys, uniter of here and hereafter,   20
Taking all hints to use them, but swiftly leaping beyond them,
A reminiscence sing.

Once Paumanok,
When the lilac-scent was in the air and Fifth-month grass was
    growing,
Up this seashore in some briers,   25
Two feathered guests from Alabama, two together,
And their nest, and four light-green eggs spotted with brown,
And every day the he-bird to and fro near at hand,

23. *Paumanok* Indian name of Long   26. *Two feathered guests* mocking
Island.   birds.

And every day the she-bird crouched on her nest, silent, with
    bright eyes,
And every day I, a curious boy, never too close, never disturbing
    them,   30
Cautiously peering, absorbing, translating.

Shine! shine! shine!
Pour down your warmth, great sun!
While we bask, we two together.

Two together!   35
Winds blow south, or winds blow north,
Day come white, or night come black,
Home, or rivers and mountains from home,
Singing all time, minding no time,
While we two keep together.   40

Till of a sudden,
Maybe killed, unknown to her mate,
One forenoon the she-bird crouched not on the nest,
Nor returned that afternoon, nor the next,
Nor ever appeared again.   45

And thenceforward all summer in the sound of the sea,
And at night under the full of the moon in calmer weather,
Over the hoarse surging of the sea,
Or flitting from brier to brier by day,
I saw, I heard at intervals the remaining one, the he-bird,   50
The solitary guest from Alabama.

Blow! blow! blow!
Blow up sea-winds along Paumanok's shore;
I wait and I wait till you blow my mate to me.

Yes, when the stars glistened,   55
All night long on the prong of a moss-scalloped stake,
Down almost amid the slapping waves,
Sat the lone singer wonderful causing tears.

He called on his mate,
He poured forth the meanings which I of all men know.   60

Yes, my brother, I know,—
The rest might not, but I have treasured every note,
For more than once dimly down to the beach gliding,
Silent, avoiding the moonbeams, blending myself with the shadows,

Recalling now the obscure shapes, the echoes, the sounds and sights
    after their sorts,   65
The white arms out in the breakers tirelessly tossing,
I, with bare feet, a child, the wind wafting my hair,
Listened long and long.

Listened to keep, to sing, now translating the notes,
Following you, my brother.   70

Soothe! soothe! soothe!
Close on its wave soothes the wave behind,
And again another behind embracing and lapping, every one close,
But my love soothes not me, not me.

Low hangs the moon, it rose late,   75
It is lagging—O I think it is heavy with love, with love.

O madly the sea pushes upon the land,
With love, with love.

O night! do I not see my love fluttering out among the breakers?
What is that little black thing I see there in the white?   80

Loud! loud! loud!
Loud I call to you, my love!
High and clear I shoot my voice over the waves,
Surely you must know who is here, is here,
You must know who I am, my love.   85

Low-hanging moon!
What is that dusky spot in your brown yellow?
O it is the shape, the shape of my mate!
O moon, do not keep her from me any longer.

Land! land! O land!   90
Whichever way I turn, O I think you could give me my mate back
    again if you only would,
For I am almost sure I see her dimly whichever way I look.

O rising stars!
Perhaps the one I want so much will rise, will rise with some of
    you.

O throat! O trembling throat!   95
Sound clearer through the atmosphere!
Pierce the woods, the earth,
Somewhere listening to catch you must be the one I want.

Shake out carols!
Solitary here, the night's carols!   100
Carols of lonesome love! death's carols!
Carols under that lagging, yellow, waning moon!
O under that moon where she droops almost down into the sea!
O reckless despairing carols!

But soft! sink low!   105
Soft! let me just murmur,
And do you wait a moment, you husky-noised sea,
For somewhere I believe I heard my mate responding to me,
So faint, I must be still, be still to listen,
But not altogether still, for then she might not come immediately
*   to me.*   110

Hither, my love!
Here I am! here!
With this just-sustained note I announce myself to you,
This gentle call is for you my love, for you.

Do not be decoyed elsewhere: 115
That is the whistle of the wind, it is not my voice,
That is the fluttering, the fluttering of the spray,
Those are the shadows of leaves.

O darkness! O in vain!
O I am very sick and sorrowful.   120

O brown halo in the sky near the moon, drooping upon the sea!
O troubled reflection in the sea!
O throat! O throbbing heart!
And I singing uselessly, uselessly all the night.

O past! O happy life! O songs of joy!   125
In the air, in the woods, over fields,
Loved! loved! loved! loved! loved!
But my mate no more, no more with me!
We two together no more.

The aria sinking.   130
All else continuing, the stars shining,
The winds blowing, the notes of the bird continuous echoing,
With angry moans the fierce old mother incessantly moaning,
On the sands of Paumanok's shore gray and rustling,
The yellow half-moon enlarged, sagging down, drooping, the face
    of the sea almost touching,   135

The boy ecstatic, with his bare feet the waves, with his hair the
    atmosphere dallying,
The love in the heart long pent, now loose, now at last tumultu-
    ously bursting,
The aria's meaning, the ears, the soul, swiftly depositing,
The strange tears down the cheeks coursing,
The colloquy there, the trio, each uttering,   140
The undertone, the savage old mother incessantly crying,
To the boy's soul's questions sullenly timing, some drowned secret
    hissing,
To the outsetting bard.

Demon or bird! (said the boy's soul)
Is it indeed toward your mate you sing? or is it really to me?   145
For I, that was a child, my tongue's use sleeping, now I have heard
    you,
Now in a moment I know what I am for, I awake,
And already a thousand singers, a thousand songs, clearer, louder
    and more sorrowful than yours,
A thousand warbling echoes have started to life within me, never
    to die.

O you singer solitary, singing by yourself, projecting me,   150
O solitary me listening, nevermore shall I cease perpetuating you,
Nevermore shall I escape, nevermore the reverberations,
Nevermore the cries of unsatisfied love be absent from me.
Never again leave me to be the peaceful child I was before what
    there in the night,
By the sea under the yellow and sagging moon,   155
The messenger there aroused, the fire, the sweet hell within,
The unknown want, the destiny of me.

O give me the clue! (It lurks in the night here somewhere)
O if I am to have so much, let me have more!

A word then, (for I will conquer it),   160
The word final, superior to all,
Subtle, sent up—what is it?—I listen;
Are you whispering it, and have been all the time, you sea-waves?
Is that it from your liquid rims and wet sands?

Whereto answering, the sea,   165
Delaying not, hurrying not,
Whispered me through the night, and very plainly before daybreak,
Lisped to me the low and delicious word death,
And again death, death, death, death,

Hissing melodious, neither like the bird nor like my aroused child's
    heart,   170
But edging near as privately for me, rustling at my feet,
Creeping thence steadily up to my ears and laving me softly all
    over,
Death, death, death, death, death.

Which I do not forget,
But fuse the song of my dusky demon and brother,   175
That he sang to me in the moonlight on Paumanok's gray beach,
With the thousand responsive songs at random,
My own songs awaked from that hour,
And with them the key, the word up from the waves,
The word of the sweetest song and all songs,   180
That strong and delicious word which, creeping to my feet,
(Or like some old crone rocking the cradle, swathed in sweet gar-
    ments, bending aside)
The sea whispered me.

THE DALLIANCE OF THE EAGLES

Skirting the river road, (my forenoon walk, my rest)
Skyward in air a sudden muffled sound, the dalliance of the eagles,
The rushing amorous contact high in space together,
The clinching interlocking claws, a living, fierce, gyrating wheel,
Four beating wings, two beaks, a swirling mass tight grappling,   5
In tumbling turning clustering loops, straight downward falling,
Till o'er the river poised, the twain yet one, a moment's lull,
A motionless still balance in the air, then parting, talons loosing,
Upward again on slow-firm pinions slanting, their separate diverse
    flight,
She hers, he his, pursuing.   10

CAVALRY CROSSING A FORD

A line in long array where they wind betwixt green islands,
They take a serpentine course, their arms flash in the sun—hark to
    the musical clank,
Behold the silvery river, in it the splashing horses loitering stop to
    drink,
Behold the brown-faced men, each group, each person a picture,
    the negligent rest on the saddles,

Some emerge on the opposite bank, others are just entering the
    ford—while,
Scarlet and blue and snowy white,
The guidon flags flutter gaily in the wind.

O CAPTAIN! MY CAPTAIN!

O Captain! my Captain! our fearful trip is done,
The ship has weathered every rack, the prize we sought is won,
The port is near, the bells I hear, the people all exulting,
While follow eyes the steady keel, the vessel grim and daring;
      But O heart! heart! heart!   5
        O the bleeding drops of red,
           Where on the deck my Captain lies,
            Fallen cold and dead.

O Captain! my Captain! rise up and hear the bells;
Rise up—for you the flag is flung—for you the bugle trills,   10
For you bouquets and ribboned wreaths—for you the shores
      a-crowding,
For you they call, the swaying mass, their eager faces turning;
      Here Captain! dear father!
        The arm beneath your head!
          It is some dream that on the deck,   15
           You've fallen cold and dead.

My Captain does not answer, his lips are pale and still,
My father does not feel my arm, he has no pulse nor will,
The ship is anchored safe and sound, its voyage closed and
      done,
From fearful trip the victor ship comes in with object won;   20
      Exult O shores, and ring O bells!
      But I with mournful tread,
        Walk the deck my Captain lies,
          Fallen cold and dead.

Captain   Abraham Lincoln.

A NOISELESS PATIENT SPIDER

A noiseless patient spider,
I marked where on a little promontory it stood isolated,
Marked how to explore the vacant vast surrounding,
It launched forth filament, filament, filament, out of itself,
Ever unreeling them, ever tirelessly speeding them.   5

And you O my soul where you stand,
Surrounded, detached, in measureless oceans of space,
Ceaselessly musing, venturing, throwing, seeking the spheres to con-
        nect them,
Till the bridge you will need be formed, till the ductile anchor
        hold,
Till the gossamer thread you fling catch somewhere, O my soul.   10

≺☼≻

MATTHEW ARNOLD
(*1822–1888*)

·

MEMORIAL VERSES
APRIL, 1850

Goethe in Weimar sleeps, and Greece,
Long since, saw Byron's struggle cease.
But one such death remained to come;
The last poetic voice is dumb—
We stand today by Wordsworth's tomb.   5

When Byron's eyes were shut in death,
We bowed our head and held our breath.
He taught us little; but our soul
Had *felt* him like the thunder's roll.
With shivering heart the strife we saw   10
Of passion with eternal law;
And yet with reverential awe
We watched the fount of fiery life
Which served for that Titanic strife.

When Goethe's death was told, we said: 15
Sunk, then, is Europe's sagest head.
Physician of the iron age,
Goethe has done his pilgrimage.
He took the suffering human race,
He read each wound, each weakness clear;   20
And struck his finger on the place,
And said: *Thou ailest here, and here!*
He looked on Europe's dying hour
Of fitful dream and feverish power;
His eye plunged down the weltering strife,   25
The turmoil of expiring life—
He said: *The end is everywhere,*
Art still has truth, take refuge there!
And he was happy, if to know
Causes of things, and far below   30
His feet to see the lurid flow
Of terror, and insane distress,
And headlong fate, be happiness.

1. *Weimar*   in central Germany; Goethe's burial place.

241

And Wordsworth!—Ah, pale ghosts, rejoice!
For never has such soothing voice 35
Been to your shadowy world conveyed,
Since erst, at morn, some wandering shade
Heard the clear song of Orpheus come
Through Hades, and the mournful gloom.
Wordsworth has gone from us—and ye, 40
Ah, may ye feel his voice as we!
He too upon a wintry clime
Had fallen—on this iron time
Of doubts, disputes, distractions, fears.
He found us when the age had bound 45
Our souls in its benumbing round;
He spoke, and loosed our heart in tears.
He laid us as we lay at birth
On the cool flowery lap of earth,
Smiles broke from us and we had ease; 50
The hills were round us, and the breeze
Went o'er the sunlit fields again;
Our foreheads felt the wind and rain.
Our youth returned; for there was shed
On spirits that had long been dead, 55
Spirits dried up and closely furled,
The freshness of the early world.

Ah! since dark days still bring to light
Man's prudence and man's fiery might,
Time may restore us in his course 60
Goethe's sage mind and Byron's force;
But where will Europe's latter hour
Again find Wordsworth's healing power?
Others will teach us how to dare,
And against fear our breast to steel; 65
Others will strengthen us to bear—
But who, ah! who, will make us feel?
The cloud of mortal destiny,
Others will front it fearlessly—
But who, like him, will put it by? 70

Keep fresh the grass upon his grave
O Rotha, with thy living wave!
Sing him thy best! for few or none
Hears thy voice right, now he is gone.

38. *Orpheus* mythical poet, whose music charmed the spirits of Hades, allowing him to redeem Eurydice.

72. *Rotha* river near Wordsworth's grave.

TO MARGUERITE

Yes! in the sea of life enisled,
With echoing straits between us thrown,
Dotting the shoreless watery wild,
We mortal millions live *alone*.
The islands feel the enclasping flow,   5
And then their endless bounds they know.

But when the moon their hollows lights,
And they are swept by balms of spring,
And in their glens, on starry nights,
The nightingales divinely sing;   10
And lovely notes, from shore to shore,
Across the sounds and channels pour—

Oh! then a longing like despair
Is to their farthest caverns sent;
For surely once, they feel, we were   15
Parts of a single continent!
Now round us spreads the watery plain—
Oh might our marges meet again!

Who ordered, that their longing's fire
Should be, as soon as kindled, cooled?   20
Who renders vain their deep desire?—
A God, a God their severance ruled!
And bade betwixt their shores to be
The unplumbed, salt, estranging sea.

THE BURIED LIFE

Light flows our war of mocking words, and yet,
Behold, with tears mine eyes are wet!
I feel a nameless sadness o'er me roll.
Yes, yes, we know that we can jest,
We know, we know that we can smile!   5
But there's a something in this breast,
To which thy light words bring no rest,
And thy gay smiles no anodyne.
Give me thy hand, and hush awhile,
And turn those limpid eyes on mine,   10
And let me read there, love! thy inmost soul.

Alas! is even love too weak
To unlock the heart, and let it speak?
Are even lovers powerless to reveal
To one another what indeed they feel?   15
I knew the mass of men concealed
Their thoughts, for fear that if revealed
They would by other men be met
With blank indifference, or with blame reproved;
I knew they lived and moved   20
Tricked in disguises, alien to the rest
Of men, and alien to themselves—and yet
The same heart beats in every human breast!

But we, my love!—doth a like spell benumb
Our hearts, our voices?—must we too be dumb?   25

Ah! well for us, if even we,
Even for a moment, can get free
Our heart, and have our lips unchained;
For that which seals them hath been deep-ordained!

Fate, which foresaw   30
How frivolous a baby man would be—
By what distractions he would be possessed,
How he would pour himself in every strife,
And well-nigh change his own identity—
That it might keep from his capricious play   35
His genuine self, and force him to obey
Even in his own despite his being's law,
Bade through the deep recesses of our breast
The unregarded river of our life
Pursue with indiscernible flow its way;   40
And that we should not see
The buried stream, and seem to be
Eddying at large in blind uncertainty,
Though driving on with it eternally.

But often, in the world's most crowded streets,   45
But often, in the din of strife,
There rises an unspeakable desire
After the knowledge of our buried life;
A thirst to spend our fire and restless force
In tracking out our true, original course;   50
A longing to inquire
Into the mystery of this heart which beats

So wild, so deep in us—to know
Whence our lives come and where they go.
And many a man in his own breast then delves,   55
But deep enough, alas! none ever mines.
And we have been on many thousand lines,
And we have shown, on each, spirit and power;
But hardly have we, for one little hour,
Been on our own line, have we been ourselves—   60
Hardly had skill to utter one of all
The nameless feelings that course through our breast,
But they course on forever unexpressed.
And long we try in vain to speak and act
Our hidden self, and what we say and do   65
Is eloquent, is well—but 'tis not true!
And then we will no more be racked
With inward striving, and demand
Of all the thousand nothings of the hour
Their stupefying power;   70
Ah yes, and they benumb us at our call!
Yet still, from time to time, vague and forlorn,
From the soul's subterranean depth upborne
As from an infinitely distant land,
Come airs, and floating echoes, and convey   75
A melancholy into all our day.

Only—but this is rare—
When a belovéd hand is laid in ours,
When, jaded with the rush and glare
Of the interminable hours,   80
Our eyes can in another's eyes read clear,
When our world-deafened ear
Is by the tones of a loved voice caressed—
A bolt is shot back somewhere in our breast,
And a lost pulse of feeling stirs again.   85
The eye sinks inward, and the heart lies plain,
And what we mean, we say, and what we would, we know.
A man becomes aware of his life's flow,
And hears its winding murmur; and he sees
The meadows where it glides, the sun, the breeze.   90

And there arrives a lull in the hot race
Wherein he doth forever chase
That flying and elusive shadow, rest.
An air of coolness plays upon his face,
And an unwonted calm pervades his breast.   95

And then he thinks he knows
The hills where his life rose,
And the sea where it goes.

PHILOMELA

Hark! ah, the nightingale—
The tawny-throated!
Hark, from that moonlit cedar what a burst!
What triumph! hark!—what pain!

O wanderer from a Grecian shore,   5
Still, after many years, in distant lands,
Still nourishing in thy bewildered brain
That wild, unquenched, deep-sunken, old-world pain—
Say, will it never heal?
And can this fragrant lawn   10
With its cool trees, and night,
And the sweet, tranquil Thames,
And moonshine, and the dew,
To thy racked heart and brain
Afford no balm?   15

Dost thou tonight behold,
Here, through the moonlight on this English grass,
The unfriendly palace in the Thracian wild?
Dost thou again peruse
With hot cheeks and seared eyes   20
The too clear web, and thy dumb sister's shame?
Dost thou once more assay
Thy flight, and feel come over thee,
Poor fugitive, the feathery change
Once more, and once more seem to make resound   25
With love and hate, triumph and agony,
Lone Daulis, and the high Cephissian vale?
Listen, Eugenia—
How thick the bursts come crowding through the leaves!
Again—thou hearest?   30
Eternal passion!
Eternal pain!

Philomela in Greek mythology, ravished by Tereus, husband of her sister Procne. Though Tereus cut out her tongue, Philomela disclosed his crime by representing it in a weaving. Escaping, she and Procne—just as they were about to be overtaken by Tereus—were changed into a nightingale and a swallow respectively.

THE SCHOLAR GYPSY

Go, for they call you, shepherd, from the hill;
 Go, shepherd, and untie the wattled cotes!
  No longer leave thy wistful flock unfed,
 Nor let thy bawling fellows rack their throats,
  Nor the cropped herbage shoot another head. 5
   But when the fields are still,
 And the tired men and dogs all gone to rest,
  And only the white sheep are sometimes seen
  Cross and recross the strips of moon-blanched green,
Come, shepherd, and again begin the quest! 10

Here, where the reaper was at work of late—
 In this high field's dark corner, where he leaves
  His coat, his basket, and his earthen cruse,
 And in the sun all morning binds the sheaves,
  Then here, at noon, comes back his stores to use— 15
   Here will I sit and wait,
 While to my ear from uplands far away
  The bleating of the folded flocks is borne,
  With distant cries of reapers in the corn—
All the live murmur of a summer's day. 20

Screened is this nook o'er the high, half-reaped field,
 And here till sundown, shepherd! will I be.
  Through the thick corn the scarlet poppies peep,
 And round green roots and yellowing stalks I see
  Pale pink convolvulus in tendrils creep; 25
   And air-swept lindens yield

Gypsy There was very lately a lad in the University of Oxford, who was by his poverty forced to leave his studies there; and at last to join himself to a company of vagabond gypsies. Among these extravagant people, by the insinuating subtilty of his carriage, he quickly got so much of their love and esteem as that they discovered to him their mystery. After he had been a pretty while well exercised in the trade, there chanced to ride by a couple of scholars, who had formerly been of his acquaintance. They quickly spied out their old friend among the gypsies; and he gave them an account of the necessity which drove him to that kind of life, and told them that the people he went with were not such impostors as they were taken for, but that they had a traditional kind of learning among them, and could do wonders by the power of imagination, their fancy binding that of others: that himself had learned much of their art, and when he had compassed the whole secret, he intended, he said, to leave their company, and give the world an account of what he had learned.—Glanvil's *Vanity of Dogmatizing*, 1661 [Arnold's note].
2. *wattled cotes* sheep enclosures made of interwoven sticks and branches.
13. *cruse* a drinking vessel.

Their scent, and rustle down their perfumed showers
  Of bloom on the bent grass where I am laid,
    And bower me from the August sun with shade;
And the eye travels down to Oxford's towers.   30

And near me on the grass lies Glanvil's book—
  Come, let me read the oft-read tale again!
    The story of the Oxford scholar poor,
  Of pregnant parts and quick inventive brain,
    Who, tired of knocking at preferment's door,   35
      One summer morn forsook
His friends, and went to learn the gypsy lore,
  And roamed the world with that wild brotherhood,
  And came, as most men deemed, to little good,
But came to Oxford and his friends no more.   40

But once, years after, in the country lanes,
  Two scholars, whom at college erst he knew,
    Met him, and of his way of life inquired;
  Whereat he answered, that the gypsy crew,
    His mates, had arts to rule as they desired   45
      The workings of men's brains,
And they can bind them to what thoughts they will.
  "And I," he said, "the secret of their art,
  When fully learned, will to the world impart;
But it needs heaven-sent moments for this skill."   50

This said, he left them, and returned no more.—
  But rumors hung about the countryside,
    That the lost Scholar long was seen to stray,
  Seen by rare glimpses, pensive and tongue-tied,
    In hat of antique shape, and cloak of gray,   55
      The same the gypsies wore.
Shepherds had met him on the Hurst in spring;
  At some lone alehouse in the Berkshire moors,
  On the warm ingle-bench, the smock-frocked boors
Had found him seated at their entering,   60

But, 'mid their drink and clatter, he would fly.
  And I myself seem half to know thy looks,
    And put the shepherds, wanderer! on thy trace;
  And boys who in lone wheatfields scare the rooks
    I ask if thou hast passed their quiet place;   65
      Or in my boat I lie

28. *bent* a kind of reedy grass.   59. *boors* country people.
57. *Hurst* hill near Oxford.

Moored to the cool bank in the summer heats,
   'Mid wide grass meadows which the sunshine fills,
   And watch the warm, green-muffled Cumner hills,
And wonder if thou haunt'st their shy retreats.   70

For most, I know, thou lov'st retired ground!
   Thee at the ferry Oxford riders blithe,
     Returning home on summer nights, have met
   Crossing the stripling Thames at Bab-lock-hithe,
     Trailing in the cool stream thy fingers wet,   75
       As the punt's rope chops round;
   And leaning backward in a pensive dream,
     And fostering in thy lap a heap of flowers
     Plucked in shy fields and distant Wychwood bowers,
   And thine eyes resting on the moonlit stream.   80

And then they land, and thou art seen no more!—
   Maidens, who from the distant hamlets come
     To dance around the Fyfield elm in May,
   Oft through the darkening fields have seen thee roam,
     Or cross a stile into the public way.   85
       Oft thou hast given them store
   Of flowers—the frail-leafed, white anemone,
     Dark bluebells drenched with dews of summer eves,
     And purple orchises with spotted leaves—
   But none hath words she can report of thee.   90

And, above Godstow Bridge, when hay time's here
   In June, and many a scythe in sunshine flames,
     Men who through those wide fields of breezy grass
   Where black-winged swallows haunt the glittering Thames,
     To bathe in the abandoned lasher pass,   95
       Have often passed thee near
   Sitting upon the river bank o'ergrown;
     Marked thine outlandish garb, thy figure spare,
     Thy dark vague eyes, and soft abstracted air—
   But, when they came from bathing, thou wast gone!   100

At some lone homestead in the Cumner hills,
   Where at her open door the housewife darns,
     Thou hast been seen, or hanging on a gate
   To watch the threshers in the mossy barns.
     Children, who early range these slopes and late   105
       For cresses from the rills,

95. *lasher*   pool formed by water flow-   106. *cresses*   watercress.
ing over a weir or small dam.

Have known thee eying, all an April day,
    The springing pastures and the feeding kine;
      And marked thee, when the stars come out and shine,
    Through the long dewy grass move slow away.   110

In autumn, on the skirts of Bagley Wood—
    Where most the gypsies by the turf-edged way
      Pitch their smoked tents, and every bush you see
    With scarlet patches tagged and shreds of gray,
      Above the forest ground called Thessaly—   115
        The blackbird, picking food,
    Sees thee, nor stops his meal, nor fears at all;
      So often has he known thee past him stray,
      Rapt, twirling in thy hand a withered spray,
    And waiting for the spark from heaven to fall.   120

And once, in winter, on the causeway chill
    Where home through flooded fields foot-travelers go,
      Have I not passed thee on the wooden bridge,
    Wrapped in thy cloak and battling with the snow,
      Thy face tow'rd Hinksey and its wintry ridge?   125
        And thou hast climbed the hill,
    And gained the white brow of the Cumner range;
      Turned once to watch, while thick the snowflakes fall,
      The line of festal light in Christ Church hall—
    Then sought thy straw in some sequestered grange.   130

But what—I dream! Two hundred years are flown
    Since first thy story ran through Oxford halls,
      And the grave Glanvil did the tale inscribe
    That thou wert wandered from the studious walls
      To learn strange arts, and join a gypsy tribe;   135
        And thou from earth art gone
    Long since, and in some quiet churchyard laid—
      Some country nook, where o'er thy unknown grave
      Tall grasses and white flowering nettles wave,
    Under a dark, red-fruited yew tree's shade.   140

—No, no, thou hast not felt the lapse of hours!
    For what wears out the life of mortal men?
      'Tis that from change to change their being rolls;
    'Tis that repeated shocks, again, again,
      Exhaust the energy of strongest souls   145
        And numb the elastic powers.

129. *Christ Church hall*   dining hall of Christ Church, an Oxford college.

Till having used our nerves with bliss and teen,
    And tired upon a thousand schemes our wit,
      To the just-pausing Genius we remit
Our worn-out life, and are—what we have been.   150

Thou hast not lived, why should'st thou perish, so?
    Thou hadst *one* aim, *one* business, *one* desire;
      Else wert thou long since numbered with the dead!
Else hadst thou spent, like other men, thy fire!
      The generations of thy peers are fled,   155
        And we ourselves shall go;
But thou possessest an immortal lot,
    And we imagine thee exempt from age
    And living as thou liv'st on Glanvil's page,
Because thou hadst—what we, alas! have not.   160

For early didst thou leave the world, with powers
    Fresh, undiverted to the world without,
      Firm to their mark, not spent on other things;
    Free from the sick fatigue, the languid doubt,
      Which much to have tried, in much been baffled, brings.   165
        O life unlike to ours!
Who fluctuate idly without term or scope,
    Of whom each strives, nor knows for what he strives,
    And each half lives a hundred different lives;
Who wait like thee, but not, like thee, in hope.   170

Thou waitest for the spark from heaven! and we,
    Light half-believers of our casual creeds,
      Who never deeply felt, nor clearly willed,
    Whose insight never has borne fruit in deeds,
      Whose vague resolves never have been fulfilled;   175
        For whom each year we see
Breeds new beginnings, disappointments new;
    Who hesitate and falter life away,
    And lose tomorrow the ground won today—
Ah! do not we, wanderer! await it too?   180

Yes, we await it!—but it still delays,
    And then we suffer! and amongst us one,
      Who most has suffered, takes dejectedly
    His seat upon the intellectual throne;
      And all his store of sad experience he   185
        Lays bare of wretched days;

147. *teen* grief.   149. *Genius* keeper of the gates of life and death.

Tells us his misery's birth and growth and signs,
  And how the dying spark of hope was fed,
  And how the breast was soothed, and how the head,
And all his hourly varied anodynes.   190

This for our wisest! and we others pine,
  And wish the long unhappy dream would end,
  And waive all claim to bliss, and try to bear;
With close-lipped patience for our only friend,
  Sad patience, too near neighbor to despair—   195
    But none has hope like thine!
Thou through the fields and through the woods dost stray,
  Roaming the countryside, a truant boy,
  Nursing thy project in unclouded joy,
And every doubt long blown by time away.   200

O born in days when wits were fresh and clear,
  And life ran gaily as the sparkling Thames;
  Before this strange disease of modern life,
With its sick hurry, its divided aims,
  Its heads o'ertaxed, its palsied hearts, was rife—   205
    Fly hence, our contact fear!
Still fly, plunge deeper in the bowering wood!
  Averse, as Dido did with gesture stern
  From her false friend's approach in Hades turn,
Wave us away, and keep thy solitude!   210

Still nursing the unconquerable hope,
  Still clutching the inviolable shade,
  With a free, onward impulse brushing through,
By night, the silvered branches of the glade—
  Far on the forest skirts, where none pursue.   215
    On some mild pastoral slope
Emerge, and resting on the moonlit paels
  Freshen thy flowers as in former years
  With dew, or listen with enchanted ears,
From the dark dingles, to the nightingales!   220

But fly our paths, our feverish contact fly!
  For strong the infection of our mental strife,
  Which, though it gives no bliss, yet spoils for rest;
And we should win thee from thy own fair life,
  Like us distracted, and like us unblest.   225
    Soon, soon thy cheer would die,

208. *Dido* Queen of Carthage who killed herself, when deserted by Aeneas. When he visits Hades, she turns away from him.
220. *dingles* deep dells or hollows.

Thy hopes grow timorous, and unfixed thy powers,
   And thy clear aims be cross and shifting made;
   And then thy glad perennial youth would fade,
Fade, and grow old at last, and die like ours.   230

Then fly our greetings, fly our speech and smiles!
   —As some grave Tyrian trader, from the sea,
   Descried at sunrise an emerging prow
Lifting the cool-haired creepers stealthily,
   The fringes of a southward-facing brow   235
      Among the Aegean isles;
And saw the merry Grecian coaster come,
   Freighted with amber grapes, and Chian wine,
   Green, bursting figs, and tunnies steeped in brine—
And knew the intruders on his ancient home,   240

The young lighthearted masters of the waves—
   And snatched his rudder, and shook out more sail;
   And day and night held on indignantly
O'er the blue Midland waters with the gale,
   Betwixt the Syrtes and soft Sicily,   245
      To where the Atlantic raves
Outside the western straits; and unbent sails
   There, where down cloudy cliffs, through sheets of foam,
   Shy traffickers, the dark Iberians come;
And on the beach undid his corded bales.   250

STANZAS FROM THE GRANDE CHARTREUSE

Through Alpine meadows soft-suffused
With rain, where thick the crocus blows,
Past the dark forges long disused,
The mule-track from Saint Laurent goes.
The bridge is crossed, and slow we ride,   5
Through forest, up the mountainside.

The autumnal evening darkens round,
The wind is up, and drives the rain;
While, hark! far down, with strangled sound
Doth the Dead Guier's stream complain,   10
Where that wet smoke, among the woods,
Over his boiling cauldron broods.

232. *Tyrian* from Tyre, the ancient Phoenician city which was a center of extensive commerce.
249. *Iberians* early inhabitants of Spain and Portugal.

Grande Chartreuse Carthusian monastery in the Alps.

Swift rush the spectral vapors white
Past limestone scars with ragged pines,
Showing—then blotting from our sight!— 15
Halt—through the cloud-drift something shines!
High in the valley, wet and drear,
The huts of Courrerie appear.

Strike leftward! cries our guide; and higher
Mounts up the stony forest-way. 20
At last the encircling trees retire;
Look! through the showery twilight grey
What pointed roofs are these advance?—
A palace of the kings of France?

Approach, for what we seek is here! 25
Alight, and sparely sup, and wait
For rest in this outbuilding near;
Then cross the sward and reach that gate.
Knock; pass the wicket! Thou art come
To the Carthusians' world-famed home. 30

The silent courts, where night and day
Into their stone-carved basins cold
The splashing icy fountains play—
The humid corridors behold!
Where, ghostlike in the deepening night, 35
Cowled forms brush by in gleaming white.

The chapel, where no organ's peal
Invests the stern and naked prayer—
With penitential cries they kneel
And wrestle; rising then, with bare 40
And white uplifted faces stand,
Passing the Host from hand to hand;

Each takes, and then his visage wan
Is buried in his cowl once more.
The cells!—the suffering Son of Man 45
Upon the wall—the knee-worn floor—
And where they sleep, that wooden bed,
Which shall their coffin be, when dead!

The library, where tract and tome
Not to feed priestly pride are there,
To hymn the conquering march of Rome, 50

Nor yet to amuse, as ours are!
They paint of souls the inner strife,
Their drops of blood, their death in life.

The garden, overgrown—yet mild,   55
See, fragrant herbs are flowering there!
Strong children of the Alpine wild
Whose culture is the brethren's care;
Of human tasks their only one,
And cheerful works beneath the sun.   60

Those halls, too, destined to contain
Each its own pilgrim-host of old,
From England, Germany, or Spain—
All are before me! I behold
The House, the Brotherhood austere!   65
—And what am I, that I am here?

For rigorous teachers seized my youth,
And purged its faith, and trimmed its fire,
Showed me the high, white star of Truth,
There bade me gaze, and there aspire.   70
Even now their whispers pierce the gloom:
What dost thou in this living tomb?

Forgive me, masters of the mind!
At whose behest I long ago
So much unlearnt, so much resigned—   75
I come not here to be your foe!
I seek these anchorites, not in ruth,
To curse and to deny your truth;

Not as their friend, or child, I speak!
But as, on some far nothern strand,   80
Thinking of his own gods, a Greek
In pity and mournful awe might stand
Before some fallen Runic stone—
For both were faiths, and both are gone.

Wandering between two worlds, one dead,   85
The other powerless to be born,
With nowhere yet to rest my head,
Like these, on earth I wait forlorn.
Their faith, my tears, the world deride—
I come to shed them at their side.   90

77. *anchorites*   religious recluses.

Oh, hide me in your gloom profound,
Ye solemn seats of holy pain!
Take me, cowled forms, and fence me round,
Till I possess my soul again;
Till free my thoughts before me roll,   95
Not chafed by hourly false control!

For the world cries your faith is now
But a dead time's exploded dream;
My melancholy, sciolists say,
Is a passed mode, an outworn theme—   100
As if the world had ever had
A faith, or sciolists been sad!

Ah, if it *be* passed, take away,
At least, the restlessness, the pain;
Be man henceforth no more a prey   105
To these outdated stings again!
The nobleness of grief is gone—
Ah, leave us not the fret alone!

But—if you cannot give us ease—
Last of the race of them who grieve   110
Here leave us to die out with these
Last of the people who believe!
Silent, while years engrave the brow;
Silent—the best are silent now.

Achilles ponders in his tent,   115
The kings of modern thought are dumb;
Silent they are, though not content,
And wait to see the future come.
They have the grief men had of yore,
But they contend and cry no more.   120

Our fathers watered with their tears
This sea of time whereon we sail,
Their voices were in all men's ears
Who passed within their puissant hail.
Still the same ocean round us raves,   125
But we stand mute, and watch the waves.

For what availed it, all the noise
And outcry of the former men?—
Say, have their sons achieved more joys,

99. *sciolists* superficial pretenders to knowledge.

Say, is life lighter now than then?   130
The sufferers died, they left their pain—
The pangs which tortured them remain.

What helps it now, that Byron bore,
With haughty scorn which mock'd the smart,
Through Europe to the Aetolian shore   135
The pageant of his bleeding heart?
That thousands counted every groan,
And Europe made his woe her own?

What boots it, Shelley! that the breeze
Carried thy lovely wail away,   140
Musical through Italian trees
Which fringe thy soft blue Spezzian bay?
Inheritors of thy distress
Have restless hearts one throb the less?

Or are we easier, to have read,   145
O Obermann! the sad, stern page,
Which tells us how thou hidd'st thy head
From the fierce tempest of thine age
In the lone brakes of Fontainebleau,
Or chalets near the Alpine snow?   150

Ye slumber in your silent grave!—
The world, which for an idle day
Grace to your mood of sadness gave,
Long since hath flung her weeds away.
The eternal trifler breaks your spell;   155
But we—we learnt your lore too well!

Years hence, perhaps, may dawn an age,
More fortunate, alas! than we,
Which without hardness will be sage,
And gay without frivolity.   160
Sons of the world, oh, speed those years;
But, while we wait, allow our tears!

Allow them! We admire with awe
The exulting thunder of your race;
You give the universe your law,   165
You triumph over time and space!
Your pride of life, your tireless powers,
We laud them, but they are not ours.

146. *Obermann* melancholy hero of an early nineteenth-century romance by
Senancour.

We are like children reared in shade
Beneath some old-world abbey wall,   170
Forgotten in a forest glade,
And secret from the eyes of all.
Deep, deep the greenwood round them waves,
Their abbey, and its close of graves!

But, where the road runs near the stream,   175
Oft through the trees they catch a glance
Of passing troops in the sun's beam—
Pennon, and plume, and flashing lance!
Forth to the world those soldiers fare,
To life, to cities, and to war!   180

And through the wood, another way,
Faint bugle notes from far are borne,
Where hunters gather, staghounds bay,
Round some fair forest lodge at morn.
Gay dames are there, in sylvan green;   185
Laughter and cries—those notes between!

The banners flashing through the trees
Make their blood dance and chain their eyes;
That bugle music on the breeze
Arrests them with a charmed surprise.   190
Banner by turns and bugle woo:
Ye shy recluses, follow too!

O children, what do ye reply?—
"Action and pleasure, will ye roam
Through these secluded dells to cry   195
And call us?—but too late ye come!
Too late for us your call ye blow,
Whose bent was taken long ago.

"Long since we pace this shadowed nave;
We watch those yellow tapers shine,   200
Emblems of hope over the grave,
In the high altar's depth divine;
The organ carries to our ear
Its accents of another sphere.

"Fenced early in this cloistral round   205
Of reverie, of shade, of prayer,
How should we grow in other ground?
How can we flower in foreign air?
—Pass, banners, pass, and bugles, cease;
And leave our desert to its peace!"   210

DOVER BEACH

The sea is calm tonight.
The tide is full, the moon lies fair
Upon the straits—on the French coast the light
Gleams and is gone; the cliffs of England stand,
Glimmering and vast, out in the tranquil bay.   5
Come to the window, sweet is the night air!
Only, from the long line of spray
Where the sea meets the moon-blanched land,
Listen! you hear the grating roar
Of pebbles which the waves draw back, and fling,   10
At their return, up the high strand,
Begin, and cease, and then again begin,
With tremulous cadence slow, and bring
The eternal note of sadness in.

Sophocles long ago   15
Heard it on the Aegean, and it brought
Into his mind the turbid ebb and flow
Of human misery; we
Find also in the sound a thought,
Hearing it by this distant northern sea.   20

The Sea of Faith
Was once, too, at the full, and round earth's shore
Lay like the folds of a bright girdle furled.
But now I only hear
Its melancholy, long, withdrawing roar,   25
Retreating, to the breath
Of the night wind, down the vast edges drear
And naked shingles of the world.

Ah, love, let us be true
To one another! for the world, which seems   30
To lie before us like a land of dreams,
So various, so beautiful, so new,
Hath really neither joy, nor love, nor light,
Nor certitude, nor peace, nor help for pain;
And we are here as on a darkling plain   35
Swept with confused alarms of struggle and flight,
Where ignorant armies clash by night.

A Selection of Eighteenth- and Early Nineteenth-Century Poems

≺ ☼ ≻

ANNE FINCH, COUNTESS OF WINCHILSEA

(*1661–1720*)

•

TO THE NIGHTINGALE

Exert thy voice, sweet harbinger of spring!
   This moment is thy time to sing,
   This moment I attend to praise,
And set my numbers to thy lays.
   Free as thine shall be my song;   5
   As thy music, short, or long.

Poets, wild as thee, were born,
   Pleasing best when unconfined,
   When to please is least designed,
Soothing but their cares to rest;   10
   Cares do still their thoughts molest,
   And still th' unhappy poet's breast,
Like thine, when best he sings, is placed against a thorn.

She begins, let all be still!
   Muse, thy promise now fulfill!   15
Sweet, oh! sweet, still sweeter yet
Can thy words such accents fit,
Canst thou syllables refine,
Melt a sense that shall retain
Still some spirit of the brain,   20
Till with sounds like these it join.
   'Twill not be! then change thy note;
   Let division shake thy throat.
Hark! division now she tries;
Yet as far the muse outflies.   25
   Cease then, prithee, cease thy tune;
   Trifler, wilt thou sing till June?

23. *division*   singing of a rapid melodic passage; warbling.

Till thy business all lies waste,
And the time of building's past!
   Thus we poets that have speech,   30
Unlike what thy forests teach,
   If a fluent vein be shown
   That's transcendent to our own,
Criticize, reform, or preach,
Or censure what we cannot reach.   35

THE TREE

Fair tree! for thy delightful shade
'Tis just that some return be made:
Sure, some return is due from me
To thy cool shadows, and to thee.
When thou to birds dost shelter give,   5
Thou music dost from them receive;
If travelers beneath thee stay,
'Till storms have worn themselves away,
That time in praising thee they spend,
And thy protecting pow'r commend: 10
The shepherd here, from scorching freed,
Tunes to thy dancing leaves his reed;
Whilst his loved nymph, in thanks, bestows
Her flow'ry chaplets on thy boughs.
Shall I then only silent be,   15
And no return be made by me?
No; let this wish upon thee wait,
And still to flourish be thy fate,
To future ages may'st thou stand
Untouched by the rash workman's hand;   20
'Till that large stock of sap is spent,
Which gives thy summer's ornament;
'Till the fierce winds, that vainly strive
To shock thy greatness whilst alive,
Shall on thy lifeless hour attend,   25
Prevent the axe, and grace thy end;
Their scattered strength together call,
And to the clouds proclaim thy fall;
Who then their ev'ning-dews may spare,
When thou no longer art their care;   30
But shalt, like ancient heroes, burn,
And some bright hearth be made thy urn.

A NOCTURNAL REVERIE

In such a night, when every louder wind
Is to its distant cavern safe confined;
And only gentle zephyr fans his wings,
And lonely Philomel, still waking, sings;
Or from some tree, famed for the owl's delight,   5
She, hollowing clear, directs the wand'rer right:
In such a night, when passing clouds give place,
Or thinly veil the heav'ns' mysterious face;
When in some river, overhung with green,
The waving moon and trembling leaves are seen;   10
When freshened grass now bears itself upright,
And makes cool banks to pleasing rest invite,
Whence springs the woodbind, and the bramble-rose,
And where the sleepy cowslip sheltered grows;
Whilst now a paler hue the foxglove takes,   15
Yet checquers still with red the dusky brakes:
When scattered glowworms, but in twilight fine,
Show trivial beauties watch their hour to shine;
Whilst Salisbury stands the test of every light,
In perfect charms, and perfect virtue bright: 20
When odors, which declined repelling day,
Through temp'rate air uninterrupted stray;
When darkened groves their softest shadows wear,
And falling waters we distinctly hear;
When through the gloom more venerable shows   25
Some ancient fabric, awful in repose,
While sunburnt hills their swarthy looks conceal,
And swelling haycocks thicken up the vale:
When the loosed horse now, as his pasture leads,
Comes slowly grazing through th' adjoining meads,   30
Whose stealing pace, and lengthened shade we fear,
Till torn up forage in his teeth we hear:
When nibbling sheep at large pursue their food,
And unmolested kine rechew the cud;
When curlews cry beneath the village walls,   35
And to her straggling brood the partridge calls;
Their shortlived jubilee the creatures keep,
Which but endures, whilst tyrant man does sleep;
When a sedate content the spirit feels,
And no fierce light disturbs, whilst it reveals;   40
But silent musings urge the mind to seek

19. *Salisbury*   a friend, the Countess of Salisbury.

Something, too high for syllables to speak;
Till the free soul to a composedness charmed,
Finding the elements of rage disarmed,
O'er all below a solemn quiet grown,   45
Joys in th' inferior world, and thinks it like her own:
In such a night let me abroad remain,
Till morning breaks, and all's confused again;
Our cares, our toils, our clamors are renewed,
Or pleasures, seldom reached, again pursued.   50

MATTHEW PRIOR
(1664–1721)

·

THE SECRETARY
WRITTEN AT THE HAGUE, IN THE YEAR 1696

While with labor assid'ous due pleasure I mix,
And in one day atone for the business of six,
In a little Dutch-chaise on a Saturday night,
On my left hand my Horace, a Nymph on my right.
No Memoire to compose, and no post-boy to move,   5
That on Sunday may hinder the softness of love;
For her, neither visits, nor parties of tea,
Nor the long-winded cant of a dull refugee.
This night and the next shall be hers, shall be mine,
To good or ill fortune the third we resign: 10
Thus scorning the world, and superior to fate,
I drive on my car in processional state;
So with Phia through Athens Pisistratus rode,
Men thought her Minerva, and him a new God.
But why should I stories of Athens rehearse,   15
Where people knew love, and were partial to verse,
Since none can with justice my pleasures oppose,
In Holland half-drowned in int'rest and prose:
By Greece and past ages, what need I be tried,
When the Hague and the present, are both on my side,   20
And is it enough, for the joys of the day;

Secretary Prior was secretary to the ambassador at the Hague.
5. *Memoire* memorandum.
13. *Pisistratus* Athenian tyrant, who tricked the populace by riding through the city with *Phia* dressed as Athena (Minerva).

To think what Anacreon, or Sappho would say.
When good Vandergoes, and his provident Vrough,
As they gaze on my triumph, do freely allow,
That search all the province, you'd find no man there is   25
So blessed as the *Englishen Heer Secretaris.*

WRITTEN IN THE BEGINNING OF MÉZERAY'S *HISTORY OF FRANCE*

Whate'er thy countrymen have done
By law and wit, by sword and gun,
     In thee is faithfully recited:
And all the living world, that view
Thy work, give thee the praises due,   5
     At once instructed and delighted.

Yet for the fame of all these deeds,
What beggar in the Invalides,
     With lameness broke, with blindness smitten,
Wished ever decently to die,   10
To have been either Mézeray,
     Or any monarch he has written?

It strange, dear author, yet it true is,
That down from Pharamond to Loüis,
     All covet life, yet call it pain: 15
All feel the ill, yet shun the cure:
Can sense this paradox endure?
     Resolve me, Cambrai or Fontaine.

The man in graver tragic known
Though his best part long since was done,   20
     Still on the stage desires to tarry;
And he who played the Harlequin,
After the jest still loads the scene,
     Unwilling to retire, though weary.

22. *Anacreon* like *Sappho,* a writer of love poetry.

8. *Invalides* hospital in Paris for disabled soldiers.
14. *Pharamond to Loüis* Pharamond, legendary first King of France; Louis XIV.
18. *Cambrai* Fénélon, Archbishop of Cambrai, French writer of the Enlightenment, wise in the ways of the world; *Fontaine* Jean de la Fontaine, author of the famous *Fables.*

JOSEPH ADDISON
(1672–1719)

·

ODE

The spacious firmament on high,
With all the blue ethereal sky,
And spangled heav'ns, a shining frame,
Their great Original proclaim:
Th' unwearied sun, from day to day,   5
Does his Creator's power display,
And publishes to every land
The work of an Almighty Hand.

Soon as the evening shades prevail,
The moon takes up the wondrous tale,   10
And nightly to the listning earth
Repeats the story of her birth:
Whilst all the stars that round her burn,
And all the planets, in their turn,
Confirm the tidings as they roll,   15
And spread the truth from pole to pole.

What though, in solemn silence, all
Move round the dark terrestrial ball?
What though nor real voice nor sound
Amid their radiant orbs be found?   20
In reason's ear they all rejoice,
And utter forth a glorious voice,
Forever singing, as they shine,
"The Hand that made us is divine."

JOHN GAY
(1685–1732)

·

FROM THE SHEPHERD'S WEEK
FRIDAY; OR THE DIRGE

BUMKINET.   GRUBBINOL.

BUMKINET

Why, Grubbinol, dost thou so wistful seem?
There's sorrow in thy look, if right I deem.
'Tis true, yon oaks with yellow tops appear,
And chilly blasts begin to nip the year;
From the tall elm a shower of leaves is born,   5
And their lost beauty riven beeches mourn.
Yet ev'n this season pleasance blithe affords,
Now the squeezed press foams with our apple hoards.
Come, let us hie, and quaff a cheery bowl,
Let cider new *wash sorrow from thy soul.*   10

GRUBBINOL

Ah Bumkinet! since thou from hence wert gone,
From these sad plains all merriment is flown;
Should I reveal my grief 'twould spoil thy cheer,
And make thine eye o'er-flow with many a tear.

BUMKINET

Hang Sorrow! Let's to yonder hut repair,   15
And with trim sonnets cast away our care.
Gillian of Croydon well thy pipe can play,
Thou sing'st most sweet, *o'er hills and far away.*
Of Patient Grissel I devise to sing,
And catches quaint shall make the valleys ring.   20
Come, Grubbinol, beneath this shelter, come,
From hence we view our flocks securely roam.

GRUBBINOL

Yes, blithesome lad, a tale I mean to sing,
But with my woe shall distant valleys ring.
The tale shall make our kidlings droop their head,   25
For woe is me!—our Blouzelind is dead.

BUMKINET

Is Blouzelinda dead? farewell my glee!
No happiness is now reserved for me.
As the wood pigeon cooes without his mate,
So shall my doleful dirge bewail her fate.   30
Of Blouzelinda fair I mean to tell,
The peerless maid that did all maids excel.
  Henceforth the morn shall dewy sorrow shed,
And evening tears upon the grass be spread;
The rolling streams with wat'ry grief shall flow,   35
And winds shall moan aloud—when loud they blow.
Henceforth, as oft as autumn shall return,
The dropping trees, whene'er it rains, shall mourn;
This season quite shall strip the country's pride,
For 'twas in autumn Blouzelinda died.   40
  Where-e'er I gad, I Blouzelind shall view,
Woods, dairy, barn, and mows our passion knew.
When I direct my eyes to yonder wood,
Fresh rising sorrow curdles in my blood.
Thither I've often been the damsel's guide,   45
When rotten sticks our fuel have supplied;
There I remember how her faggots large,
Were frequently these happy shoulders' charge.
Sometimes this crook drew hazel boughs adown,
And stuffed her apron wide with nuts so brown;   50
Or when her feeding hogs had missed their way,
Or wallowing 'mid a feast of acorns lay;
Th' untoward creatures to the sty I drove,
And whistled all the way—or told my love.
  If by the dairy's hatch I chance to hie,   55
I shall her goodly countenance espy,
For there her goodly countenance I've seen,
Set off with kerchief starched and pinners clean.
Sometimes, like wax, she rolls the butter round,
Or with the wooden lily prints the pound.   60
Whilome I've seen her skim the clotted cream,
And press from spongy curds the milky stream.
But now, alas! these ears shall hear no more
The whining swine surround the dairy door,
No more her care shall fill the hollow tray,   65
To fat the guzzling hogs with floods of whey.
Lament, ye swine, in gruntings spend your grief,
For you, like me, have lost your sole relief.
  When in the barn the sounding flail I ply,

Where from his sieve the chaff was wont to fly,   70
The poultry there will seem around to stand,
Waiting upon her charitable hand.
No succor meet the poultry now can find,
For they, like me, have lost their Blouzelind.

    Whenever by yon barley mow I pass,   75
Before my eyes will trip the tidy lass.
I pitched the sheaves (oh could I do so now)
Which she in rows piled on the growing mow.
There ev'ry deal my heart by love was gained,
There the sweet kiss my courtship has explained.   80
Ah Blouzelind! that mow I ne'er shall see,
But thy memorial will revive in me.

    Lament, ye fields, and rueful symptoms show,
Henceforth let not the smelling primrose grow;
Let weeds instead of butter-flowers appear,   85
And meads, instead of daisies, hemlock bear;
For cowslips sweet let dandelions spread,
For Blouzelinda, blithesome maid, is dead!
Lament ye swains, and o'er her grave bemoan,
And spell ye right this verse upon her stone: 90
Here Blouzelinda *lies—Alas, alas!*
Weep shepherds—and remember flesh is grass.

GRUBBINOL

    Albeit thy songs are sweeter to mine ear,
Than to the thirsty cattle rivers clear;
Or winter porridge to the lab'ring youth,   95
Or buns and sugar to the damsel's tooth;
Yet Blouzelinda's name shall tune my lay,
Of her I'll sing forever and for aye.

    When Blouzelind expired, the weather's bell
Before the drooping flock tolled forth her knell;   100
The solemn death-watch clicked the hour she died,
And shrilling crickets in the chimney cried;
The boding raven on her cottage sate,
And with hoarse croaking warned us of her fate;
The lambkin, which her wonted tendance bred,   105
Dropped on the plains that fatal instant dead;
Swarmed on a rotten stick the bees I spied,
Which erst I saw when goody Dobson died.

    How shall I, void of tears, her death relate,
While on her dearling's bed her mother sate!   110
These words the dying Blouzelinda spoke,
And *of the dead let none the will revoke.*

"Mother," quoth she, "let not the poultry need,
And give the goose wherewith to raise her breed,
Be these my sister's care—and ev'ry morn   115
Amid the ducklings let her scatter corn;
The sickly calf that's housed, be sure to tend,
Feed him with milk, and from bleak colds defend.
Yet e'er I die—see, mother, yonder shelf,
There secretly I've hid my worldly pelf.   120
Twenty good shillings in a rag I laid,
Be ten the Parson's, for my sermon paid.
The rest is yours—my spinning-wheel and rake,
Let Susan keep for her dear sister's sake;
My new straw hat that's trimly lined with green,   125
Let Peggy wear, for she's a damsel clean.
My leathern bottle, long in harvests tried,
Be Grubbinol's—this silver ring beside:
Three silver pennies, and a ninepence bent,
A token kind, to Bumkinet is sent."   130
Thus spoke the maiden, while her mother cried,
And peaceful, like the harmless lamb, she died.

  To show their love, the neighbors far and near,
Followed with wistful look the damsel's bier.
Sprigged rosemary the lads and lasses bore,   135
While dismally the Parson walked before.
Upon her grave the rosemary they threw,
The daisy, butter-flower and endive blue.

  After the good man warned us from his text,
That none could tell whose turn would be the next;   140
He said, that heav'n would take her soul, no doubt,
And spoke the hour-glass in her praise—quite out.

  To her sweet mem'ry flow'ry garlands strung,
O'er her now empty seat aloft were hung.
With wicker rods we fenced her tomb around,   145
To ward from man and beast the hallowed ground,
Lest her new grave the Parson's cattle raze,
For both his horse and cow the churchyard graze.

  Now we trudged homeward to her mother's farm,
To drink new cider mulled, with ginger warm.   150
For gaffer Tread-well told us by the by,
Excessive sorrow is exceeding dry.

  While bulls bear horns upon their curléd brow,
Or lasses with soft strokings milk the cow;
While paddling ducks the standing lake desire,   155
Or batt'ning hogs roll in the sinking mire;
While moles the crumbled earth in hillocks raise,

So long shall swains tell Blouzelinda's praise.
  Thus wailed the louts in melancholy strain,
'Till bonny Susan sped across the plain;   160
They seized the lass in apron clean arrayed,
And to the ale-house forced the willing maid;
In ale and kisses they forget their cares,
And Susan Blouzelinda's loss repairs.

THOMAS GRAY
(*1716–1771*)

·

SONNET ON THE DEATH OF
MR. RICHARD WEST

In vain to me the smiling mornings shine,
And redd'ning Phoebus lifts his golden fire.
The birds in vain their amorous descant join;
Or cheerful fields resume their green attire.
These ears, alas! for other notes repine,   5
A different object do these eyes require.
My lonely anguish melts no heart but mine;
And in my breast the imperfect joys expire.
Yet morning smiles the busy race to cheer,
And new-born pleasure brings to happier men.   10
The fields to all their wonted tribute bear,
To warm their little loves the birds complain;
I fruitless mourn to him, that cannot hear,
And weep the more, because I weep in vain.

WILLIAM COLLINS
(*1721–1759*)

·

ODE TO EVENING

If aught of oaten stop, or pastoral song,
May hope, chaste Eve, to soothe thy modest ear,
  Like thy own solemn springs,

Thy springs and dying gales,
O nymph reserved, while now the bright-haired sun   5
Sits in yon western tent, whose cloudy skirts,
   With brede ethereal wove,
   O'erhang his wavy bed;
Now air is hushed, save where the weak-eyed bat,
With short shrill shrieks flits by on leathern wing,   10
   Or where the beetle winds
   His small but sullen horn,
As oft he rises 'midst the twilight path,
Against the pilgrim borne in heedless hum;
   Now teach me, maid composed,   15
   To breathe some softened strain,
Whose numbers, stealing through thy dark'ning vale,
May not unseemly with its stillness suit,
   As musing slow, I hail
   Thy genial loved return!   20
For when thy folding star arising shows
His paly circlet, at his warning lamp
   The fragrant Hours, and elves
   Who slept in flowers the day,
And many a nymph who wreaths her brows with sedge,   25
And sheds the freshening dew, and lovelier still,
   The pensive Pleasures sweet,
   Prepare thy shadowy car.
Then lead, calm Vot'ress, where some sheety lake
Cheers the lone heath, or some time-hallowed pile   30
   Or upland fallows gray
   Reflect its last cool gleam.
But when chill blust'ring winds, or driving rain,
Forbid my willing feet, be mine the hut
   That from the mountain's side   35
   Views wilds, and swelling floods,
And hamlets brown, and dim-discovered spires,
And hears their simple bell, and marks o'er all
   Thy dewy fingers draw
   The gradual dusky veil.   40
While Spring shall pour his showers, as oft he wont,
And bathe thy breathing tresses, meekest Eve;
   While Summer loves to sport
   Beneath thy ling'ring light;
While sallow Autumn fills thy lap with leaves;   45
Or Winter, yelling through the troublous air,
   Affrights thy shrinking train,
   And rudely rends thy robes;

So long, sure-found beneath the sylvan shed,
Shall Fancy, Friendship, Science, rose-lipped Health,   50
   Thy gentlest influence own,
   And hymn thy favorite name!

ODE WRITTEN IN THE BEGINNING OF THE YEAR 1746

How sleep the brave who sink to rest
By all their country's wishes blest!
When Spring, with dewy fingers cold,
Returns to deck their hallowed mold,
She there shall dress a sweeter sod   5
Than Fancy's feet have ever trod.

By fairy hands their knell is rung,
By forms unseen their dirge is sung;
There Honor comes, a pilgrim gray,
To bless the turf that wraps their clay,   10
And Freedom shall awhile repair,
To dwell a weeping hermit there!

MARK AKENSIDE
(1721–1770)
·

INSCRIPTION: FOR A GROTTO

To me, whom in their lays the shepherds call
Actaea, daughter of the neighboring stream,
This cave belongs. The fig-tree and the vine,
Which o'er the rocky entrance downward shoot,
Were placed by Glycon. He with cowslips pale,   5
Primrose, and purple lychnis, decked the green
Before my threshold, and my shelving walls
With honeysuckle covered. Here at noon,
Lulled by the murmur of my rising fount,
I slumber; here my clustering fruits I tend,   10
Or from the humid flowers, at break of day,
Fresh garlands weave, and chase from all my bounds
Each thing impure or noxious. Enter in,

O stranger, undismayed. Nor bat nor toad
Here lurks; and if thy breast of blameless thoughts   15
Approve thee, not unwelcome shalt thou tread
My quiet mansion—chiefly, if thy name
Wise Pallas and the immortal Muses own.

CHRISTOPHER SMART
(1722–1771)

·

ON A BED OF GUERNSEY LILIES
WRITTEN IN SEPTEMBER, 1763

Ye beauties! O how great the sum
  Of sweetness that ye bring,
On what a charity ye come
  To bless the latter spring!
How kind the visit that ye pay,   5
Like strangers on a rainy day,
  When heartiness despaired of guests:
No neighbor's praise your pride alarms,
No rival flower surveys your charms,
  Or heightens, or contests!   10

Lo, through her works gay nature grieves
  How brief she is and frail,
As ever o'er the falling leaves
  Autumnal winds prevail.
Yet still the philosophic mind   15
Consolatory food can find,
  And hope her anchorage maintain:
We never are deserted quite;
'Tis by succession of delight
  That love supports his reign.   20

16. *approve*   testify (to your having "blameless thoughts").

SAMUEL TAYLOR COLERIDGE
(*1772–1834*)

.

THIS LIME-TREE BOWER MY PRISON
ADDRESSED TO CHARLES LAMB, OF THE INDIA HOUSE, LONDON

*In the June of 1797 some long-expected friends paid a visit to the
author's cottage; and on the morning of their arrival, he met with an
accident, which disabled him from walking during the whole time of
their stay. One evening, when they had left him for a few hours, he
composed the following lines in the garden-bower.*

Well, they are gone, and here must I remain,
This lime-tree bower my prison! I have lost
Beauties and feelings, such as would have been
Most sweet to my remembrance even when age
Had dimmed mine eyes to blindness! They, meanwhile,   5
Friends, whom I never more may meet again,
On springy heath, along the hilltop edge,
Wander in gladness, and wind down, perchance,
To that still roaring dell, of which I told;
The roaring dell, o'erwooded, narrow, deep,   10
And only speckled by the midday sun;
Where its slim trunk the ash from rock to rock
Flings arching like a bridge;—that branchless ash,
Unsunned and damp, whose few poor yellow leaves
Ne'er tremble in the gale, yet tremble still,   15
Fanned by the water-fall! and there my friends
Behold the dark green file of long lank weeds,
That all at once (a most fantastic sight!)
Still nod and drip beneath the dripping edge
Of the blue clay-stone.

                        Now, my friends emerge   20
Beneath the wide wide Heaven—and view again
The many-steepled tract magnificent
Of hilly fields and meadows, and the sea,
With some fair bark, perhaps, whose sails light up
The slip of smooth clear blue betwixt two Isles   25
Of purple shadow! Yes! they wander on

In gladness all; but thou, methinks, most glad,
My gentle-hearted Charles! for thou hast pined
And hungered after Nature, many a year,
In the great City pent, winning thy way   30
With sad yet patient soul, through evil and pain
And strange calamity! Ah! slowly sink
Behind the western ridge, thou glorious sun!
Shine in the slant beams of the sinking orb,
Ye purple heath-flowers! richlier burn, ye clouds!   35
Live in the yellow light, ye distant groves!
And kindle, thou blue ocean! So my friend
Struck with deep joy may stand, as I have stood,
Silent with swimming sense; yea, gazing round
On the wide landscape, gaze till all doth seem   40
Less gross than bodily; and of such hues
As veil the Almighty Spirit, when yet he makes
Spirits perceive his presence.

                        A delight
Comes sudden on my heart, and I am glad
As I myself were there! Nor in this bower,   45
This little lime-tree bower, have I not marked
Much that has soothed me. Pale beneath the blaze
Hung the transparent foliage; and I watched
Some broad and sunny leaf, and loved to see
The shadow of the leaf and stem above   50
Dappling its sunshine! And that walnut-tree
Was richly tinged, and a deep radiance lay
Full on the ancient ivy, which usurps
Those fronting elms, and now, with blackest mass
Makes their dark branches gleam a lighter hue   55
Through the late twilight: and though now the bat
Wheels silent by, and not a swallow twitters,
Yet still the solitary humble-bee
Sings in the bean-flower! Henceforth I shall know
That Nature ne'er deserts the wise and pure;   60
No plot so narrow, be but Nature there,
No waste so vacant, but may well employ
Each faculty of sense, and keep the heart
Awake to Love and Beauty! and sometimes
'Tis well to be bereft of promised good,   65
That we may lift the soul, and contemplate
With lively joy the joys we cannot share.
My gentle-hearted Charles! when the last rook
Beat its straight path along the dusky air

Homewards, I blest it! deeming its black wing   70
(Now a dim speck, now vanishing in light)
Had crossed the mighty orb's dilated glory,
While thou stood'st gazing; or, when all was still,
Flew creeking o'er thy head, and had a charm
For thee, my gentle-hearted Charles, to whom   75
No sound is dissonant which tells of Life.

FROST AT MIDNIGHT

The Frost performs its secret ministry,
Unhelped by any wind. The owlet's cry
Came loud—and hark, again! loud as before.
The inmates of my cottage, all at rest,
Have left me to that solitude, which suits   5
Abstruser musings: save that at my side
My cradled infant slumbers peacefully.
'Tis calm indeed! so calm, that it disturbs
And vexes meditation with its strange
And extreme silentness. Sea, hill, and wood,   10
This populous village! Sea, and hill, and wood,
With all the numberless goings-on of life,
Inaudible as dreams! the thin blue flame
Lies on my low-burnt fire, and quivers not;
Only that film, which fluttered on the grate,   15
Still flutters there, the sole unquiet thing.
Methinks its motion in this hush of nature
Gives it dim sympathies with me who live,
Making it a companionable form,
Whose puny flaps and freaks the idling Spirit   20
By its own moods interprets, everywhere
Echo or mirror seeking of itself,
And makes a toy of Thought.

                              But O! how oft,
How oft, at school, with most believing mind,
Presageful, have I gazed upon the bars,   25
To watch that fluttering *stranger!* and as oft
With unclosed lids, already had I dreamt
Of my sweet birthplace, and the old church tower,
Whose bells, the poor man's only music, rang

15. *film* "In all parts of the Kingdom   absent friend" (Coleridge).
these films are called *strangers* and are   25. *bars* of the fireplace.
supposed to portend the arrival of some

From morn to evening, all the hot Fair-day, 30
So sweetly, that they stirred and haunted me
With a wild pleasure, falling on mine ear
Most like articulate sounds of things to come!
So gazed I, till the soothing things, I dreamt,
Lulled me to sleep, and sleep prolonged my dreams! 35
And so I brooded all the following morn,
Awed by the stern preceptor's face, mine eye
Fixed with mock study on my swimming book:
Save if the door half opened, and I snatched
A hasty glance, and still my heart leaped up, 40
For still I hoped to see the *stranger's* face,
Townsman, or aunt, or sister more beloved,
My playmate when we both were clothed alike!

   Dear Babe, that sleepest cradled by my side,
Whose gentle breathings, heard in this deep calm, 45
Fill up the interspersèd vacancies
And momentary pauses of the thought!
My babe so beautiful! it thrills my heart
With tender gladness, thus to look at thee,
And think that thou shalt learn far other lore, 50
And in far other scenes! For I was reared
In the great city, pent 'mid cloisters dim,
And saw nought lovely but the sky and stars.
But *thou*, my babe! shalt wander like a breeze
By lakes and sandy shores, beneath the crags 55
Of ancient mountain, and beneath the clouds,
Which image in their bulk both lakes and shores
And mountain crags: so shalt thou see and hear
The lovely shapes and sounds intelligible
Of that eternal language, which thy God 60
Utters, who from eternity doth teach
Himself in all, and all things in himself.
Great universal Teacher! he shall mold
Thy spirit, and by giving make it ask.

   Therefore all seasons shall be sweet to thee, 65
Whether the summer clothe the general earth
With greenness, or the redbreast sit and sing
Betwixt the tufts of snow on the bare branch
Of mossy apple tree, while the nigh thatch
Smokes in the sun-thaw; whether the eave-drops fall 70
Heard only in the trances of the blast,

Or if the secret ministry of frost
Shall hang them up in silent icicles,
Quietly shining to the quiet moon.

A SUNSET

Upon the mountain's edge with light touch resting,
There a brief while the globe of splendor sits
   And seems a creature of the earth; but soon
    More changeful than the moon,
To wane fantastic his great orb submits,   5
Or cone or mow of fire: till sinking slowly
Even to a star at length he lessens wholly.

Abrupt, as spirits vanish, he is sunk!
A soul-like breeze possesses all the wood.
   The boughs, the sprays have stood   10
As motionless as stands the ancient trunk!
But every leaf through all the forest flutters,
And deep the cavern of the fountain mutters.

TO NATURE

It may indeed be fantasy, when I
   Essay to draw from all created things
   Deep, heartfelt, inward joy that closely clings;
And trace in leaves and flowers that round me lie
Lessons of love and earnest piety.   5
   So let it be; and if the wide world rings
   In mock of this belief, it brings
Nor fear, nor grief, nor vain perplexity.
So will I build my altar in the fields,
   And the blue sky my fretted dome shall be,   10
And the sweet fragrance that the wild flower yields
   Shall be the incense I will yield to Thee,
Thee only God! and thou shalt not despise
Even me, the priest of this poor sacrifice.

—<☼>—

GEORGE GORDON, LORD BYRON
(1788–1824)

·

THE GIRL OF CADIZ

Oh never talk again to me
  Of northern climes and British ladies;
It has not been your lot to see,
  Like me, the lovely Girl of Cadiz.
Although her eye be not of blue,   5
  Nor fair her locks, like English lasses,
How far its own expressive hue
  The languid azure eye surpasses!

Prometheus-like from heaven she stole
  The fire that through those silken lashes   10
In darkest glances seems to roll,
  From eyes that cannot hide their flashes:
And as along her bosom steal
  In lengthened flow her raven tresses,
You'd swear each clustering lock could feel,   15
  And curled to give her neck caresses.

Our English maids are long to woo,
  And frigid even in possession;
And if their charms be fair to view,
  Their lips are slow at love's confession;   20
But, born beneath a brighter sun,
  For love ordained the Spanish maid is,
And who—when fondly, fairly won—
  Enchants you like the Girl of Cadiz?

The Spanish maid is no coquette,   25
  Nor joys to see a lover tremble
And if she love, or if she hate,
  Alike she knows not to dissemble.
Her heart can ne'er be bought or sold—
  Howe'er it beats, it beats sincerely;   30
And, though it will not bend to gold,
  'Twill love you long and love you dearly.

The Spanish girl that meets your love
  Ne'er taunts you with a mock denial,
For every thought is bent to prove   35
  Her passion in the hour of trial.
When thronging foemen menace Spain,
  She dares the deed and shares the danger;
And should her lover press the plain,
  She hurls the spear, her love's avenger.   40

And when, beneath the evening star,
  She mingles in the gay Bolero,
Or sings to her attuned guitar
  Of Christian knight or Moorish hero,
Or counts her beads with fairy hand   45
  Beneath the twinkling rays of Hesper,
Or joins Devotion's choral band,
  To chant the sweet and hallowed vesper;—

In each her charms the heart must move
  Of all who venture to behold her;   50
Then let not maids less fair reprove
  Because her bosom is not colder:
Through many a clime 'tis mine to roam
  Where many a soft and melting maid is,
But none abroad, and few at home,   55
  May match the dark-eyed Girl of Cadiz.

SHE WALKS IN BEAUTY

She walks in beauty, like the night
  Of cloudless climes and starry skies;
And all that's best of dark and bright
  Meet in her aspect and her eyes:
Thus mellowed to that tender light   5
  Which heaven to gaudy day denies.

One shade the more, one ray the less,
  Had half impaired the nameless grace
Which waves in every raven tress,
  Or softly lightens o'er her face;   10
Where thoughts serenely sweet express,
  How pure, how dear their dwelling place.

And on that cheek, and o'er that brow,
  So soft, so calm, yet eloquent,

The smiles that win, the tints that glow,   15
  But tell of days in goodness spent,
A mind at peace with all below,
  A heart whose love is innocent!

SO WE'LL GO NO MORE A-ROVING

So we'll go no more a-roving
  So late into the night,
Though the heart be still as loving,
  And the moon be still as bright.

For the sword outwears its sheath,   5
  And the soul wears out the breast,
And the heart must pause to breathe,
  And Love itself have rest.

Though the night was made for loving,
  And the day returns too soon,   10
Yet we'll go no more a-roving
  By the light of the moon.

PERCY BYSSHE SHELLEY
(1792–1822)

.

STANZAS WRITTEN IN DEJECTION,
NEAR NAPLES

The sun is warm, the sky is clear,
  The waves are dancing fast and bright,
Blue·isles and snowy mountains wear
  The purple noon's transparent might,
  The breath of the moist earth is light,   5
Around its unexpanded buds;
  Like many a voice of one delight,
The winds, the birds, the ocean floods,
The City's voice itself, is soft like Solitude's.

I see the Deep's untrampled floor   10
  With green and purple seaweeds strown;

I see the waves upon the shore,
  Like light dissolved in star-showers, thrown:
  I sit upon the sands alone—
The lightning of the noontide ocean   15
  Is flashing round me, and a tone
  Arises from its measured motion;
How sweet! did any heart now share in my emotion.

Alas! I have nor hope nor health,
  Nor peace within nor calm around,   20
Nor that content surpassing wealth
  The sage in meditation found,
  And walked with inward glory crowned—
Nor fame, nor power, nor love, nor leisure.
  Others I see whom these surround—   25
  Smiling they live, and call life pleasure;
To me that cup has been dealt in another measure.

Yet now despair itself is mild,
  Even as the winds and waters are;
I could lie down like a tired child,   30
  And weep away the life of care
  Which I have borne and yet must bear,
Till death like sleep might steal on me,
  And I might feel in the warm air
My cheek grow cold, and hear the sea   35
Breathe o'er my dying brain its last monotony.

Some might lament that I were cold,
  As I, when this sweet day is gone,
Which my lost heart, too soon grown old,
  Insults with this untimely moan;   40
  They might lament—for I am one
Whom men love not—and yet regret,
  Unlike this day, which, when the sun
Shall on its stainless glory set,
Will linger, though enjoyed, like joy in memory yet.   45

ENGLAND IN 1819

An old, mad, blind, despised, and dying king—
Princes, the dregs of their dull race, who flow
Through public scorn—mud from a muddy spring;
Rulers who neither see, nor feel, nor know,

---

22. *Sage*   Marcus Aurelius, Roman   1. *King*   George III, who ruled 1760–
Emperor and Stoic philosopher, author   1820.
of *Meditations*.

But leechlike to their fainting country cling,   5
Till they drop, blind in blood, without a blow;
A people starved and stabbed in the untilled field—
An army, which liberticide and prey
Makes as a two-edged sword to all who wield;
Golden and sanguine laws which tempt and slay;   10
Religion Christless, Godless—a book sealed;
A Senate—Time's worst statute unrepealed—
Are graves, from which a glorious phantom may
Burst, to illumine our tempestuous day.

ODE TO THE WEST WIND

I

O wild West Wind, thou breath of Autumn's being,
Thou, from whose unseen presence the leaves dead
Are driven, like ghosts from an enchanter fleeing,

Yellow, and black, and pale, and hectic red,
Pestilence-stricken multitudes: O thou,   5
Who chariotest to their dark wintry bed

The wingéd seeds, where they lie cold and low,
Each like a corpse within its grave, until
Thine azure sister of the Spring shall blow

Her clarion o'er the dreaming earth, and fill   10
(Driving sweet buds like flocks to feed in air)
With living hues and odors plain and hill:

Wild Spirit, which art moving everywhere;
Destroyer and preserver; hear, oh, hear!

II

Thou on whose stream, mid the steep sky's commotion,   15
Loose clouds like earth's decaying leaves are shed,
Shook from the tangled boughs of Heaven and Ocean,

Angels of rain and lightning: there are spread
On the blue surface of thine aëry surge,
Like the bright hair uplifted from the head   20

Of some fierce Maenad, even from the dim verge
Of the horizon to the zenith's height,
The locks of the approaching storm. Thou dirge

21. *Maenad* one of the women followers of Bacchus, inspired by the god to ecstatic frenzy.

Of the dying year, to which this closing night
Will be the dome of a vast sepulchre,   25
Vaulted with all thy congregated might

Of vapors, from whose solid atmosphere
Black rain, and fire, and hail will burst: oh, hear!

III

Thou who didst waken from his summer dreams
The blue Mediterranean, where he lay,   30
Lulled by the coil of his crystálline streams,

Beside a pumice isle in Baiae's bay,
And saw in sleep old palaces and towers
Quivering within the wave's intenser day,

All overgrown with azure moss and flowers   35
So sweet, the sense faints picturing them! Thou
For whose path the Atlantic's level powers

Cleave themselves into chasms, while far below
The sea-blooms and the oozy woods which wear
The sapless foliage of the ocean, know   40

Thy voice, and suddenly grow gray with fear,
And tremble and despoil themselves: oh, hear!

IV

If I were a dead leaf thou mightest bear,
If I were a swift cloud to fly with thee;
A wave to pant beneath thy power, and share   45

The impulse of thy strength, only less free
Than thou, O uncontrollable! If even
I were as in my boyhood, and could be

The comrade of thy wanderings over Heaven,
As then, when to outstrip thy skyey speed   50
Scarce seemed a vision; I would ne'er have striven

As thus with thee in prayer in my sore need.
Oh, lift me as a wave, a leaf, a cloud!
I fall upon the thorns of life! I bleed!

32. *Baiae's bay* near Naples, the site of a Roman town, "the ruins of its antique grandeur standing in the transparent sea" (Shelley).

A heavy weight of hours has chained and bowed   55
One too like thee; tameless, and swift, and proud.

V

Make me thy lyre, even as the forest is:
What if my leaves are falling like its own!
The tumult of thy mighty harmonies

Will take from both a deep, autumnal tone,   60
Sweet though in sadness. Be thou, Spirit fierce,
My spirit! Be thou me, impetuous one!

Drive my dead thoughts over the universe
Like withered leaves to quicken a new birth!
And, by the incantation of this verse,   65

Scatter, as from an unextinguished hearth
Ashes and sparks, my words among mankind!
Be through my lips to unawakened earth

The trumpet of a prophecy! O Wind,
If Winter comes, can Spring be far behind?   70

LINES: WHEN THE LAMP
IS SHATTERED

I

When the lamp is shattered
The light in the dust lies dead—
When the cloud is scattered
The rainbow's glory is shed.
When the lute is broken,   5
Sweet tones are remembered not;
When the lips have spoken,
Loved accents are soon forgot.

II

As music and splendor
Survive not the lamp and the lute,   10
The heart's echoes render
No song when the spirit is mute—
No song but sad dirges,
Like the wind through a ruined cell,
Or the mournful surges   15
That ring the dead seaman's knell.

III

When hearts have once mingled
Love first leaves the well-built nest;
  The weak one is singled
To endure what it once possessed.   20
  O Love! who bewailest
The frailty of all things here,
  Why choose you the frailest
For your cradle, your home, and your bier?

IV

Its passions will rock thee   25
As the storms rock the ravens on high;
  Bright reason will mock thee,
Like the sun from a wintry sky.
  From thy nest every rafter
Will rot, and thine eagle home   30
  Leave thee naked to laughter,
When leaves fall and cold winds come.

RALPH WALDO EMERSON
(1803–1882)

·

URIEL

It fell in the ancient periods
  Which the brooding soul surveys,
Or ever the wild Time coined itself
  Into calendar months and days.

This was the lapse of Uriel,   5
Which in Paradise befell.
Once, among the Pleiads walking,
Seyd overheard the young gods talking;
And the treason, too long pent,
To his ears was evident.   10
The young deities discussed
Laws of form, and meter just,
Orb, quintessence, and sunbeams,

Uriel in Milton's *Paradise Lost,* the   8. *Seyd*   the poet.
archangel of the sun.

What subsisteth, and what seems.
One, with low tones that decide,   15
And doubt and reverend use defied,
With a look that solved the sphere,
And stirred the devils everywhere,
Gave his sentiment divine
Against the being of a line.   20
"Line in nature is not found;
Unit and universe are round;
In vain produced, all rays return;
Evil will bless, and ice will burn."
As Uriel spoke with piercing eye,   25
A shudder ran around the sky;
The stern old war-gods shook their heads,
The seraphs frowned from myrtle-beds;
Seemed to the holy festival
The rash word boded ill to all;   30
The balance-beam of Fate was bent;
The bounds of good and ill were rent;
Strong Hades could not keep his own,
But all slid to confusion.

A sad self-knowledge, withering, fell   35
On the beauty of Uriel;
In heaven once eminent, the god
Withdrew, that hour, into his cloud;
Whether doomed to long gyration
In the sea of generation,   40
Or by knowledge grown too bright
To hit the nerve of feebler sight.
Straightway, a forgetting wind
Stole over the celestial kind
And their lips the secret kept,   45
If in ashes the fire-seed slept.
But now and then, truth-speaking things
Shamed the angels' veiling wings;
And, shrilling from the solar course,
Or from fruit of chemic force,   50
Procession of a soul in matter,
Or the speeding change of water,
Or out of the good of evil born,

21–24. *"Line . . . burn"* compare the doctrine of unity in *Brahma,* p. 288. 39–40. *long gyration . . . generation* according to neoplatonic doctrine every soul "must make periods of ascent from and descent into generation, and this forever and ever" (Proclus).

Came Uriel's voice of cherub scorn,
And a blush tinged the upper sky, 55
And the gods shook, they knew not why.

BRAHMA

If the red slayer think he slays,
  Or if the slain think he is slain,
They know not well the subtle ways
  I keep, and pass, and turn again.

Far or forgot to me is near; 5
  Shadow and sunlight are the same;
The vanished gods to me appear;
  And one to me are shame and fame.

They reckon ill who leave me out;
  When me they fly, I am the wings; 10
I am the doubter and the doubt,
  And I the hymn the Brahmin sings.

The strong gods pine for my abode,
  And pine in vain the sacred Seven,
But thou, meek lover of the good! 15
  Find me, and turn thy back on heaven.

DAYS

Daughters of Time, the hypocritic Days,
Muffled and dumb like barefoot dervishes,
And marching single in an endless file,
Bring diadems and fagots in their hands.
To each they offer gifts after his will, 5
Bread, kingdoms, stars, and sky that holds them all.
I, in my pleached garden, watched the pomp,
Forgot my morning wishes, hastily
Took a few herbs and apples, and the Day
Turned and departed silent. I, too late, 10
Under her solemn fillet saw the scorn.

Brahma Hindu god, the creator of the universe. The subject of the poem is the Hindu "doctrine of the absolute unity."
12. *Brahmin* Hindu of the highest or priestly caste.
13. *strong gods* Indra, god of the sky; Ami, god of fire; Yama, god of death.
14. *Seven* the Maharshis or highest saints.
16. *heaven* ". . . the soul seeks . . . resolution into being above form, out of Tartarus and into heaven—liberation from nature" (Emerson). Emerson opposed the "living" heaven to the conventional one.

≺ ☼ ≻

HENRY DAVID THOREAU
(1812–1862)

·

SMOKE IN WINTER

The sluggish smoke curls up from some deep dell,
The stiffened air exploring in the dawn,
And making slow acquaintance with the day;
Delaying now upon its heavenward course,
In wreathéd loiterings dallying with itself,   5
With as uncertain purpose and slow deed,
As its half-wakened master by the hearth,
Whose mind still slumbering and sluggish thoughts
Have not yet swept into the onward current
Of the new day;—and now it streams afar,   10
The while the chopper goes with step direct,
And mind intent to swing the early axe.
   First in the dusky dawn he sends abroad
His early scout, his emissary, smoke,
The earliest, latest pilgrim from the roof,   15
To feel the frosty air, inform the day;
And while he crouches still beside the hearth,
Nor musters courage to unbar the door,
It has gone down the glen with the light wind,
And o'er the plain unfurled its venturous wreath,   20
Draped the tree tops, loitered upon the hill,
And warmed the pinions of the early bird;
And now, perchance, high in the crispy air,
Has caught sight of the day o'er the earth's edge,
And greets its master's eye at his low door,   25
As some refulgent cloud in the upper sky.

HAZE

Woof of the sun, ethereal gauze,
Woven of Nature's richest stuffs,
Visible heat, air-water, and dry sea,
Last conquest of the eye;
Toil of the day displayed, sun-dust,   5
Aerial surf upon the shores of earth,

Ethereal estuary, frith of light,
Breakers of air, billows of heat,
Fine summer spray on inland seas;
Bird of the sun, transparent-winged   10
Owlet of noon, soft-pinioned,
From heath or stubble rising without song,—
Establish thy serenity o'er the fields.

CONSCIENCE

Conscience is instinct bred in the house,
Feeling and Thinking propagate the sin
By an unnatural breeding in and in.
I say, Turn it out doors,
Into the moors.   5
I love a life whose plot is simple,
And does not thicken with every pimple,
A soul so sound no sickly conscience binds it,
That makes the universe no worse than't finds it.
I love an earnest soul,   10
Whose mighty joy and sorrow
Are not drowned in a bowl,
And brought to life tomorrow;
That lives one tragedy,
And not seventy;   15
A conscience worth keeping,
Laughing not weeping;
A conscience wise and steady,
And forever ready;
Not changing with events,   20
Dealing in compliments;
A conscience exercised about
Large things, where one *may* doubt.
I love a soul not all of wood,
Predestinated to be good,   25
But true to the backbone
Unto itself alone,
And false to none;
Born to its own affairs,
Its own joys and own cares;   30
By whom the work which God begun
Is finished, and not undone;
Taken up where he left off,

Whether to worship or to scoff;
If not good, why then evil,   35
If not good god, good devil.
Goodness! you hypocrite, come out of that,
Live your life, do your work, then take your hat.
I have no patience towards
Such conscientious cowards.   40
Give me simple laboring folk,
Who love their work,
Whose virtue is a song
To cheer God along.

THE ATLANTIDES

The smothered streams of love, which flow
More bright than Phlegethon, more low,
Island us ever, like the sea,
In an Atlantic mystery.
Our fabled shores none ever reach,   5
No mariner has found our beach,
Scarcely our mirage now is seen,
And neighboring waves with floating green,
Yet still the oldest charts contain
Some dotted outline of our main;   10
In ancient times midsummer days
Unto the western islands' gaze,
To Teneriffe and the Azores,
Have shown our faint and cloud-like shores.

But sink not yet, ye desolate isles,   15
Anon your coast with commerce smiles,
And richer freights ye'll furnish far
Than Africa or Malabar.
Be fair, be fertile evermore,
Ye rumored but untrodden shore,   20
Princes and monarchs will contend
Who first unto your land shall send,
And pawn the jewels of the crown
To call your distant soil their own.

2. *Phlegethon*   the river of fire in Hades.

≺☼≻

ROBERT BROWNING
(*1812–1889*)

·

THE BISHOP ORDERS HIS TOMB AT SAINT PRAXED'S CHURCH

ROME, 15—

Vanity, saith the preacher, vanity!
Draw round my bed: is Anselm keeping back?
Nephews—sons mine . . . ah God, I know not! Well—
She, men would have to be your mother once,
Old Gandolf envied me, so fair she was!   5
What's done is done, and she is dead beside,
Dead long ago, and I am Bishop since,
And as she died so must we die ourselves,
And thence ye may perceive the world's a dream.
Life, how and what is it? As here I lie   10
In this state chamber, dying by degrees,
Hours and long hours in the dead night, I ask
"Do I live, am I dead?" Peace, peace seems all.
Saint Praxed's ever was the church for peace;
And so, about this tomb of mine. I fought   15
With tooth and nail to save my niche, ye know:
—Old Gandolf cozened me, despite my care;
Shrewd was that snatch from out the corner south
He graced his carrion with, God curse the same!
Yet still my niche is not so cramped but thence   20
One sees the pulpit o' the epistle side,
And somewhat of the choir, those silent seats,
And up into the aery dome where live
The angels, and a sunbeam's sure to lurk:
And I shall fill my slab of basalt there,   25
And 'neath my tabernacle take my rest,
With those nine columns round me, two and two,
The odd one at my feet where Anselm stands:
Peach-blossom marble all, the rare, the ripe

Church   Church of S. Prassede in
Rome, particularly remarkable for its
mosaics.
3. *Nephews* common euphemism for
sons of Renaissance churchmen.

17. *cozened* cheated.
21. *epistle side* to the right of the
altar, where the epistle is read during
divine service.
26. *tabernacle* canopy.

As fresh-poured red wine of a mighty pulse.   30
—Old Gandolf with his paltry onion-stone,
Put me where I may look at him! True peach,
Rosy and flawless: how I earned the prize!
Draw close: that conflagration of my church
—What then? So much was saved if aught were missed!   35
My sons, ye would not be my death? Go dig
The white-grape vineyard where the oil-press stood,
Drop water gently till the surface sink,
And if ye find . . . Ah God, I know not, I! . . .
Bedded in store of rotten fig leaves soft,   40
And corded up in a tight olive-frail,
Some lump, ah God, of *lapis lazuli*,
Big as a Jew's head cut off at the nape,
Blue as a vein o'er the Madonna's breast . . .
Sons, all have I bequeathed you, villas, all,   45
That brave Frascati villa with its bath,
So, let the blue lump poise between my knees,
Like God the Father's globe on both his hands
Ye worship in the Jesu Church so gay,
For Gandolf shall not choose but see and burst!   50
Swift as a weaver's shuttle fleet our years:
Man goeth to the grave, and where is he?
Did I say basalt for my slab, sons? Black—
'Twas ever antique-black I meant! How else
Shall ye contrast my frieze to come beneath?   55
The bas-relief in bronze ye promised me,
Those Pans and Nymphs ye wot of, and perchance
Some tripod, thyrsus, with a vase or so,
The Saviour at his sermon on the mount,
Saint Praxed in a glory, and one Pan   60
Ready to twitch the Nymph's last garment off,
And Moses with the tables . . . but I know
Ye mark me not! What do they whisper thee,
Child of my bowels, Anselm? Ah, ye hope
To revel down my villas while I gasp   65
Bricked o'er with beggar's moldy travertine
Which Gandolf from his tomb-top chuckles at!
Nay, boys, ye love me—all of jasper, then!

30. *pulse* strength.
31. *onion-stone* marble made of thin layers.
41. *olive-frail* olive basket.
46. *Frascati* hill town near Rome with splendid villas.
49. *Jesu* Il Jesu, Jesuit church in Rome, in gorgeous baroque style.
58. *tripod* a Greek three-legged vessel. There was a most famous one at the oracle of Delphi; *thyrsus* a staff carried by followers of Bacchus.
66. *travertine* a common Italian building stone.

'Tis jasper ye stand pledged to, lest I grieve
My bath must needs be left behind, alas!   70
One block, pure green as a pistachio nut,
There's plenty jasper somewhere in the world—
And have I not Saint Praxed's ear to pray
Horses for ye, and brown Greek manuscripts,
And mistresses with great smooth marbly limbs?   75
—That's if ye carve my epitaph aright,
Choice Latin, picked phrase, Tully's every word,
No gaudy ware like Gandolf's second line—
Tully, my masters? Ulpian serves his need!
And then how I shall lie through centuries,   80
And hear the blessed mutter of the mass,
And see God made and eaten all day long,
And feel the steady candle flame, and taste
Good strong thick stupefying incense-smoke!
For as I lie here, hours of the dead night,   85
Dying in state and by such slow degrees,
I fold my arms as if they clasped a crook,
And stretch my feet forth straight as stone can point,
And let the bedclothes, for a mortcloth, drop
Into great laps and folds of sculptor's-work: 90
And as yon tapers dwindle, and strange thoughts
Grow, with a certain humming in my ears,
About the life before I lived this life,
And this life too, popes, cardinals, and priests,
Saint Praxed at his sermon on the mount,   95
Your tall pale mother with her talking eyes,
And new-found agate urns as fresh as day,
And marble's language, Latin pure, discreet
—Aha, ELUCESCEBAT quoth our friend?
No Tully, said I, Ulpian at the best!   100
Evil and brief hath been my pilgrimage.
All *lapis*, all, sons! Else I give the Pope
My villas! Will ye ever eat my heart?
Ever your eyes were as a lizard's quick,
They glitter like your mother's for my soul,   105
Or ye would heighten my impoverished frieze,
Piece out its starved design, and fill my vase
With grapes, and add a vizor and a Term,
And to the tripod ye would tie a lynx

77. *Tully*   Marcus Tullius Cicero, master of the best Latin style.
79. *Ulpian*   Dominius Ulpianus, died 228 A.D., whose style was regarded as degenerate.

89. *mortcloth*   cloth to cover the dead.
99. *Elucescebat*   "he was famous."
108. *Term*   a pillar adorned with a head or bust.

That in his struggle throws the thyrsus down,   110
To comfort me on my entablature
Whereon I am to lie till I must ask
"Do I live, am I dead?" There, leave me, there!
For ye have stabbed me with ingratitude
To death—ye wish it—God, ye wish it! Stone—   115
Gritstone, a-crumble! Clammy squares which sweat
As if the corpse they keep were oozing through—
And no more *lapis* to delight the world!
Well go! I bless ye. Fewer tapers there,
But in a row: and, going, turn your backs   120
—Aye, like departing altar-ministrants,
And leave me in my church, the church for peace,
That I may watch at leisure if he leers—
Old Gandolf, at me, from his onion-stone,
As still he envied me, so fair she was!   125

EMILY BRONTË
(*1818–1848*)

·

REMEMBRANCE

Cold in the earth—and the deep snow piled above thee,
   Far, far removed, cold in the dreary grave!
Have I forgot, my only Love, to love thee,
   Severed at last by Time's all-severing wave?

Now, when alone, do my thoughts no longer hover   5
   Over the mountains, on that northern shore,
Resting their wings where heath and fern leaves cover
   Thy noble heart for ever, ever more?

Cold in the earth—and fifteen wild Decembers,
   From those brown hills, have melted into spring;   10
Faithful, indeed, is the spirit that remembers
   After such years of change and suffering!

Sweet Love of youth, forgive, if I forget thee,
   While the world's tide is bearing me along;
Other desires and other hopes beset me,   15
   Hopes which obscure, but cannot do thee wrong!

No later light has lightened up my heaven,
  No second morn has ever shone for me;
All my life's bliss from thy dear life was given,
  All my life's bliss is in the grave with thee.   20

But when the days of golden dreams had perished,
  And even Despair was powerless to destroy,
Then did I learn how existence could be cherished,
  Strengthened and fed without the aid of joy.

Then did I check the tears of useless passion—   25
  Weaned my young soul from yearning after thine;
Sternly denied its burning wish to hasten
  Down to that tomb already more than mine.

And, even yet, I dare not let it languish,
  Dare not indulge in memory's rapturous pain;   30
Once drinking deep of that divinest anguish,
  How could I seek the empty world again?

⤜☼⤛

THOMAS HARDY
(1840–1928)

·

NEUTRAL TONES

We stood by a pond that winter day,
And the sun was white, as though chidden of God,
And a few leaves lay on the starving sod;
    —They had fallen from an ash, and were gray.

Your eyes on me were as eyes that rove 5
Over tedious riddles of years ago;
And some words played between us to and fro
    On which lost the more by our love.

The smile on your mouth was the deadest thing
Alive enough to have strength to die; 10
And a grin of bitterness swept thereby
    Like an ominous bird a-wing. . . .

Since then, keen lessons that love deceives,
And wrings with wrong, have shaped to me
Your face, and the God-cursed sun, and a tree, 15
    And a pond edged with grayish leaves.

A BROKEN APPOINTMENT

    You did not come,
And marching Time drew on, and wore me numb.—
Yet less for loss of your dear presence there
Than that I thus found lacking in your make
That high compassion which can overbear 5
Reluctance for pure loving kindness' sake
Grieved I, when, as the hope-hour stroked its sum,
    You did not come.

    You love not me,
And love alone can lend you loyalty; 10
—I know and knew it.   But, unto the store
Of human deeds divine in all but name,
Was it not worth a little hour or more

To add yet this: Once you, a woman, came
To soothe a time-torn man; even though it be   15
        You love not me?

THE DARKLING THRUSH

I leant upon a coppice gate
        When Frost was specter-gray,
And Winter's dregs made desolate
        The weakening eye of day.
The tangled bine-stems scored the sky   5
        Like strings of broken lyres,
And all mankind that haunted nigh
        Had sought their household fires.

The land's sharp features seemed to be
        The Century's corpse outleant,   10
His crypt the cloudy canopy,
        The wind his death-lament.
The ancient pulse of germ and birth
        Was shrunken hard and dry,
And every spirit upon earth   15
        Seemed fervorless as I.

At once a voice arose among
        The bleak twigs overhead
In a full-hearted evensong
        Of joy illimited;   20
An aged thrush, frail, gaunt, and small,
        In blast-beruffled plume,
Had chosen thus to fling his soul
        Upon the growing gloom.

So little cause for carolings   25
        Of such ecstatic sound
Was written on terrestrial things
        Afar or nigh around,
That I could think there trembled through
        His happy good-night air   30
Some blessed Hope, whereof he knew
        And I was unaware.

DECEMBER 1900.

ON THE DEPARTURE PLATFORM

We kissed at the barrier; and passing through
She left me, and moment by moment got
Smaller and smaller, until to my view
     She was but a spot;

A wee white spot of muslin fluff   5
That down the diminishing platform bore
Through hustling crowds of gentle and rough
     To the carriage door.

Under the lamplight's fitful glowers,
Behind dark groups from far and near,   10
Whose interests were apart from ours,
     She would disappear,

Then show again, till I ceased to see
That flexible form, that nebulous white;
And she who was more than my life to me   15
     Had vanished quite. . . .

We have penned new plans since that fair fond day,
And in season she will appear again—
Perhaps in the same soft white array—
     But never as then!   20

—"And why, young man, must eternally fly
A joy you'll repeat, if you love her well?"
—O friend, nought happens twice thus; why,
     I cannot tell!

THE CONVERGENCE OF THE TWAIN
(LINES ON THE LOSS OF THE "TITANIC")

     In a solitude of the sea
     Deep from human vanity,
And the Pride of Life that planned her, stilly couches she.

     Steel chambers, late the pyres
     Of her salamandrine fires,   5
Cold currents thrid, and turn to rhythmic tidal lyres.

Over the mirrors meant
To glass the opulent
The sea-worm crawls—grotesque, slimed, dumb, indifferent.

Jewels in joy designed   10
To ravish the sensuous mind
Lie lightless, all their sparkles bleared and black and blind.

Dim moon-eyed fishes near
Gaze at the gilded gear
And query: "What does this vaingloriousness down here?" . . . 15

Well: while was fashioning
This creature of cleaving wing,
The Immanent Will that stirs and urges everything

Prepared a sinister mate
For her—so gaily great—   20
A Shape of Ice, for the time far and dissociate.

And as the smart ship grew
In stature, grace, and hue,
In shadowy silent distance grew the Iceberg too.

Alien they seemed to be: 25
No mortal eye could see
The intimate welding of their later history.

Or sign that they were bent
By paths coincident
On being anon twin halves of one august event,   30

Till the Spinner of the Years
Said "Now!" And each one hears,
And consummation comes, and jars two hemispheres.

AFTER A JOURNEY

Hereto I come to view a voiceless ghost;
    Whither, O whither will its whim now draw me?
Up the cliff, down, till I'm lonely, lost,
    And the unseen waters' ejaculations awe me.
Where you will next be there's no knowing,   5
    Facing round about me everywhere,
        With your nut-colored hair,
And gray eyes, and rose-flush coming and going.

Yes: I have re-entered your olden haunts at last;
 Through the years, through the dead scenes I have tracked
   you;   10
What have you now found to say of our past—
 Scanned across the dark space wherein I have lacked you?
Summer gave us sweets, but autumn wrought division?
 Things were not lastly as firstly well
  With us twain, you tell?   15
But all's closed now, despite Time's derision.

I see what you are doing: you are leading me on
 To the spots we knew when we haunted here together,
The waterfall, above which the mist-bow shone
 At the then fair hour in the then fair weather, 20
And the cave just under, with a voice still so hollow
 That it seems to call out to me from forty years ago,
  When you were all aglow,
And not the thin ghost that I now frailly follow!

Ignorant of what there is flitting here to see, 25
 The waked birds preen and the seals flop lazily,
Soon you will have, Dear, to vanish from me,
 For the stars close their shutters and the dawn whitens hazily.
Trust me, I mind not, though Life lours,
 The bringing me here; nay, bring me here again! 30
  I am just the same as when
Our days were a joy, and our paths through flowers.

THE OXEN

 Christmas Eve, and twelve of the clock.
  "Now they are all on their knees,"
 An elder said as we sat in a flock
  By the embers in hearthside ease.

 We pictured the meek mild creatures where 5
  They dwelt in their strawy pen,
 Nor did it occur to one of us there
  To doubt they were kneeling then.

 So fair a fancy few would weave
  In these years! Yet, I feel, 10
 If someone said on Christmas Eve,
  "Come; see the oxen kneel,

"In the lonely barton by yonder coomb
Our childhood used to know,"
I should go with him in the gloom,   15
Hoping it might be so.

MIDNIGHT ON THE GREAT WESTERN

In the third-class seat sat the journeying boy,
And the roof-lamp's oily flame
Played down on his listless form and face,
Bewrapt past knowing to what he was going,
Or whence he came.   5

In the band of his hat the journeying boy
Had a ticket stuck; and a string
Around his neck bore the key of his box,
That twinkled gleams of the lamp's sad beams
Like a living thing.   10

What past can be yours, O journeying boy
Towards a world unknown,
Who calmly, as if incurious quite
On all at stake, can undertake
This plunge alone?   15

Knows your soul a sphere, O journeying boy,
Our rude realms far above,
Whence with spacious vision you mark and mete
This region of sin that you find you in,
But are not of?   20

13. *barton* farmyard; *coomb* narrow ravine.

THE FALLOW DEER AT
THE LONELY HOUSE

One without looks in tonight
    Through the curtain-chink
From the sheet of glistening white;
One without looks in tonight
    As we sit and think   5
    By the fender-brink.

We do not discern those eyes
    Watching in the snow;
Lit by lamps of rosy dyes
We do not discern those eyes   10
    Wondering, aglow,
    Fourfooted, tiptoe.

6. *fender-brink* edge of the low metal frame around a fireplace.

GERARD MANLEY HOPKINS
(*1844–1889*)

·

GOD'S GRANDEUR

The world is charged with the grandeur of God.
 It will flame out, like shining from shook foil;
 It gathers to a greatness, like the ooze of oil
Crushed. Why do men then now not reck his rod?
Generations have trod, have trod, have trod;   5
 And all is seared with trade; bleared, smeared with toil;
 And wears man's smudge and shares man's smell: the soil
Is bare now, nor can foot feel, being shod.

And for all this, nature is never spent;
 There lives the dearest freshness deep down things; 10
And though the last lights off the black West went
 Oh, morning, at the brown brink eastward, springs—
Because the Holy Ghost over the bent
 World broods with warm breast and with ah! bright wings.

THE STARLIGHT NIGHT

Look at the stars! look, look up at the skies!
 O look at all the fire-folk sitting in the air!
 The bright boroughs, the circle-citadels there!
Down in dim woods the diamond delves! the elves'-eyes!
The grey lawns cold where gold, where quickgold lies! 5
 Wind-beat whitebeam! airy abeles set on a flare!
 Flake-doves sent floating forth at a farmyard scare!—
Ah well! it is all a purchase, all is a prize.

Buy then! bid then!—What?—Prayer, patience, alms, vows.
 Look, look: a May-mess, like on orchard boughs! 10
 Look! March-bloom, like on mealed-with-yellow sallows!

2. *foil* "I mean foil in its sense of leaf or tinsel . . . Shaken goldfoil gives off broad glows like sheet lightning . . ." (Hopkins).

4. *delves* pits, caves.
6. *whitebeam* tree having large leaves with white silky hairs on the underside; *abeles* white poplars.
10. *May-mess* cf. "a mess of greens."
11. *sallows* European broad-leaved willows.

These are indeed the barn; withindoors house
The shocks. This piece-bright paling shuts the spouse
Christ home, Christ and his mother and all his hallows.

THE WINDHOVER
TO CHRIST OUR LORD

I caught this morning morning's minion, king-
dom of daylight's dauphin, dapple-dawn-drawn Falcon, in his
riding
Of the rolling level underneath him steady air, and striding
High there, how he rung upon the rein of a wimpling wing
In his ecstasy! then off, off forth on swing,   5
As a skate's heel sweeps smooth on a bow-bend: the hurl and
gliding
Rebuffed the big wind. My heart in hiding
Stirred for a bird,—the achieve of, the mastery of the thing!

Brute beauty and valor and act, oh, air, pride, plume, here
Buckle! AND the fire that breaks from thee then, a billion   10
Times told lovelier, more dangerous, O my chevalier!

No wonder of it: shéer plód makes plough down sillion
Shine, and blue-bleak embers, ah my dear,
Fall, gall themselves, and gash gold-vermilion.

PIED BEAUTY

Glory be to God for dappled things—
For skies of couple-color as a brinded cow;
For rose-moles all in stipple upon trout that swim;
Fresh-firecoal chestnut-falls; finches' wings;
Landscape plotted and pieced—fold, fallow, and plough;   5
And áll trádes, their gear and tackle and trim.

All things counter, original, spare, strange;
Whatever is fickle, freckled (who knows how?)
With swift, slow; sweet, sour; adazzle, dim;
He fathers-forth whose beauty is past change: 10
Praise him.

4. *rung upon the rein* a term of horse-manship: the curving flight of the bird is compared to the circular motion of a horse at the end of the trainer's rein; *wimpling* (1) beautifully curved, and pleated quill over quill and (2) swinging, fluttering.
12. *sillion* furrow.
13. *embers* of a coal fire.

2. *brinded* brindled, streaked.

IN THE VALLEY OF THE ELWY

I remember a house where all were good
  To me, God knows, deserving no such thing:
  Comforting smell breathed at very entering,
Fetched fresh, as I suppose, off some sweet wood.
That cordial air made those kind people a hood   5
  All over, as a bevy of eggs the mothering wing
  Will, or mild nights the new morsels of spring:
Why, it seemed of course; seemed of right it should.

Lovely the woods, waters, meadows, combes, vales,
All the air things wear that build this world of Wales; 10
  Only the inmate does not correspond:
God, lover of souls, swaying considerate scales,
Complete thy creature dear O where it fails,
  Being mighty a master, being a father and fond.

THE CANDLE INDOORS

Some candle clear burns somewhere I come by.
I muse at how its being puts blissful back
With yellowy moisture mild night's blear-all black,
Or to-fro tender trambeams truckle at the eye.
By that window what task what fingers ply,   5
I plod wondering, a-wanting, just for lack
Of answer the eagerer a-wanting Jessy or Jack
There God to aggrándize, God to glorify.—
Come you indoors, come home; your fading fire
Mend first and vital candle in close heart's vault: 10
You there are master, do your own desire;
What hinders? Are you beam-blind, yet to a fault
In a neighbor deft-handed? Are you that liar
And, cast by conscience out, spendsavour salt?

1. *house* in the valley of the Elwy.
9. *combes* narrow, ravine-like valleys.

4. *trambeams* a *tram* a continuous line of timber; *beams* here, of the lines of light that seem to run to the eye from the candle; they *truckle,* that is, obey the eye as it moves.

SPRING AND FALL
TO A YOUNG CHILD

Márgarét, are you gríeving
Over Goldengrove unleaving?
Leáves, líke the things of man, you
With your fresh thoughts care for, can you?
Áh! ás the heart grows older   5
It will come to such sights colder
By and by, nor spare a sigh
Though worlds of wanwood leafmeal lie;
And yet you wíll weep and know why.
Now no matter, child, the name: 10
Sórrow's spríngs áre the same.
Nor mouth had, no nor mind, expressed
What heart heard of, ghost guessed:
It ís the blight man was born for,
It is Margaret you mourn for.   15

(CARRION COMFORT)

Not, I'll not, carrion comfort, Despair, not feast on thee;
Not untwist—slack they may be—these last strands of man
In me ór, most weary, cry *I can no more*. I can;
Can something, hope, wish day come, not choose not to be.
But ah, but O thou terrible, why wouldst thou rude on me   5
Thy wring-world right foot rock? lay a lionlimb against me? scan
With darksome devouring eyes my bruisèd bones? and fan,
O in turns of tempest, me heaped there; me frantic to avoid thee
    and flee?

  Why? That my chaff might fly; my grain lie, sheer and clear.
Nay in all that toil, that coil, since (seems) I kissed the rod,   10
Hand rather, my heart lo! lapped strength, stole joy, would laugh,
    chéer.
Cheer whom though? the hero whose heaven-handling flung me,
    fóot tród
Me? or me that fought him? O which one? is it each one? That
    night, that year
Of now done darkness I wretch lay wrestling with (my God!) my
    God.

13. *ghost* spirit.

NO WORST, THERE IS NONE

No worst, there is none. Pitched past pitch of grief,
More pangs will, schooled at forepangs, wilder wring.
Comforter, where, where is your comforting?
Mary, mother of us, where is your relief?
My cries heave, herds-long, huddle in a main, a chief   5
Woe, world-sorrow; on an age-old anvil wince and sing—
Then lull, then leave off. Fury had shrieked "No ling-
ering! Let me be fell: force I must be brief."

O the mind, mind has mountains; cliffs of fall
Frightful, sheer, no-man-fathomed. Hold them cheap   10
May who ne'er hung there. Nor does long our small
Durance deal with that steep or deep. Here! creep,
Wretch, under a comfort serves in a whirlwind: all
Life death does end and each day dies with sleep.

(THOU ART INDEED JUST, LORD)

*Justus quidem tu es, Domine, si disputem tecum: verumtamen justa
loquar ad te: Quare via impiorum prosperatur? etc.*

Thou art indeed just, Lord, if I contend
With thee; but, sir, so what I plead is just.
Why do sinners' ways prosper? and why must
Disappointment all I endeavor end?
    Wert thou my enemy, O thou my friend,   5
How wouldst thou worse, I wonder, than thou dost
Defeat, thwart me? Oh, the sots and thralls of lust
Do in spare hours more thrive than I that spend,
Sir, life upon thy cause. See, banks and brakes
Now, leavèd how thick! lacèd they are again   10
With fretty chervil, look, and fresh wind shakes
Them; birds build—but not I build; no, but strain,
Time's eunuch, and not breed one work that wakes.
Mine, O thou lord of life, send my roots rain.

---

8. *force* perforce.

Justus . . . etc. from *Jeremiah* xii.1,
in the Latin version of the Vulgate;
translated in the first three lines of the
poem.

11. *chervil* herb of the carrot family,
with divided leaves; *fretty* as if orna-
mented with openwork.

WILLIAM BUTLER YEATS
(1865–1939)

·

THE FOLLY OF BEING COMFORTED

One that is ever kind said yesterday:
"Your well-belovéd's hair has threads of gray,
And little shadows come about her eyes;
Time can but make it easier to be wise
Though now it seem impossible, and so   5
Patience is all that you have need of."
                                        No,
I have not a crumb of comfort, not a grain.
Time can but make her beauty over again:
Because of that great nobleness of hers
The fire that stirs about her, when she stirs,   10
Burns but more clearly. O she had not these ways
When all the wild summer was in her gaze.
O heart! O heart! if she'd but turn her head,
You'd know the folly of being comforted.

NO SECOND TROY

Why should I blame her that she filled my days
With misery, or that she would of late
Have taught to ignorant men most violent ways,
Or hurled the little streets upon the great,
Had they but courage equal to desire?   5
What could have made her peaceful with a mind
That nobleness made simple as a fire,
With beauty like a tightened bow, a kind
That is not natural in an age like this,
Being high and solitary and most stern?   10
Why, what could she have done, being what she is?
Was there another Troy for her to burn?

The Folly of Being Comforted   the text
printed here is from *Later Poems,* 1924.
1. *her*   an allusion to Yeats's love,
Maud Gonne, active in the Irish revolu-
tionary movement.

309

THE MAGI

Now as at all times I can see in the mind's eye,
In their stiff, painted clothes, the pale unsatisfied ones
Appear and disappear in the blue depth of the sky
With all their ancient faces like rain-beaten stones,
And all their helms of silver hovering side by side,   5
And all their eyes still fixed, hoping to find once more,
Being by Calvary's turbulence unsatisfied,
The uncontrollable mystery on the bestial floor.

MEN IMPROVE WITH THE YEARS

I am worn out with dreams;
A weather-worn, marble triton
Among the streams;
And all day long I look
Upon this lady's beauty   5
As though I had found in a book
A pictured beauty,
Pleased to have filled the eyes
Or the discerning ears,
Delighted to be but wise,   10
For men improve with the years;
And yet, and yet,
Is this my dream, or the truth?
O would that we had met
When I had my burning youth!   15
But I grow old among dreams,
A weather-worn, marble triton
Among the streams.

THE FISHERMAN

Although I can see him still,
The freckled man who goes
To a grey place on a hill
In grey Connemara clothes
At dawn to cast his flies,   5
It's long since I began

The Magi "I had noticed . . . how all thought among us is frozen into 'something other than human life'" (Yeats).

2. triton the merman of Greek myth-ology; a common sculptured figure for a fountain.

4. Connemara a region in Galway, Ireland.

To call up to the eyes
This wise and simple man.
All day I'd looked in the face
What I had hoped 'twould be   10
To write for my own race
And the reality;
The living men that I hate,
The dead man that I loved,
The craven man in his seat,   15
The insolent unreproved,
And no knave brought to book
Who has won a drunken cheer,
The witty man and his joke
Aimed at the commonest ear,   20
The clever man who cries
The catch-cries of the clown,
The beating down of the wise
And great Art beaten down.

Maybe a twelvemonth since   25
Suddenly I began,
In scorn of this audience,
Imagining a man,
And his sun-freckled face,
And grey Connemara cloth,   30
Climbing up to a place
Where stone is dark under froth,
And the down-turn of his wrist
When the flies drop in the stream;
A man who does not exist,   35
A man who is but a dream;
And cried, 'Before I am old
I shall have written him one
Poem maybe as cold
And passionate as the dawn.'   40

EASTER 1916

I have met them at close of day
Coming with vivid faces
From counter or desk among gray

---

12. *reality* referring to Yeats's disheartening experience with the Irish literary and theatrical audience.
14. *man* John Synge, playwright; his *Playboy of the Western World* caused a riot when it was first produced.

Easter 1916 written after an insurrection of Irish nationalists on Easter Monday, 1916. Fifteen men were executed by the English, including the four commemorated here (lines 24–38; **75, 76**).

Eighteenth-century houses.
I have passed with a nod of the head   5
Or polite meaningless words,
Or have lingered awhile and said
Polite meaningless words,
And thought before I had done
Of a mocking tale or a gibe   10
To please a companion
Around the fire at the club,
Being certain that they and I
But lived where motley is worn:
All changed, changed utterly: 15
A terrible beauty is born.

That woman's days were spent
In ignorant good-will,
Her nights in argument
Until her voice grew shrill.   20
What voice more sweet than hers
When, young and beautiful,
She rode to harriers?
This man had kept a school
And rode our wingéd horse;   25
This other his helper and friend
Was coming into his force;
He might have won fame in the end,
So sensitive his nature seemed,
So daring and sweet his thought.   30
This other man I had dreamed
A drunken, vainglorious lout.
He had done most bitter wrong
To some who are near my heart,
Yet I number him in the song;   35
He, too, has resigned his part
In the casual comedy;
He, too, has been changed in his turn,
Transformed utterly:
A terrible beauty is born.   40

Hearts with one purpose alone
Through summer and winter seem

17. *woman* Countess Markiewicz, imprisoned for life for her part in the Easter rising.
24. *man* Patrick Pearse, teacher of Gaelic.
26. *other* Thomas MacDonagh, a writer.
31. *man* John MacBride, husband of Maud Gonne.

Enchanted to a stone
To trouble the living stream.
The horse that comes from the road,   45
The rider, the birds that range
From cloud to tumbling cloud,
Minute by minute they change;
A shadow of cloud on the stream
Changes minute by minute;   50
A horse-hoof slides on the brim,
And a horse plashes within it;
The long-legged moor-hens dive,
And hens to moor-cocks call;
Minute by minute they live: 55
The stone's in the midst of all.

Too long a sacrifice
Can make a stone of the heart.
O when may it suffice?
That is Heaven's part, our part   60
To murmur name upon name,
As a mother names her child
When sleep at last has come
On limbs that had run wild.
What is it but nightfall?   65
No, no, not night but death;
Was it needless death after all?
For England may keep faith
For all that is done and said.
We know their dream; enough   70
To know they dreamed and are dead;
And what if excess of love
Bewildered them till they died?
I write it out in a verse—
MacDonagh and MacBride   75
And Connolly and Pearse
Now and in time to be,
Wherever green is worn,
Are changed, changed utterly:
A terrible beauty is born.   80

SEPTEMBER 25, 1916

76. *Connolly*   James Connolly, Pearse's partner in the insurrection.

ON A POLITICAL PRISONER

She that but little patience knew,
From childhood on, had now so much
A gray gull lost its fear and flew
Down to her cell and there alit,
And there endured her fingers' touch   5
And from her fingers ate its bit.

Did she in touching that lone wing
Recall the years before her mind
Became a bitter, an abstract thing,
Her thought some popular enmity: 10
Blind and leader of the blind
Drinking the foul ditch where they lie?

When long ago I saw her ride
Under Ben Bulben to the meet,
The beauty of her countryside   15
With all youth's lonely wildness stirred,
She seemed to have grown clean and sweet
Like any rock-bred, sea-borne bird:

Sea-borne, or balanced on the air
When first it sprang out of the nest   20
Upon some lofty rock to stare
Upon the cloudy canopy,
While under its storm-beaten breast
Cried out the hollows of the sea.

THE SECOND COMING

Turning and turning in the widening gyre
The falcon cannot hear the falconer;
Things fall apart; the center cannot hold;
Mere anarchy is loosed upon the world,
The blood-dimmed tide is loosed, and everywhere   5
The ceremony of innocence is drowned;
The best lack all conviction, while the worst
Are full of passionate intensity.

Prisoner   Countess Markiewicz; see
Easter 1916, line 17 and note.
14. *Ben Bulben*   mountain near which
Yeats lived in his younger years.

1. *gyre*   a spiral; cf. *Sailing to Byzantium,* p. 317, line 19 (also, a symbol
for a cycle of history).

Surely some revelation is at hand;
Surely the Second Coming is at hand.   10
The Second Coming! Hardly are those words out
When a vast image out of *Spiritus Mundi*
Troubles my sight: somewhere in sands of the desert
A shape with lion body and the head of a man,
A gaze blank and pitiless as the sun,   15
Is moving its slow thighs, while all about it
Reel shadows of the indignant desert birds.
The darkness drops again; but now I know
That twenty centuries of stony sleep
Were vexed to nightmare by a rocking cradle,   20
And what rough beast, its hour come round at last,
Slouches towards Bethlehem to be born?

A PRAYER FOR MY DAUGHTER

Once more the storm is howling, and half hid
Under this cradle-hood and coverlid
My child sleeps on. There is no obstacle
But Gregory's wood and one bare hill
Whereby the haystack- and roof-leveling wind,   5
Bred on the Atlantic, can be stayed;
And for an hour I have walked and prayed
Because of the great gloom that is in my mind.

I have walked and prayed for this young child an hour
And heard the sea-wind scream upon the tower,   10
And under the arches of the bridge, and scream
In the elms above the flooded stream;
Imagining in excited reverie
That the future years had come,
Dancing to a frenzied drum,   15
Out of the murderous innocence of the sea.

May she be granted beauty and yet not
Beauty to make a stranger's eye distraught,
Or hers before a looking-glass, for such,
Being made beautiful overmuch,   20
Consider beauty a sufficient end,

---

12. *Spiritus Mundi* spirit or soul of
the universe, in which all individual
souls are connected; also, the Great
Memory; for Yeats, nearly equal to the
subconscious.

4. *Gregory*   Lady Gregory, Yeats's
friend and literary associate.
13. *reverie*   on this vision (lines 14–
16) see *The Second Coming*, especially
lines 4–6.

Lose natural kindness and maybe
The heart-revealing intimacy
That chooses right, and never find a friend.

Helen being chosen found life flat and dull   25
And later had much trouble from a fool,
While that great Queen, that rose out of the spray,
Being fatherless could have her way
Yet chose a bandy-leggèd smith for man.
It's certain that fine women eat   30
A crazy salad with their meat
Whereby the Horn of Plenty is undone.

In courtesy I'd have her chiefly learned;
Hearts are not had as a gift but hearts are earned
By those that are not entirely beautiful;   35
Yet many, that have played the fool
For beauty's very self, has charm made wise,
And many a poor man that has roved,
Loved and thought himself beloved,
From a glad kindness cannot take his eyes.   40

May she become a flourishing hidden tree
That all her thoughts may like the linnet be,
And have no business but dispensing round
Their magnanimities of sound,
Nor but in merriment begin a chase,   45
Nor but in merriment a quarrel.
O may she live like some green laurel
Rooted in one dear perpetual place.

My mind, because the minds that I have loved,
The sort of beauty that I have approved,   50
Prosper but little, has dried up of late,
Yet knows that to be choked with hate
May well be of all evil chances chief.
If there's no hatred in a mind
Assault and battery of the wind   55
Can never tear the linnet from the leaf.

An intellectual hatred is the worst,
So let her think opinions are accursed.
Have I not seen the loveliest woman born

26. *fool*   Paris, who carried off Helen
of Troy.
27. *Queen*   Aphrodite, goddess of
beauty, who chose the crippled "smith,"
Hephaestus, for her lover.
59. *woman*   Maud Gonne; see *No Second Troy*, line 1, note; and *Easter 1916*, line 31, note.

Out of the mouth of Plenty's horn,   60
Because of her opinionated mind
Barter that horn and every good
By quiet natures understood
For an old bellows full of angry wind?

Considering that, all hatred driven hence,   65
The soul recovers radical innocence
And learns at last that it is self-delighting,
Self-appeasing, self-affrighting,
And that its own sweet will is Heaven's will;
She can, though every face should scowl   70
And every windy quarter howl
Or every bellows burst, be happy still.

And may her bridegroom bring her to a house
Where all's accustomed, ceremonious;
For arrogance and hatred are the wares   75
Peddled in the thoroughfares.
How but in custom and in ceremony
Are innocence and beauty born?
Ceremony's a name for the rich horn,
And custom for the spreading laurel tree.   80

SAILING TO BYZANTIUM

That is no country for old men. The young
In one another's arms, birds in the trees
—Those dying generations—at their song,
The salmon-falls, the mackerel-crowded seas,
Fish, flesh, or fowl, commend all summer long   5
Whatever is begotten, born, and dies.
Caught in that sensual music all neglect
Monuments of unaging intellect.

An aged man is but a paltry thing,
A tattered coat upon a stick, unless   10
Soul clap its hands and sing, and louder sing
For every tatter in its mortal dress,
Nor is there singing school but studying
Monuments of its own magnificence;
And therefore I have sailed the seas and come   15
To the holy city of Byzantium.

Byzantium capital of the Eastern Roman Empire, the "holy city" of the Greek Orthodox Church, noted for the extreme purity of its intellectual life and for its relatively unnaturalistic art. 1. *That* Ireland, but also like "Byzantium," more than an actual place.

O sages standing in God's holy fire
As in the gold mosaic of a wall,
Come from the holy fire, perne in a gyre,
And be the singing-masters of my soul.   20
Consume my heart away; sick with desire
And fastened to a dying animal
It knows not what it is; and gather me
Into the artifice of eternity.

Once out of nature I shall never take   25
My bodily form from any natural thing,
But such a form as Grecian goldsmiths make
Of hammered gold and gold enameling
To keep a drowsy Emperor awake;
Or set upon a golden bough to sing   30
To lords and ladies of Byzantium
Of what is past, or passing, or to come.

LEDA AND THE SWAN

A sudden blow: the great wings beating still
Above the staggering girl, her thighs caressed
By the dark webs, her nape caught in his bill,
He holds her helpless breast upon his breast.

How can those terrified vague fingers push   5
The feathered glory from her loosening thighs?
And how can body, laid in that white rush,
But feel the strange heart beating where it lies?

A shudder in the loins engenders there
The broken wall, the burning roof and tower   10
And Agamemnon dead.
                Being so caught up,
So mastered by the brute blood of the air,
Did she put on his knowledge with his power
Before the indifferent beak could let her drop?

17. *sages* figures in the mosaics of Saint Sophia ("Holy Wisdom").
19. *perne* spool; on *gyre* see *The Second Coming*, line 1, note.
27. *form* "in the Emperor's palace at Byzantium [there] was a tree made of gold and silver, and artificial birds that sang" (Yeats).

Swan Leda, loved by Zeus in the form of a swan, became the mother of Helen of Troy.
11. *Agamemnon* the leader of the Greek expedition against Troy.

AFTER LONG SILENCE

Speech after long silence; it is right,
All other lovers being estranged or dead,
Unfriendly lamplight hid under its shade,
The curtains drawn upon unfriendly night,
That we descant and yet again descant   5
Upon the supreme theme of Art and Song:
Bodily decrepitude is wisdom; young
We loved each other and were ignorant.

ROBERT FROST
(1874–1963)

·

MOWING

There was never a sound beside the wood but one,
And that was my long scythe whispering to the ground.
What was it it whispered? I knew not well myself;
Perhaps it was something about the heat of the sun,
Something, perhaps, about the lack of sound—   5
And that was why it whispered and did not speak.
It was no dream of the gift of idle hours,
Or easy gold at the hand of fay or elf:
Anything more than the truth would have seemed too weak
To the earnest love that laid the swale in rows,   10
Not without feeble-pointed spikes of flowers
(Pale orchises), and scared a bright green snake.
The fact is the sweetest dream that labor knows.
My long scythe whispered and left the hay to make.

A SERVANT TO SERVANTS

I didn't make you know how glad I was
To have you come and camp here on our land.
I promised myself to get down some day
And see the way you lived, but I don't know!
With a houseful of hungry men to feed   5
I guess you'd find. . . . It seems to me
I can't express my feelings any more
Than I can raise my voice or want to lift
My hand (oh, I can lift it when I have to).
Did ever you feel so? I hope you never.   10
It's got so I don't even know for sure
Whether I *am* glad, sorry, or anything.
There's nothing but a voice-like left inside
That seems to tell me how I ought to feel,
And would feel if I wasn't all gone wrong.   15
You take the lake. I look and look at it.
I see it's a fair, pretty sheet of water.
I stand and make myself repeat out loud
The advantages it has, so long and narrow,

Like a deep piece of some old running river   20
Cut short off at both ends. It lies five miles
Straight away through the mountain notch
From the sink window where I wash the plates,
And all our storms come up toward the house,
Drawing the slow waves whiter and whiter and whiter.   25
It took my mind off doughnuts and soda biscuit
To step outdoors and take the water dazzle
A sunny morning, or take the rising wind
About my face and body and through my wrapper,
When a storm threatened from the Dragon's Den,   30
And a cold chill shivered across the lake.
I see it's a fair, pretty sheet of water,
Our Willoughby! How did you hear of it?
I expect, though, everyone's heard of it.
In a book about ferns? Listen to that!   35
You let things more like feathers regulate
Your going and coming. And you like it here?
I can see how you might. But I don't know!
It would be different if more people came,
For then there would be business. As it is,   40
The cottages Len built, sometimes we rent them,
Sometimes we don't. We've a good piece of shore
That ought to be worth something, and may yet.
But I don't count on it as much as Len.
He looks on the bright side of everything,   45
Including me. He thinks I'll be all right
With doctoring. But it's not medicine—
Lowe is the only doctor's dared to say so—
It's rest I want—there, I have said it out—
From cooking meals for hungry hired men   50
And washing dishes after them—from doing
Things over and over that just won't stay done.
By good rights I ought not to have so much
Put on me, but there seems no other way.
Len says one steady pull more ought to do it.   55
He says the best way out is always through.
And I agree to that, or in so far
As that I can see no way out but through—
Leastways for me—and then they'll be convinced.
It's not that Len don't want the best for me.   60
It was his plan our moving over in
Beside the lake from where that day I showed you
We used to live—ten miles from anywhere.
We didn't change without some sacrifice,

But Len went at it to make up the loss.   65
His work's a man's, of course, from sun to sun,
But he works when he works as hard as I do—
Though there's small profit in comparisons.
(Women and men will make them all the same.)
But work ain't all. Len undertakes too much.   70
He's into everything in town. This year
It's highways, and he's got too many men
Around him to look after that make waste.
They take advantage of him shamefully,
And proud, too, of themselves for doing so.   75
We have four here to board, great good-for-nothings,
Sprawling about the kitchen with their talk
While I fry their bacon. Much they care!
No more put out in what they do or say
Than if I wasn't in the room at all.   80
Coming and going all the time, they are:
I don't learn what their names are, let alone
Their characters, or whether they are safe
To have inside the house with doors unlocked.
I'm not afraid of them, though, if they're not   85
Afraid of me. There's two can play at that.
I have my fancies: it runs in the family.
My father's brother wasn't right. They kept him
Locked up for years back there at the old farm.
I've been away once—yes, I've been away.   90
The State Asylum. I was prejudiced;
I wouldn't have sent anyone of mine there;
You know the old idea—the only asylum
Was the poorhouse, and those who could afford,
Rather than send their folks to such a place,   95
Kept them at home; and it does seem more human.
But it's not so: the place is the asylum.
There they have every means proper to do with,
And you aren't darkening other people's lives—
Worse than no good to them, and they no good   100
To you in your condition; you can't know
Affection or the want of it in that state.
I've heard too much of the old-fashioned way.
My father's brother, he went mad quite young.
Some thought he had been bitten by a dog,   105
Because his violence took on the form
Of carrying his pillow in his teeth;
But it's more likely he was crossed in love,
Or so the story goes. It was some girl.

Anyway all he talked about was love.   110
They soon saw he would do someone a mischief
If he wa'n't kept strict watch of, and it ended
In father's building him a sort of cage,
Or room within a room, of hickory poles,
Like stanchions in the barn, from floor to ceiling,—   115
A narrow passage all the way around.
Anything they put in for furniture
He'd tear to pieces, even a bed to lie on.
So they made the place comfortable with straw,
Like a beast's stall, to ease their consciences.   120
Of course they had to feed him without dishes.
They tried to keep him clothed, but he paraded
With his clothes on his arm—all of his clothes.
Cruel—it sounds. I s'pose they did the best
They knew. And just when he was at the height,   125
Father and mother married, and mother came,
A bride, to help take care of such a creature,
And accommodate her young life to his.
That was what marrying father meant to her.
She had to lie and hear love things made dreadful   130
By his shouts in the night. He'd shout and shout
Until the strength was shouted out of him,
And his voice died down slowly from exhaustion.
He'd pull his bars apart like bow and bowstring,
And let them go and make them twang until   135
His hands had worn them smooth as any oxbow.
And then he'd crow as if he thought that child's play
The only fun he had. I've heard them say, though,
They found a way to put a stop to it.
He was before my time—I never saw him;   140
But the pen stayed exactly as it was
There in the upper chamber in the ell,
A sort of catch-all full of attic clutter.
I often think of the smooth hickory bars.
It got so I would say—you know, half fooling—   145
'It's time I took my turn upstairs in jail'—
Just as you will till it becomes a habit.
No wonder I was glad to get away.
Mind you, I waited till Len said the word.
I didn't want the blame if things went wrong.   150
I was glad though, no end, when we moved out,
And I looked to be happy, and I was,
As I said, for a while—but I don't know!
Somehow the change wore out like a prescription.

And there's more to it than just window-views   155
And living by a lake. I'm past such help—
Unless Len took the notion, which he won't,
And I won't ask him—it's not sure enough.
I s'pose I've got to go the road I'm going:
Other folks have to, and why shouldn't I?   160
I almost think if I could do like you,
Drop everything and live out on the ground—
But it might be, come night, I shouldn't like it,
Or a long rain. I should soon get enough,
And be glad of a good roof overhead.   165
I've lain awake thinking of you, I'll warrant,
More than you have yourself, some of these nights.
The wonder was the tents weren't snatched away
From over you as you lay in your beds.
I haven't courage for a risk like that.   170
Bless you, of course, you're keeping me from work,
But the thing of it is, I need to *be* kept.
There's work enough to do—there's always that;
But behind's behind. The worst that you can do
Is set me back a little more behind.   175
I sha'n't catch up in this world, anyway.
I'd *rather* you'd not go unless you must.

AFTER APPLE-PICKING

My long two-pointed ladder's sticking through a tree
Toward heaven still,
And there's a barrel that I didn't fill
Beside it, and there may be two or three
Apples I didn't pick upon some bough.   5
But I am done with apple-picking now.
Essence of winter sleep is on the night,
The scent of apples: I am drowsing off.
I cannot rub the strangeness from my sight
I got from looking through a pane of glass   10
I skimmed this morning from the drinking trough
And held against the world of hoary grass.
It melted, and I let it fall and break.
But I was well
Upon my way to sleep before it fell,   15
And I could tell
What form my dreaming was about to take.

Magnified apples appear and disappear,
Stem end and blossom end,
And every fleck of russet showing clear.   20
My instep arch not only keeps the ache,
It keeps the pressure of a ladder-round.
I feel the ladder sway as the boughs bend.
And I keep hearing from the cellar bin
The rumbling sound   25
Of load on load of apples coming in.
For I have had too much
Of apple-picking: I am overtired
Of the great harvest I myself desired.
There were ten thousand thousand fruit to touch,   30
Cherish in hand, lift down, and not let fall.
For all
That struck the earth,
No matter if not bruised or spiked with stubble,
Went surely to the cider-apple heap   35
As of no worth.
One can see what will trouble
This sleep of mine, whatever sleep it is.
Were he not gone,
The woodchuck could say whether it's like his   40
Long sleep, as I describe its coming on,
Or just some human sleep.

THE OVEN BIRD

There is a singer everyone has heard,
Loud, a mid-summer and a mid-wood bird,
Who makes the solid tree trunks sound again.
He says that leaves are old and that for flowers
Mid-summer is to spring as one to ten.   5
He says the early petal-fall is past
When pear and cherry bloom went down in showers
On sunny days a moment overcast;
And comes that other fall we name the fall.
He says the highway dust is over all.   10
The bird would cease and be as other birds
But that he knows in singing not to sing.
The question that he frames in all but words
Is what to make of a diminished thing.

The Oven Bird   the oven bird seems to say "teacher-teacher."

FOR ONCE, THEN, SOMETHING

Others taunt me with having knelt at well-curbs
Always wrong to the light, so never seeing
Deeper down in the well than where the water
Gives me back in a shining surface picture
Me myself in the summer heaven godlike   5
Looking out of a wreath of fern and cloud puffs.
Once, when trying with chin against a well-curb,
I discerned, as I thought, beyond the picture,
Through the picture, a something white, uncertain,
Something more of the depths—and then I lost it.   10
Water came to rebuke the too clear water.
One drop fell from a fern, and lo, a ripple
Shook whatever it was lay there at bottom,
Blurred it, blotted it out. What was that whiteness?
Truth? A pebble of quartz? For once, then, something.

SPRING POOLS

These pools that, though in forests, still reflect
The total sky almost without defect,
And like the flowers beside them, chill and shiver,
Will like the flowers beside them soon be gone,
And yet not out by any brook or river,   5
But up by roots to bring dark foliage on.

The trees that have it in their pent-up buds
To darken nature and be summer woods—
Let them think twice before they use their powers
To blot out and drink up and sweep away   10
These flowery waters and these watery flowers
From snow that melted only yesterday.

ONCE BY THE PACIFIC

The shattered water made a misty din.
Great waves looked over others coming in,
And thought of doing something to the shore
That water never did to land before.
The clouds were low and hairy in the skies,   5
Like locks blown forward in the gleam of eyes.

You could not tell, and yet it looked as if
The shore was lucky in being backed by cliff,
The cliff in being backed by continent;
It looked as if a night of dark intent   10
Was coming, and not only a night, an age.
Someone had better be prepared for rage.
There would be more than ocean-water broken
Before God's last *Put out the Light* was spoken.

ACQUAINTED WITH THE NIGHT

I have been one acquainted with the night.
I have walked out in rain—and back in rain.
I have outwalked the furthest city light.

I have looked down the saddest city lane.
I have passed by the watchman on his beat   5
And dropped my eyes, unwilling to explain.

I have stood still and stopped the sound of feet
When far away an interrupted cry
Came over houses from another street,

But not to call me back or say good-by;   10
And further still at an unearthly height,
One luminary clock against the sky

Proclaimed the time was neither wrong nor right.
I have been one acquainted with the night.

THE INVESTMENT

Over back where they speak of life as staying
('You couldn't call it living, for it ain't'),
There was an old, old house renewed with paint,
And in it a piano loudly playing.

Out in the plowed ground in the cold a digger,   5
Among unearthed potatoes standing still,
Was counting winter dinners, one a hill,
With half an ear to the piano's vigor.

All that piano and new paint back there,
Was it some money suddenly come into?   10
Or some extravagance young love had been to?
Or old love on an impulse not to care—

Not to sink under being man and wife,
But get some color and music out of life?

DESIGN

I found a dimpled spider, fat and white,
On a white heal-all, holding up a moth
Like a white piece of rigid satin cloth—
Assorted characters of death and blight
Mixed ready to begin the morning right,   5
Like the ingredients of a witches' broth—
A snow-drop spider, a flower like a froth,
And dead wings carried like a paper kite.

What had that flower to do with being white,
The wayside blue and innocent heal-all?   10
What brought the kindred spider to that height,
Then steered the white moth thither in the night?
What but design of darkness to appall?—
If design govern in a thing so small.

THE SILKEN TENT

She is as in a field a silken tent
At midday when a sunny summer breeze
Has dried the dew and all its ropes relent,
So that in guys it gently sways at ease,
And its supporting central cedar pole,   5
That is its pinnacle to heavenward
And signifies the sureness of the soul,
Seems to owe naught to any single cord,
But strictly held by none, is loosely bound
By countless silken ties of love and thought   10
To everything on earth the compass round,
And only by one's going slightly taut
In the capriciousness of summer air
Is of the slightest bondage made aware.

ALL REVELATION

A head thrusts in as for the view,
But where it is it thrusts in from
Or what it is it thrusts into
By that Cyb'laean avenue,
And what can of its coming come,   5

And whither it will be withdrawn,
And what take hence or leave behind,
These things the mind has pondered on
A moment and still asking gone.
Strange apparition of the mind!   10

But the impervious geode
Was entered, and its inner crust
Of crystals with a ray cathode
At every point and facet glowed
In answer to the mental thrust.   15

Eyes seeking the response of eyes
Bring out the stars, bring out the flowers,
Thus concentrating earth and skies
So none need be afraid of size.
All revelation has been ours.   20

COME IN

As I came to the edge of the woods,
Thrush music—hark!
Now if it was dusk outside,
Inside it was dark.

Too dark in the woods for a bird   5
By sleight of wing
To better its perch for the night,
Though it still could sing.

The last of the light of the sun
That had died in the west   10
Still lived for one song more
In a thrush's breast.

4. *Cyb'laean*   adjective from Cybele, goddess of earth.
13. *cathode* apparently   referring   to   the use of x-rays and cathode rays to study crystals in order to determine their nature.

Far in the pillared dark
Thrush music went—
Almost like a call to come in   15
To the dark and lament.

But no, I was out for stars:
I would not come in.
I meant not even if asked,
And I hadn't been.   20

DIRECTIVE

Back out of all this now too much for us,
Back in a time made simple by the loss
Of detail, burned, dissolved, and broken off
Like graveyard marble sculpture in the weather,
There is a house that is no more a house   5
Upon a farm that is no more a farm
And in a town that is no more a town.
The road there, if you'll let a guide direct you
Who only has at heart your getting lost,
May seem as if it should have been a quarry—   10
Great monolithic knees the former town
Long since gave up pretence of keeping covered.
And there's a story in a book about it:
Besides the wear of iron wagon wheels
The ledges show lines ruled southeast northwest,   15
The chisel work of an enormous Glacier
That braced his feet against the Arctic Pole.
You must not mind a certain coolness from him
Still said to haunt this side of Panther Mountain.
Nor need you mind the serial ordeal   20
Of being watched from forty cellar holes
As if by eye pairs out of forty firkins.
As for the woods' excitement over you
That sends light rustle rushes to their leaves,
Charge that to upstart inexperience.   25
Where were they all not twenty years ago?
They think too much of having shaded out
A few old pecker-fretted apple trees.
Make yourself up a cheering song of how
Someone's road home from work this once was,   30
Who may be just ahead of you on foot
Or creaking with a buggy load of grain.

The height of the adventure is the height
Of country where two village cultures faded
Into each other. Both of them are lost.   35
And if you're lost enough to find yourself
By now, pull in your ladder road behind you
And put a sign up CLOSED to all but me.
Then make yourself at home. The only field
Now left's no bigger than a harness gall.   40
First there's the children's house of make believe,
Some shattered dishes underneath a pine,
The playthings in the playhouse of the children.
Weep for what little things could make them glad.
Then for the house that is no more a house,   45
But only a belilaced cellar hole,
Now slowly closing like a dent in dough.
This was no playhouse but a house in earnest.
Your destination and your destiny's
A brook that was the water of the house,   50
Cold as a spring as yet so near its source,
Too lofty and original to rage.
(We know the valley streams that when aroused
Will leave their tatters hung on barb and thorn.)
I have kept hidden in the instep arch   55
Of an old cedar at the waterside
A broken drinking goblet like the Grail
Under a spell so the wrong ones can't find it,
So can't get saved, as Saint Mark says they mustn't.
(I stole the goblet from the children's playhouse.)   60
Here are your waters and your watering place.
Drink and be whole again beyond confusion.

59. *Saint Mark* *Mark* viii.35.

WALLACE STEVENS
(1879–1955)

.

THE SNOW MAN

One must have a mind of winter
To regard the frost and the boughs
Of the pine-trees crusted with snow;

And have been cold a long time
To behold the junipers shagged with ice,   5
The spruces rough in the distant glitter

Of the January sun; and not to think
Of any misery in the sound of the wind,
In the sound of a few leaves,

Which is the sound of the land   10
Full of the same wind
That is blowing in the same bare place

For the listener, who listens in the snow,
And, nothing himself, beholds
Nothing that is not there and the nothing that is.   15

SUNDAY MORNING

Complacencies of the peignoir, and late
Coffee and oranges in a sunny chair,
And the green freedom of a cockatoo
Upon a rug mingle to dissipate
The holy hush of ancient sacrifice.   5
She dreams a little, and she feels the dark
Encroachment of that old catastrophe,
As a calm darkens among water-lights.
The pungent oranges and bright, green wings
Seem things in some procession of the dead,   10
Winding across wide water, without sound.
The day is like wide water, without sound,
Stilled for the passing of her dreaming feet
Over the seas, to silent Palestine,
Dominion of the blood and sepulchre.   15

1. *peignoir*   a loose dressing-gown.

Why should she give her bounty to the dead?
What is divinity if it can come
Only in silent shadows and in dreams?
Shall she not find in comforts of the sun,
In pungent fruit and bright, green wings, or else   20
In any balm or beauty of the earth,
Things to be cherished like the thought of heaven?
Divinity must live within herself:
Passions of rain, or moods in falling snow;
Grievings in loneliness, or unsubdued   25
Elations when the forest blooms; gusty
Emotions on wet roads on autumn nights;
All pleasures and all pains, remembering
The bough of summer and the winter branch.
These are the measures destined for her soul.   30

Jove in the clouds had his inhuman birth.
No mother suckled him, no sweet land gave
Large-mannered motions to his mythy mind.
He moved among us, as a muttering king,
Magnificent, would move among his hinds,   35
Until our blood, commingling, virginal,
With heaven, brought such requital to desire
The very hinds discerned it, in a star.
Shall our blood fail? Or shall it come to be
The blood of paradise? And shall the earth   40
Seem all of paradise that we shall know?
The sky will be much friendlier then than now,
A part of labor and a part of pain,
And next in glory to enduring love,
Not this dividing and indifferent blue.   45

She says, "I am content when wakened birds,
Before they fly, test the reality
Of misty fields, by their sweet questionings;
But when the birds are gone, and their warm fields
Return no more, where, then, is paradise?"   50
There is not any haunt of prophecy,
Nor any old chimera of the grave,
Neither the golden underground, nor isle
Melodious, where spirits gat them home,
Nor visionary south, nor cloudy palm   55
Remote on heaven's hill, that has endured
As April's green endures; or will endure

35. *hinds* farm-servants.

Like her remembrance of awakened birds,
Or her desire for June and evening, tipped
By the consummation of the swallow's wings.   60

She says, "But in contentment I still feel
The need of some imperishable bliss."
Death is the mother of beauty; hence from her,
Alone, shall come fulfillment to our dreams
And our desires. Although she strews the leaves   65
Of sure obliteration on our paths,
The path sick sorrow took, the many paths
Where triumph rang its brassy phrase, or love
Whispered a little out of tenderness,
She makes the willow shiver in the sun   70
For maidens who were wont to sit and gaze
Upon the grass, relinquished to their feet.
She causes boys to pile new plums and pears
On disregarded plate. The maidens taste
And stray impassioned in the littering leaves.   75

Is there no change of death in paradise?
Does ripe fruit never fall? Or do the boughs
Hang always heavy in that perfect sky,
Unchanging, yet so like our perishing earth,
With rivers like our own that seek for seas   80
They never find, the same receding shores
That never touch with inarticulate pang?
Why set the pear upon those river-banks
Or spice the shores with odors of the plum?
Alas, that they should wear our colors there,   85
The silken weavings of our afternoons,
And pick the strings of our insipid lutes!
Death is the mother of beauty, mystical,
Within whose burning bosom we devise
Our earthly mothers waiting, sleeplessly.   90

Supple and turbulent, a ring of men
Shall chant in orgy on a summer morn.
Their boisterous devotion to the sun,
Not as a god, but as a god might be,
Naked among them, like a savage source.   95
Their chant shall be a chant of paradise,
Out of their blood, returning to the sky;
And in their chant shall enter, voice by voice,

The windy lake wherein their lord delights,
The trees, like serafin, and echoing hills,   100
That choir among themselves long afterward.
They shall know well the heavenly fellowship
Of men that perish and of summer morn.
And whence they came and whither they shall go
The dew upon their feet shall manifest.   105

She hears, upon that water without sound,
A voice that cries, "The tomb in Palestine
Is not the porch of spirits lingering.
It is the grave of Jesus, where he lay."
We live in an old chaos of the sun,   110
Or old dependency of day and night,
Or island solitude, unsponsored, free,
Of that wide water, inescapable.
Deer walk upon our mountains, and the quail
Whistle about us their spontaneous cries;   115
Sweet berries ripen in the wilderness;
And, in the isolation of the sky,
At evening, casual flocks of pigeons make
Ambiguous undulations as they sink,
Downward to darkness, on extended wings.   120

THE DEATH OF A SOLDIER

Life contracts and death is expected,
As in a season of autumn.
The soldier falls.

He does not become a three-days personage,
Imposing his separation,   5
Calling for pomp.   .

Death is absolute and without memorial,
As in a season of autumn,
When the wind stops,

When the wind stops and, over the heavens,   10
The clouds go, nevertheless,
In their direction.

THE IDEA OF ORDER AT KEY WEST

She sang beyond the genius of the sea.
The water never formed to mind or voice,
Like a body wholly body, fluttering
Its empty sleeves; and yet its mimic motion
Made constant cry, caused constantly a cry,   5
That was not ours although we understood,
Inhuman, of the veritable ocean.

The sea was not a mask. No more was she.
The song and water were not medleyed sound
Even if what she sang was what she heard,   10
Since what she sang was uttered word by word.
It may be that in all her phrases stirred
The grinding water and the gasping wind;
But it was she and not the sea we heard.

For she was the maker of the song she sang.   15
The ever-hooded, tragic-gestured sea
Was merely a place by which she walked to sing.
Whose spirit is this? we said, because we knew
It was the spirit that we sought and knew
That we should ask this often as she sang.   20

If it was only the dark voice of the sea
That rose, or even colored by many waves;
If it was only the outer voice of sky
And cloud, of the sunken coral water-walled,
However clear, it would have been deep air,   25
The heaving speech of air, a summer sound
Repeated in a summer without end
And sound alone. But it was more than that,
More even than her voice, and ours, among
The meaningless plungings of water and the wind,   30
Theatrical distances, bronze shadows heaped
On high horizons, mountainous atmospheres
Of sky and sea.   It was her voice that made
The sky acutest at its vanishing.
She measured to the hour its solitude.   35
She was the single artificer of the world
In which she sang. And when she sang, the sea,

Whatever self it had, became the self
That was her song, for she was the maker. Then we,
As we beheld her striding there alone,   40
Knew that there never was a world for her
Except the one she sang and, singing, made.

Ramon Fernandez, tell me, if you know,
Why, when the singing ended and we turned
Toward the town, tell why the glassy lights,   45
The lights in the fishing boats at anchor there,
As the night descended, tilting in the air,
Mastered the night and portioned out the sea,
Fixing emblazoned zones and fiery poles,
Arranging, deepening, enchanting night.   50

Oh! Blessed rage for order, pale Ramon,
The maker's rage to order words of the sea,
Words of the fragrant portals, dimly-starred,
And of ourselves and of our origins,
In ghostlier demarcations, keener sounds.   55

THE SUN THIS MARCH

The exceeding brightness of this early sun
Makes me conceive how dark I have become,

And re-illumines things that used to turn
To gold in broadest blue, and be a part

Of a turning spirit in an earlier self.   5
That, too, returns from out the winter's air,

Like an hallucination come to daze
The corner of the eye. Our element,

Cold is our element and winter's air
Brings voices as of lions coming down.   10

Oh! Rabbi, rabbi, fend my soul for me
And true savant of this dark nature be.

THE SENSE OF THE
SLEIGHT-OF-HAND MAN

One's grand flights, one's Sunday baths,
One's tootings at the weddings of the soul
Occur as they occur. So bluish clouds
Occurred above the empty house and the leaves
Of the rhododendrons rattled their gold,   5
As if someone lived there. Such floods of white
Came bursting from the clouds. So the wind
Threw its contorted strength around the sky.

Could you have said the bluejay suddenly
Would swoop to earth? It is a wheel, the rays   10
Around the sun. The wheel survives the myths.
The fire eye in the clouds survives the gods.
To think of a dove with an eye of grenadine
And pines that are cornets, so it occurs,
And a little island full of geese and stars: 15
It may be that the ignorant man, alone,
Has any chance to mate his life with life
That is the sensual, pearly spouse, the life
That is fluent in even the wintriest bronze.

THE WORLD AS MEDITATION

*J'ai passé trop de temps à travailler mon violon, à voyager. Mais l'exercice
essentiel du compositeur—la méditation—rien ne l'a jamais suspendu en
moi . . . Je vis un rêve permanent, qui ne s'arrête ni nuit ni jour.*
                                                    —GEORGES ENESCO

Is it Ulysses that approaches from the east,
The interminable adventurer? The trees are mended.
That winter is washed away. Someone is moving

On the horizon and lifting himself up above it.
A form of fire approaches the cretonnes of Penelope,   5
Whose mere savage presence awakens the world in which she
    dwells.

J'ai passé . . . ni jour "I have spent too much time working at my violin and traveling. But nothing has ever kept me from the essential exercise of the composer—meditation . . . I live a permanent dream, which stops neither night nor day."
1. *Ulysses* in the *Odyssey,* Penelope resists other suitors awaiting her husband's return.

She has composed, so long, a self with which to welcome him,
Companion to his self for her, which she imagined,
Two in a deep-founded sheltering, friend and dear friend.

The trees had been mended, as an essential exercise   10
In an inhuman meditation, larger than her own.
No winds like dogs watched over her at night.

She wanted nothing he could not bring her by coming alone.
She wanted no fetchings. His arms would be her necklace
And her belt, the final fortune of their desire.   15

But was it Ulysses? Or was it only the warmth of the sun
On her pillow? The thought kept beating in her like her heart.
The two kept beating together. It was only day.

It was Ulysses and it was not. Yet they had met,
Friend and dear friend and a planet's encouragement.   20
The barbarous strength within her would never fail.

She would talk a little to herself as she combed her hair,
Repeating his name with its patient syllables,
Never forgetting him that kept coming constantly so near.

FINAL SOLILOQUY OF THE
INTERIOR PARAMOUR

Light the first light of evening, as in a room
In which we rest and, for small reason, think
The world imagined is the ultimate good.

This is, therefore, the intensest rendezvous.
It is in that thought that we collect ourselves,   5
Out of all the indifferences, into one thing:

Within a single thing, a single shawl
Wrapped tightly round us, since we are poor, a warmth,
A light, a power, the miraculous influence.

Here, now, we forget each other and ourselves.   10
We feel the obscurity of an order, a whole,
A knowledge, that which arranged the rendezvous.

Within its vital boundary, in the mind.
We say God and the imagination are one . . .
How high that highest candle lights the dark.   15

Out of this same light, out of the central mind,
We make a dwelling in the evening air,
In which being there together is enough.

THOMAS STEARNS ELIOT
(*1888–1965*)

·

THE LOVE SONG OF
J. ALFRED PRUFROCK

S'io credesse che mia risposta fosse
A persona che mai tornasse al mondo,
Questa fiamma staria senza piu scosse.
Ma perciocche giammai di questo fondo
Non torno vivo alcun, s'i'odo il vero,
Senza tema d'infamia ti rispondo.

Let us go then, you and I,
When the evening is spread out against the sky
Like a patient etherized upon a table;
Let us go, through certain half-deserted streets,
The muttering retreats   5
Of restless nights in one-night cheap hotels
And sawdust restaurants with oyster shells:
Streets that follow like a tedious argument
Of insidious intent
To lead you to an overwhelming question . . .   10
Oh, do not ask, "What is it?"
Let us go and make our visit.

In the room the women come and go
Talking of Michelangelo.

The yellow fog that rubs its back upon the windowpanes,   15
The yellow smoke that rubs its muzzle on the windowpanes
Licked its tongue into the corners of the evening,
Lingered upon the pools that stand in drains,
Let fall upon its back the soot that falls from chimneys,
Slipped by the terrace, made a sudden leap,   20
And seeing that it was a soft October night,
Curled once about the house, and fell asleep.

S'io credesse . . . rispondo "If I be- the truth) I answer you without fear of
lieved that my reply would be to any- infamy" (Dante, *Inferno,* xxvii, 61–
one who would ever return to the world, 66). In this passage, Guido da Monte-
this flame would remain without more feltro, enclosed in flames, admits his
movement. But since no one ever re- crimes to Dante.
turns alive from these depths (if I hear

And indeed there will be time
For the yellow smoke that slides along the street,
Rubbing its back upon the windowpanes;   25
There will be time, there will be time
To prepare a face to meet the faces that you meet;
There will be time to murder and create,
And time for all the works and days of hands
That lift and drop a question on your plate;   30
Time for you and time for me,
And time yet for a hundred indecisions,
And for a hundred visions and revisions,
Before the taking of a toast and tea.

In the room the women come and go   35
Talking of Michelangelo.

And indeed there will be time
To wonder, "Do I dare?" and, "Do I dare?"
Time to turn back and descend the stair,
With a bald spot in the middle of my hair—   40
(They will say: "How his hair is growing thin!")
My morning coat, my collar mounting firmly to the chin,
My necktie rich and modest, but asserted by a simple pin—
(They will say: "But how his arms and legs are thin!")
Do I dare   45
Disturb the universe?
In a minute there is time
For decisions and revisions which a minute will reverse.

For I have known them all already, known them all—
Have known the evenings, mornings, afternoons,   50
I have measured out my life with coffee spoons;
I know the voices dying with a dying fall
Beneath the music from a farther room.
   So how should I presume?

And I have known the eyes already, known them all—   55
The eyes that fix you in a formulated phrase,
And when I am formulated, sprawling on a pin,
When I am pinned and wriggling on the wall,
Then how should I begin
To spit out all the butt-ends of my days and ways?   60
   And how should I presume?

And I have known the arms already, known them all—
Arms that are braceleted and white and bare

(But in the lamplight, downed with light brown hair!)
Is it perfume from a dress   65
That makes me so digress?
Arms that lie along a table, or wrap about a shawl.
   And should I then presume?
   And how should I begin?

             .   .   .

Shall I say, I have gone at dusk through narrow streets   70
And watched the smoke that rises from the pipes
Of lonely men in shirt-sleeves, leaning out of windows? . . .

I should have been a pair of ragged claws
Scuttling across the floors of silent seas.

             .   .   .

And the afternoon, the evening, sleeps so peacefully!   75
Smoothed by long fingers,
Asleep . . . tired . . . or it malingers,
Stretched on the floor, here beside you and me.
Should I, after tea and cakes and ices,
Have the strength to force the moment to its crisis?   80
But though I have wept and fasted, wept and prayed,
Though I have seen my head (grown slightly bald) brought in
      upon a platter,
I am no prophet—and here's no great matter;
I have seen the moment of my greatness flicker,
And I have seen the eternal Footman hold my coat, and snicker,   85
And in short, I was afraid.

And would it have been worth it, after all,
After the cups, the marmalade, the tea,
Among the porcelain, among some talk of you and me,
Would it have been worth while,   90
To have bitten off the matter with a smile,
To have squeezed the universe into a ball
To roll it toward some overwhelming question,
To say: "I am Lazarus, come from the dead,
Come back to tell you all, I shall tell you all"—   95
If one, settling a pillow by her head,
   Should say: "That is not what I meant at all.
   That is not it, at all."

83. *prophet* John the Baptist's head,   94. *Lazarus* raised from the dead by
at the request of Salome, "brought in   Christ (*John* xii.1–18).
upon a platter."

And would it have been worth it, after all,
Would it have been worth while,   100
After the sunsets and the dooryards and the sprinkled streets,
After the novels, after the teacups, after the skirts that trail along
    the floor—
And this, and so much more?—
It is impossible to say just what I mean!
But as if a magic lantern threw the nerves in patterns on a
    screen: 105
Would it have been worth while
If one, settling a pillow or throwing off a shawl,
And turning toward the window, should say:
    "That is not it at all,
    That is not what I meant, at all."   110

                           .   .   .

No! I am not Prince Hamlet, nor was meant to be;
Am an attendant lord, one that will do
To swell a progress, start a scene or two,
Advise the prince; no doubt, an easy tool,
Deferential, glad to be of use,   115
Politic, cautious, and meticulous;
Full of high sentence, but a bit obtuse;
At times, indeed, almost ridiculous—
Almost, at times, the Fool.

I grow old . . . I grow old . . .   120
I shall wear the bottoms of my trousers rolled.

Shall I part my hair behind? Do I dare to eat a peach?
I shall wear white flannel trousers, and walk upon the beach.
I have heard the mermaids singing, each to each.

I do not think that they will sing to me.   125

I have seen them riding seaward on the waves
Combing the white hair of the waves blown back
When the wind blows the water white and black.

We have lingered in the chambers of the sea
By sea-girls wreathed with seaweed red and brown   130
Till human voices wake us, and we drown.

THE BOSTON EVENING TRANSCRIPT

The readers of the *Boston Evening Transcript*
Sway in the wind like a field of ripe corn.

When evening quickens faintly in the street,
Wakening the appetites of life in some
And to others bringing the *Boston Evening Transcript*,   5
I mount the steps and ring the bell, turning
Wearily, as one would turn to nod good-bye to Rochefoucauld,
If the street were time and he at the end of the street,
And I say, "Cousin Harriet, here is the *Boston Evening Transcript*."

LA FIGLIA CHE PIANGE
O quam te memorem virgo . . .

Stand on the highest pavement of the stair—
Lean on a garden urn—
Weave, weave the sunlight in your hair—
Clasp your flowers to you with a pained surprise—
Fling them to the ground and turn   5
With a fugitive resentment in your eyes:
But weave, weave the sunlight in your hair.

So I would have had him leave,
So I would have had her stand and grieve,
So he would have left   10
As the soul leaves the body torn and bruised,
As the mind deserts the body it has used.
I should find
Some way incomparably light and deft,
Some way we both should understand,   15
Simple and faithless as a smile and shake of the hand.

She turned away, but with the autumn weather
Compelled my imagination many days,
Many days and many hours:
Her hair over her arms and her arms full of flowers.   20

7. *Rochefoucauld* seventeenth-century French master of the worldly and wise epigram.

La Figlia che Piange "young girl weeping," a figure in a posture of sor-row on a grave monument.

O quam te memorem virgo . . . "By what name should I call thee, O maiden" (Aeneas to Venus, *Aeneid* I, 327).

And I wonder how they should have been together!
I should have lost a gesture and a pose.
Sometimes these cogitations still amaze
The troubled midnight and the noon's repose.

GERONTION

Thou hast nor youth nor age
But as it were an after dinner sleep
Dreaming of both.

Here I am, an old man in a dry month,
Being read to by a boy, waiting for rain.
I was neither at the hot gates
Nor fought in the warm rain
Nor knee deep in the salt marsh, heaving a cutlass,   5
Bitten by flies, fought.
My house is a decayed house,
And the Jew squats on the window sill, the owner,
Spawned in some estaminet of Antwerp,
Blistered in Brussels, patched and peeled in London.   10
The goat coughs at night in the field overhead;
Rocks, moss, stonecrop, iron, merds.
The woman keeps the kitchen, makes tea,
Sneezes at evening, poking the peevish gutter.
                              I an old man,
A dull head among windy spaces.   15

Signs are taken for wonders. "We would see a sign!"
The word within a word, unable to speak a word,
Swaddled with darkness. In the juvescence of the year
Came Christ the tiger

In depraved May, dogwood and chestnut, flowering judas,   20
To be eaten, to be divided, to be drunk
Among whispers; by Mr. Silvero
With caressing hands, at Limoges
Who walked all night in the next room;

By Hakagawa, bowing among the Titians;   25
By Madame de Tornquist, in the dark room

Thou hast . . . of both Shakespeare, *Measure for Measure,* III, i, *32–34.*
3. *hot gates* a translation of Thermopylae, the battle in which a small number of Spartans for a while held off the Persian army.
9. *estaminet* café.

16. *"We would see a sign" Matthew* xii.38.
18. *juvescence* see "juvenescence," the state of being young.
23. *Limoges* French center for enamels and china.

Shifting the candles; Fraülein von Kulp
Who turned in the hall, one hand on the door.
                                    Vacant shuttles
Weave the wind. I have no ghosts,
An old man in a draughty house   30
Under a windy knob.
After such knowledge, what forgiveness? Think now
History has many cunning passages, contrived corridors
And issues, deceives with whispering ambitions,
Guides us by vanities. Think now   35
She gives when our attention is distracted
And what she gives, gives with such supple confusions
That the giving famishes the craving. Gives too late
What's not believed in, or if still believed,
In memory only, reconsidered passion. Gives too soon   40
Into weak hands, what's thought can be dispensed with
Till the refusal propagates a fear. Think
Neither fear nor courage saves us. Unnatural vices
Are fathered by our heroism. Virtues
Are forced upon us by our impudent crimes.   45
These tears are shaken from the wrath-bearing tree.

The tiger springs in the new year. Us he devours. Think at last
We have not reached conclusion, when I
Stiffen in a rented house. Think at last
I have not made this show purposelessly   50
And it is not by any concitation
Of the backward devils.
I would meet you upon this honestly.
I that was near your heart was removed therefrom
To lose beauty in terror, terror in inquisition.   55
I have lost my passion: why should I need to keep it
Since what is kept must be adulterated?
I have lost my sight, smell, hearing, taste and touch:
How should I use them for your closer contact?

These with a thousand small deliberations   60
Protract the profit of their chilled delirium,
Excite the membrane, when the sense has cooled,
With pungent sauces, multiply variety
In a wilderness of mirrors. What will the spider do,
Suspend its operations, will the weevil   65
Delay? De Bailhache, Fresca, Mrs. Cammel, whirled
Beyond the circuit of the shuddering Bear

51. *concitation* stirring up.   67. *Bear* Big Dipper.

In fractured atoms. Gull against the wind, in the windy straits
Of Belle Isle, or running on the Horn,   70
White feathers in the snow, the Gulf claims,
And an old man driven by the Trades
To a sleepy corner.

                                    Tenants of the house,
Thoughts of a dry brain in a dry season.

SWEENEY AMONG THE NIGHTINGALES

ὤμοι, πέπληγμαι καιρίαν πληγὴν ἔσω.

Apeneck Sweeney spreads his knees
Letting his arms hang down to laugh,
The zebra stripes along his jaw
Swelling to maculate giraffe.

The circles of the stormy moon   5
Slide westward toward the River Plate,
Death and the Raven drift above
And Sweeney guards the hornéd gate.

Gloomy Orion and the Dog
Are veiled; and hushed the shrunken seas;   10
The person in the Spanish cape
Tries to sit on Sweeney's knees

Slips and pulls the tablecloth
Overturns a coffee cup,
Reorganized upon the floor   15
She yawns and draws a stocking up;

The silent man in mocha brown
Sprawls at the window sill and gapes;
The waiter brings in oranges
Bananas figs and hothouse grapes;   20

The silent vertebrate in brown
Contracts and concentrates, withdraws;
Rachel *née* Rabinovitch
Tears at the grapes with murderous paws;

Greek epigraph from Aeschylus, *Aga-*
memnon. These are Agamemnon's words
when murdered by his wife, Clytem-
nestra: "Ah, I am struck a deadly
blow and deep within."
4. *maculate* spotted.

7. *Raven* Corvus, a southern constel-
lation.
8. *horned gate* gates of Hades which
only allow true dreams to pass through
them.

She and the lady in the cape   25
Are suspect, thought to be in league;
Therefore the man with heavy eyes
Declines the gambit, shows fatigue,

Leaves the room and reappears
Outside the window, leaning in,   30
Branches of wistaria
Circumscribe a golden grin;

The host with someone indistinct
Converses at the door apart,
The nightingales are singing near   35
The Convent of the Sacred Heart,

And sang within the bloody wood
When Agamemnon cried aloud,
And let their liquid siftings fall
To stain the stiff dishonored shroud.   40

JOURNEY OF THE MAGI

"A cold coming we had of it,
Just the worst time of the year
For a journey, and such a long journey:
The ways deep and the weather sharp,
The very dead of winter."   5
And the camels galled, sore-footed, refractory,
Lying down in the melting snow.
There were times we regretted
The summer palaces on slopes, the terraces,
And the silken girls bringing sherbet.   10
Then the camel men cursing and grumbling
And running away, and wanting their liquor and women,
And the night-fires going out, and the lack of shelters,
And the cities hostile and the towns unfriendly
And the villages dirty and charging high prices: 15
A hard time we had of it.
At the end we preferred to travel all night,
Sleeping in snatches,
With the voices singing in our ears, saying
That this was all folly.   20

Magi the three wise men who journeyed to pay tribute to the infant
Jesus.

Then at dawn we came down to a temperate valley,
Wet, below the snow line, smelling of vegetation;
With a running stream and a water mill beating the darkness,
And three trees on the low sky,
And an old white horse galloped away in the meadow.   25
Then we came to a tavern with vine-leaves over the lintel,
Six hands at an open door dicing for pieces of silver,
And feet kicking the empty wineskins.
But there was no information, and so we continued
And arrived at evening, not a moment too soon   30
Finding the place; it was (you may say) satisfactory.

All this was a long time ago, I remember,
And I would do it again, but set down
This set down
This: were we led all that way for   35
Birth or Death? There was a Birth, certainly,
We had evidence and no doubt. I had seen birth and death,
But had thought they were different; this Birth was
Hard and bitter agony for us, like Death, our death.
We returned to our places, these Kingdoms,   40
But no longer at ease here, in the old dispensation,
With an alien people clutching their gods.
I should be glad of another death.

FROM CORIOLAN

I. TRIUMPHAL MARCH

Stone, bronze, stone, steel, stone, oakleaves horses' heels
Over the paving.
And the flags. And the trumpets. And so many eagles.
How many? Count them. And such a press of people.
We hardly knew ourselves that day, or knew the City.   5
This is the way to the temple, and we so many crowding the way.
So many waiting, how many waiting? what did it matter, on such
     a day?
Are they coming? No, not yet. You can see some eagles. And hear
     the trumpets.
Here they come. Is he coming?

Coriolan Caius Marcius Coriolanus, according to Plutarch and Shakespeare's play a Roman military hero of the fifth century B.C. Though the plebeians acclaimed his victories, they later banished him from Rome for his extreme patrician sympathies and scorn of the plebs.

The natural wakeful life of our Ego is a perceiving.   10
We can wait with our stools and our sausages.
What comes first? Can you see? Tell us. It is

    5,800,000 rifles and carbines,
      102,000 machine guns,
        28,000 trench mortars,   15
      53,000 field and heavy guns,
I cannot tell how many projectiles, mines and fuses,
      13,000 aeroplanes,
      24,000 aeroplane engines,
      50,000 ammunition waggons,   20
now 55,000 army waggons,
      11,000 field kitchens,
      1,150 field bakeries.

What a time that took. Will it be he now? No,
Those are the golf club Captains, these the Scouts,   25
And now the *société gymnastique de Poissy*
And now come the Mayor and the Liverymen.
   Look
There he is now, look:
There is no interrogation in his eyes   30
Or in the hands, quiet over the horse's neck,
And the eyes watchful, waiting, perceiving, indifferent.
O hidden under the dove's wing, hidden in the turtle's breast,
Under the palmtree at noon, under the running water
At the still point of the turning world. O hidden.   35

Now they go up to the temple. Then the sacrifice.
Now come the virgins bearing urns, urns containing

Dust
Dust
Dust of dust, and now   40
Stone, bronze, stone, steel, stone, oakleaves, horses' heels
Over the paving.

That is all we could see. But how many eagles! and how many
      trumpets!
(And Easter Day, we didn't get to the country,
So we took young Cyril to church. And they rang a bell   45
And he said right out loud, *crumpets.*)
          Don't throw away that sausage,

It'll come in handy. He's artful. Please, will you
Give us a light?
Light   50
Light
Et les soldats faisaient la haie? ILS LA FAISAIENT.

MARINA

Quis hic locus, quae regio, quae mundi plaga?

What seas what shores what gray rocks and what islands
What water lapping the bow
And scent of pine and the woodthrush singing through the fog
What images return
O my daughter.   5

Those who sharpen the tooth of the dog, meaning
Death
Those who glitter with the glory of the hummingbird, meaning
Death
Those who sit in the sty of contentment, meaning   10
Death
Those who suffer the ecstasy of the animals, meaning
Death

Are become unsubstantial, reduced by a wind,
A breath of pine, and the woodsong fog   15
By this grace dissolved in place

What is this face, less clear and clearer
The pulse in the arm, less strong and stronger—
Given or lent? more distant than stars and nearer than the eye

Whispers and small laughter between leaves and hurrying feet   20
Under sleep, where all the waters meet.

Bowsprit cracked with ice and paint cracked with heat.
I made this, I have forgotten
And remember.

52. *Et les . . . faisaient* "And the soldiers formed a cordon? They did."

Marina in Shakespeare's *Pericles,* the daughter who is lost at sea and finally restored to her penitent father.
Quis hic . . . plaga? "What place is this, what land, what quarter of the globe?" These are the first words of Hercules in Seneca's *Hercules Furens,* as he awakens from a fit of madness during which he has killed his own children and begins to realize the enormity of what he has done.

The rigging weak and the canvas rotten   25
Between one June and another September.
Made this unknowing, half conscious, unknown, my own.
The garboard strake leaks, the seams need calking.
This form, this face, this life
Living to live in a world of time beyond me; let me   30
Resign my life for this life, my speech for that unspoken,
The awakened, lips parted, the hope, the new ships.

What seas what shores what granite islands towards my timbers
And woodthrush calling through the fog
My daughter.   35

A Selection of Later Nineteenth- and Twentieth-Century Poems

ROBERT BRIDGES
(1844–1930)

NIGHTINGALES

Beautiful must be the mountains whence ye come,
And bright in the fruitful valleys the streams wherefrom
    Ye learn your song:
Where are those starry woods? O might I wander there,
  Among the flowers, which in that heavenly air   5
    Bloom the year long!

Nay, barren are those mountains and spent the streams:
Our song is the voice of desire, that haunts our dreams,
    A throe of the heart,
Whose pining visions dim, forbidden hopes profound,   10
  No dying cadence nor long sigh can sound,
    For all our art.

Alone, aloud in the raptured ear of men
We pour our dark nocturnal secret; and then,
    As night is withdrawn   15
From these sweet-springing meads and bursting boughs of May,
  Dream, while the innumerable choir of day
    Welcome the dawn.

≺ ☼ ≻

ERNEST DOWSON
(1867–1900)

·

NON SUM QUALIS ERAM BONAE SUB REGNO CYNARAE

Last night, ah, yesternight, betwixt her lips and mine
There fell thy shadow, Cynara! thy breath was shed
Upon my soul between the kisses and the wine;
And I was desolate and sick of an old passion,
 Yea, I was desolate and bowed my head: 5
I have been faithful to thee, Cynara! in my fashion.

All night upon mine heart I felt her warm heart beat,
Night-long within mine arms in love and sleep she lay;
Surely the kisses of her bought red mouth were sweet;
But I was desolate and sick of an old passion,   10
 When I awoke and found the dawn was gray:
I have been faithful to thee, Cynara! in my fashion.

I have forgot much, Cynara! gone with the wind,
Flung roses, roses riotously with the throng,
Dancing, to put thy pale, lost lilies out of mind;   15
But I was desolate and sick of an old passion,
 Yea, all the time, because the dance was long:
I have been faithful to thee, Cynara! in my fashion.

I cried for madder music and for stronger wine,
But when the feast is finished and the lamps expire,   20
Then falls thy shadow, Cynara! the night is thine;
And I am desolate and sick of an old passion,
 Yea hungry for the lips of my desire:
I have been faithful to thee, Cynara! in my fashion.

Non . . . Cynarae "I am not what I was under the rule of good Cynara"; from Horace (*Odes,* IV, i), in which the poet prays that Venus not disturb him, because he is older and not what he was when he loved the girl Cynara.

EDWIN ARLINGTON ROBINSON
(*1869–1935*)

·

EROS TURANNOS

She fears him, and will always ask
   What fated her to choose him;
She meets in his engaging mask
   All reasons to refuse him;
But what she meets and what she fears   5
Are less than are the downward years,
Drawn slowly to the foamless weirs
   Of age, were she to lose him.

Between a blurred sagacity
   That once had power to sound him,   10
And Love, that will not let him be
   The Judas that she found him,
Her pride assuages her almost,
As if it were alone the cost.—
He sees that he will not be lost,   15
   And waits and looks around him.

A sense of ocean and old trees
   Envelops and allures him;
Tradition, touching all he sees,
   Beguiles and reassures him;   20
And all her doubts of what he says
Are dimmed with what she knows of days—
Till even prejudice delays
   And fades, and she secures him.

The falling leaf inaugurates   25
   The reign of her confusion;
The pounding wave reverberates
   The dirge of her illusion;
And home, where passion lived and died,
Becomes a place where she can hide,   30
While all the town and harbor side
   Vibrate with her seclusion.

We tell you, tapping on our brows,
  The story as it should be,—
As if the story of a house   35
  Were told, or ever could be;
We'll have no kindly veil between
Her visions and those we have seen,—
As if we guessed what hers have been,
  Or what they are or would be.   40

Meanwhile we do no harm; for they
  That with a god have striven,
Not hearing much of what we say,
  Take what the god has given;
Though like waves breaking it may be   45
Or like a changed familiar tree,
Or like a stairway to the sea
  Where down the blind are driven.

FOR A DEAD LADY

No more with overflowing light
Shall fill the eyes that now are faded,
Nor shall another's fringe with night
Their woman-hidden world as they did.
No more shall quiver down the days   5
The flowing wonder of her ways,
Whereof no language may requite
The shifting and the many-shaded.

The grace, divine, definitive,
Clings only as a faint forestalling;   10
The laugh that love could not forgive
Is hushed, and answers to no calling;
The forehead and the little ears
Have gone where Saturn keeps the years;
The breast where roses could not live   15
Has done with rising and with falling.

The beauty, shattered by the laws
That have creation in their keeping,

No longer trembles at applause,
Or over children that are sleeping;   20
And we who delve in beauty's lore
Know all that we have known before
Of what inexorable cause
Makes Time so vicious in his reaping.

DAVID HERBERT
LAWRENCE
(1885–1930)

·

PIANO

Softly, in the dusk, a woman is singing to me;
Taking me back down the vista of years, till I see
A child sitting under the piano, in the boom of the tingling strings
And pressing the small, poised feet of a mother who smiles as she
  sings.

In spite of myself, the insidious mastery of song   5
Betrays me back, till the heart of me weeps to belong
To the old Sunday evenings at home, with winter outside
And hymns in the cozy parlor, the tinkling piano our guide.

So now it is vain for the singer to burst into clamor
With the great black piano appassionato. The glamour   10
Of childish days is upon me, my manhood is cast
Down in the flood of remembrance, I weep like a child for the past.

HUMMING-BIRD

I can imagine, in some otherworld
Primeval-dumb, far back
In that most awful stillness, that only gasped and hummed,
Humming-birds raced down the avenues.

Before anything had a soul,   5
While life was a heave of Matter, half inanimate,
This little bit chipped off in brilliance
And went whizzing through the slow, vast, succulent stems.

I believe there were no flowers then,
In the world where the humming-bird flashed ahead of creation.   10
I believe he pierced the slow vegetable veins with his long beak.

Probably he was big
As mosses, and little lizards, they say, were once big.
Probably he was a jabbing, terrifying monster.

We look at him through the wrong end of the telescope of
    Time,
                                                                15
Luckily for us.

WILLIAM CARLOS WILLIAMS
(1883–1963)

·

THE YOUNG HOUSEWIFE

At ten A.M. the young housewife
moves about in negligee behind
the wooden walls of her husband's house.
I pass solitary in my car.

Then again she comes to the curb   5
to call the ice-man, fish-man, and stands
shy, uncorseted, tucking in
stray ends of hair, and I compare her
to a fallen leaf.

The noiseless wheels of my car   10
rush with a crackling sound over
dried leaves as I bow and pass smiling.

A NEGRO WOMAN

carrying a bunch of marigolds
            wrapped
                        in an old newspaper:
She carries them upright,
            bareheaded,   5

                    the bulk
of her thighs
            causing her to waddle
                as she walks
looking into   10
            the store window which she passes
                on her way.
What is she
            but an ambassador
                    from another world   15
a world of pretty marigolds
        of two shades
                which she announces
not knowing what she does
            other   20
                    than walk the streets
holding the flowers upright
        as a torch
                so early in the morning.

MARIANNE MOORE
(b. 1887)

·

WHAT ARE YEARS?

    What is our innocence,
what is our guilt? All are
    naked, none is safe. And whence
is courage: the unanswered question,
the resolute doubt,—   5
dumbly calling, deafly listening—that
in misfortune, even death,
        encourages others
        and in its defeat, stirs

    the soul to be strong? He   10
sees deep and is glad, who
    accedes to mortality
and in his imprisonment rises
upon himself as
the sea in a chasm, struggling to be   15

free and unable to be,
  in its surrendering
  finds its continuing.

  So he who strongly feels,
behaves. The very bird,   20
  grown taller as he sings, steels
his form straight up. Though he is captive,
his mighty singing
says, satisfaction is a lowly
thing, how pure a thing is joy.   25
  This is mortality,
  this is eternity.

NEVERTHELESS

  you've seen a strawberry
    that's had a struggle; yet
    was, where the fragments met,

  a hedgehog or a star-
    fish for the multitude   5
    of seeds. What better food

than apple-seeds—the fruit
    within the fruit—locked in
    like counter-curved twin

hazel-nuts? Frost that kills   10
    the little rubber-plant-
    leaves of *kok-saghyz*-stalks, can't

harm the roots; they still grow
    in frozen ground. Once where
    there was a prickly-pear-   15

leaf clinging to barbed wire,
    a root shot down to grow
    in earth two feet below;

as carrots form mandrakes
    or a ram's-horn root some-   20
    times. Victory won't come

to me unless I go
    to it; a grape-tendril
    ties a knot in knots till

knotted thirty times,—so   25
    the bound twig that's under-
    gone and over-gone, can't stir.

The weak overcomes its
    menace, the strong over-
    comes itself. What is there   30

like fortitude! What sap
    went through that little thread
    to make the cherry red!

JOHN CROWE RANSOM
(*b. 1888*)

·

HERE LIES A LADY

Here lies a lady of beauty and high degree.
Of chills and fever she died, of fever and chills,
The delight of her husband, her aunt, an infant of three,
And of medicos marveling sweetly on her ills.

For either she burned, and her confident eyes would blaze,   5
And her fingers fly in a manner to puzzle their heads—
What was she making? Why, nothing; she sat in a maze
Of old scraps of laces, snipped into curious shreds—

Or this would pass, and the light of her fire decline
Till she lay discouraged and cold, like a thin stalk white and
    blown,   10
And would not open her eyes, to kisses, to wine;
The sixth of these states was her last; the cold settled down.

Sweet ladies, long may ye bloom, and toughly I hope ye may thole,
But was she not lucky? In flowers and lace and mourning,
In love and great honor we bade God rest her soul   15
After six little spaces of chill, and six of burning.

PIAZZA PIECE

—I am a gentleman in a dustcoat trying
To make you hear. Your ears are soft and small
And listen to an old man not at all,
They want the young men's whispering and sighing.
But see the roses on your trellis dying   5
And hear the spectral singing of the moon;
For I must have my lovely lady soon,
I am a gentleman in a dustcoat trying.

—I am a lady young in beauty waiting
Until my truelove comes, and then we kiss.   10
But what grey man among the vines is this
Whose words are dry and faint as in a dream?
Back from my trellis, Sir, before I scream!
I am a lady young in beauty waiting.

WYSTAN HUGH AUDEN
(*b. 1907*)

·

MUSÉE DES BEAUX ARTS

About suffering they were never wrong,
The Old Masters: how well they understood
Its human position; how it takes place
While someone else is eating or opening a window or just walking
    dully along;
How, when the aged are reverently, passionately waiting   5
For the miraculous birth, there always must be
Children who did not specially want it to happen, skating
On a pond at the edge of the wood:
They never forgot
That even the dreadful martyrdom must run its course   10
Anyhow in a corner, some untidy spot
Where the dogs go on with their doggy life and the torturer's
    horse
Scratches its innocent behind on a tree.

Musée des Beaux Arts   Museum of Fine Arts.

In Brueghel's *Icarus*, for instance: how everything turns away
Quite leisurely from the disaster; the ploughman may   15
Have heard the splash, the forsaken cry,
But for him it was not an important failure; the sun shone
As it had to on the white legs disappearing into the green
Water; and the expensive delicate ship that must have seen
Something amazing, a boy falling out of the sky,   20
Had somewhere to get to and sailed calmly on.

SIR, NO MAN'S ENEMY

Sir, no man's enemy, forgiving all
But will his negative inversion, be prodigal:
Send to us power and light, a sovereign touch
Curing the intolerable neural itch,
The exhaustion of weaning, the liar's quinsy,   5
And the distortions of ingrown virginity.
Prohibit sharply the rehearsed response
And gradually correct the coward's stance;
Cover in time with beams those in retreat
That, spotted, they turn though the reverse were great;   10
Publish each healer that in city lives
Or country houses at the end of drives;
Harrow the house of the dead; look shining at
New styles of architecture, a change of heart.

Index